EXTERNAL DEBT

Definition, Statistical Coverage and Methodology

A Report by
an International Working Group
on External Debt Statistics
of:
THE WORLD BANK
INTERNATIONAL MONETARY FUND
BANK FOR INTERNATIONAL SETTLEMENTS
ORGANISATION FOR ECONOMIC CO-OPERATION AND DEVELOPMENT

PARIS 1988

Readers are invited to send comments or questions on the text of this publication to the organisation concerned. Those of a more general nature should be addressed to:

The International Working Group
on External Debt Statistics

c/o The Bureau of Statistics
International Monetary Fund
Washington, DC 20431
United States

Publié en français sous le titre:

L'ENDETTEMENT
INTERNATIONAL
Définition,
couverture statistique
et méthodologie

The rapid expansion of the debt of developing countries in recent years has inevitably increased the importance attached to reliable and timely international statistics on the subject – not that precise data were needed to demonstrate the existence of a problem, but rather because only detailed statistics could show just how fast it was growing, how it related to other economic aggregates, which countries were affected and to what extent, what forms of debt were involved, how the burdens could be shared, and so on. These were all questions which took on political as well as analytical importance when debt went beyond the stage of bilateral – often private – negotiation to become a subject of international concern. Progress towards agreement on action called for at least a minimum of agreement on the precise meaning of the reported magnitudes.

It was against this background that the International Working Group on External Debt Statistics was set up. The aim of the Group (as it will be referred to for convenience from now on) was to promote convergence of debt recording practices, building on the existing bilateral co-operation between the four international organisations whose activities in the area of external debt data provide much of the subject matter of this book (together with certain others not specifically dealt with).

These four organisations are: the Bank for International Settlements (BIS); the International Monetary Fund (IMF); the Organisation for Economic Co-operation and Development (OECD); and the World Bank. The first meeting of the Group was held in March 1984.

The present volume is therefore partly a "progress report" on what the Group has achieved in its fairly short existence, with one chapter devoted to outstanding issues. It is also intended to provide the user of debt statistics published by these organisations with a comparative description of the statistics collected by them, how they are obtained, why they take the form they do, and how they relate to each other.

Perhaps the most important progress made by the Group has been agreement on a "core definition" of external debt. The background to the definition and the definition itself will be described in detail in Part I (Chapters I and II). The special emphasis placed on this core definition reflects not only the progress it represents towards common practices in reporting debt, but its utility, in the context of this report, as a framework for highlighting the particular features of the individual organisations' systems. The chapters on the individual organisations are constructed largely in terms of the extent to which their statistics conform to those that would be obtained by full application of the core definition. It should be stressed, however, that not all the organisations aim at full coverage of countries' external debt; some focus on certain elements only.

This means that the descriptions of the individual organisations' debt statistics in Part II (Chapters IV to VII) can be presented in a uniform format in order to facilitate direct comparison. For example, users who find that the inclusion or exclusion of a particular type of claim makes the data from one organisation less suitable for their purposes can refer to the section with the same title and number in the other chapters in Part II to see whether the statistics published by other organisations meet their needs better. For the most important differences, the reader can also consult the synoptic tables at the end of Part II. However, the summary nature of the information that can be contained in such tables means that they should be treated as a guide to, not a substitute for, the detailed description given in the organisation chapters themselves.

The report is structured as follows: Part I deals with the formulation of the "core definition" (Chapters I and II) and reviews outstanding issues (Chapter III); Chapters IV to VII in Part II describe the four reporting organisations' statistical activities (BIS, IMF, OECD, World Bank), reproducing specimen tables from their main publications. The synoptic tables will be found at the end of Part II. The book also contains: technical appendices, for the benefit of readers requiring additional detail; a glossary of the terms used, indicating differences in usage by individual organisations; and an annotated bibliography.

TABLE OF CONTENTS

Part I

DEFINING EXTERNAL DEBT

Chapter I

SEEKING A COMMON DEFINITION OF EXTERNAL DEBT

1. THE OBJECTIVE

The first consideration in formulating a definition of countries' external debt is that it should respect the requirements of a wide range of users. Major users include: banks and export credit guarantee agencies for their work on risk analysis; officials involved in international financial co-operation, especially those concerned with the negotiation of debt agreements; and economic analysts in general. These and other potential users must find statistics derived from the definition relevant and realistic.

At the same time, it has to be recognised that statistics used in the assessment of external debt have already been collected and published for many years by a number of organisations, each with its own constraints and objectives. While any statistical system should be geared to the needs of the final user, the organisations are themselves among those users, and any definition is therefore bound to take into account their own practical needs.

The definition should also embody an internally consistent methodological approach to the concept of debt, capable of being articulated into some of the broader statistical systems dealing with financial stocks and flows.

It must also take into account, as far as possible, the practical problems involved in the reporting, aggregation and presentation of the statistics obtained.

This last aspect will be raised at various points in later chapters, but it will be useful, before proceeding in Chapter II to the definition adopted by the Group, to discuss briefly the historical background to the role and purposes of the existing systems, and the methodological framework in which the definition is placed.

2. THE ORGANISATIONS INVOLVED

The four organisations whose activities in the field of debt statistics are described in detail in this book had been collecting data on debt or debt-related aggregates for many years before external debt emerged in the early 1980s as a topic of major international importance in its own right. But they had been doing so in different ways, viewing the exercise from different standpoints and using the data for different purposes. In some cases, the information on debt was not originally collected as such, but was a by-product of more broadly-based statistical systems. None of the organisations on its own could be said to be producing comprehensive information on external debt.

The organisations are differently constituted and have different mandates. The focus is in some cases on creditor countries, in others on both debtors and creditors; their membership consists variously of governments or central banks, restricted to particular groups of countries or more universal; some collect data from the creditor side, the others mainly from the debtors. These differences have implications for timeliness and coverage. They may also result in data that are not easily reconcilable.

Realisation of the need for progress in this field led, in the first place, to bilateral collaboration between organisations collecting complementary information, enabling the published figures to provide a more comprehensive measure of external debt – for example, figures from the banking sector obtained by the BIS were pooled with those on official and officially-supported private export credits collected by the OECD. Other examples of productive collaboration took the form of patient behind-the-scenes efforts to improve the quality of the data. This was true of the work jointly undertaken by the World Bank and the OECD to compare detailed loan-by-loan information provided by debtors and creditors. Work of this kind was a step forward, but the process inevitably identified and drew attention to the questions raised by differences in definitions, approaches and compilation methods used by the organisations.

The four organisations whose work on debt statistics is described in this book and which have been the prime movers in the attempt to move towards a common approach are:

- The BIS, an organisation whose members include the world's major central banks, involved in debt statistics largely because of the monetary authorities' concern about the commercial banks' involvement in international lending and the stability of the international financial system;
- The IMF, an international monetary and financial organisation with worldwide membership covering both developed and developing countries, whose concern with debt stems in large part from its task of ensuring the effective operation of the international monetary system, but also from its role in providing financial support and advice to countries in balance-of-payments difficulties;
- The OECD, composed of the the main market-economy industrial countries, whose interest in debt arises from its activities in the field of international financial co-operation, especially with the developing countries;
- The World Bank, with a worldwide membership of both industrial and developing countries, which collects and uses debt statistics for operational and analytical purposes related to its function as the main international development institution supplying technical and financial assistance to developing countries.

These four are by no means the only institutions interested in debt statistics or involved in their collection. They are, however, the only international organisations actively involved in collecting and publishing comprehensive original-source data of this kind.

14

None of the four organisations is authorised to publish all the debt information collected. It is only after various aggregation processes have been carried out that the results can be made available to the public. It should not be inferred, therefore, from the fact that a particular type of information is collected by an organisation that this is information which can be freely made available by the organisation concerned.

The work of the Group set up by the four organisations covers a wide range of topics relating to the practical measurement of external debt and debt-related aggregates. Clearly, however, progress in many of these fields, especially those where the aim is to move closer towards a common approach by the different organisations, is only possible if there is at least minimum agreement on what constitutes debt itself.

This was one of the considerations providing the starting-point for the formulation of the core definition of debt. Before discussing this definition, it is useful to examine some of the more general considerations involved in the concept of external debt, and how this statistical aggregate relates to some of the major international reporting systems.

3. RELATING EXTERNAL DEBT TO OTHER STATISTICAL SYSTEMS

For accurate measurement of any economic variable it is necessary to have a clear concept of what is to be measured. The development of a concept implies establishing boundaries which include what is to be measured and exclude all else. One method of ensuring that this is done consistently is to construct a comprehensive framework which gives guidance with respect to the definition and classification of all related variables. Existing examples of such frameworks are: national accounts; flow of funds; and balance of payments.

Unlike national accounts and balance-of-payments concepts, external debt has never been defined in a manner which has been agreed by compilers and analysts. Furthermore, the different definitions employed by international organisations and other compilers and users of data indicate that no single concept is appropriate for all uses. This points to the need for an agreed benchmark for the concept of external debt. One criterion guiding the Group's work has been compatibility with existing well-structured systems.

The term "debt" implies a liability, represented by a financial instrument or other formal equivalent. The United Nations' System of National Accounts (SNA) defines financial assets and liabilities as:

- "the gold, currency, and other claims on (and obligations of) other parties owned by an economic agent; or the claims on (or obligations of) an economic agent owned by other parties."

With the exception of gold and, by convention, IMF special drawing rights (SDRs), a fundamental characteristic of financial instruments is the existence of a contractual creditor/debtor relationship, i.e., one agent's liability is another agent's asset. Analysis

15

of the economic impact of financial transactions is facilitated by reference to the characteristics of the different classes of financial instrument. The SNA has identified 12 categories of financial instrument, as listed in Figure 1.

Figure 1. **Financial instruments**

Financial Assets	Financial Liabilities
1. Gold and IMF SDRs	
2. Currency and transferable deposits	2. Currency and transferable deposits
3. Other deposits	3. Other deposits
4. Bills and bonds, short-term	4. Bills and bonds, short-term
5. Bonds, long-term	5. Bonds, long-term
6. Short-term loans, not elsewhere classified (nec)	6. Short-term loans (nec)
7. Long-term loans (nec)	7. Long-term loans (nec)
8. Trade credit and advances	8. Trade credit and advances
9. Net equity of households on life insurance, pension funds	9. Net equity of households on life insurance, pension funds
10. Other accounts receivable	10. Other accounts payable
11. Corporate equities	11. Corporate equities
12. Proprietors' net equity in enterprises	12. Proprietors' net equity in enterprises

As debt is a liability concept, the focus is on all instruments except gold and SDRs. The instruments vary widely in the nature of the liability involved, but instruments 2 to 8, unlike equity, involve a clear contractual obligation to pay a fixed or pre-determined variable amount of income and/or an amount of principal. These instruments may differ substantially in terms of maturity – ranging from demand deposits to perpetual bonds – and in negotiability, but all involve a contractual payment obligation which differs from that incurred by equity issuers. Instruments 9 and 10 may also include some items of a contractual nature, but cannot be included "en bloc" on the same footing as the earlier items. It is perhaps also worth noting, in connection with the future work outlined in Chapter III, how the pairing of instruments in Figure 1 may be used to measure net indebtedness.

There is no clear rule within the SNA framework for defining debt. The broadest view of debt would include all instruments that represent financial liabilities, irrespective of the type of payment or repayment involved. The heterogeneous nature of the various instruments, however, suggests a narrower grouping of them for inclusion in a limited debt concept.

Transactions in different instruments will have varying impacts on the economy. Grouping instruments according to their impact provides an analytical basis for subdividing the whole category, saying in effect that some liabilities are more "debt" than others. However, since all financial liabilities share some common characteristics, it is clear that no one grouping of instruments will serve all requirements of analysis and policy. The work of the Group, in focusing on the nature of the payment liability, has involved reviewing instruments to see how far they carry clear contractual obligations to pay, as these have a direct, unavoidable and measurable impact on the economy.

This work therefore draws on the SNA for a consistent treatment of all financial instruments used in an economy's transactions; to obtain the basis for measuring only external transactions, and thus for external debt, it draws on the IMF balance-of-payments (BOP) system. These two systems are consistent and interrelated[1]: balance-of-payments accounting provides criteria to distinguish foreign assets and liabilities from domestic for each major class of financial instrument defined by the SNA. External debt is a sub-set of foreign liabilities in both the SNA and BOP systems of accounts.

Balance-of-payments accounts are broadly divided between current-account operations, which cover goods, services, income and unrequited transfers, and capital-account operations, which comprise transactions in foreign assets and liabilities (Figure 2).

The balance-of-payments accounts identify foreign operations on the basis of residence of the transactor; foreign liabilities are therefore those owed to non-residents. Residence (as opposed to currency, ownership, nationality or another basis) was chosen as the criterion for distinguishing foreign from domestic because it provides a clear rule for identifying those transactors whose main economic interest lies within an economy. Further, the residence criterion defined in the IMF's Balance of Payments Manual is identical to that employed in the SNA.

Figure 2. **Balance of payments**

	Debit	Credit
Current Account		
Merchandise		
Other goods, services and income		
Private unrequited transfers		
Official unrequited transfers		
Capital Account		
Capital, excluding reserves		
Direct investment		
Portfolio investment		
Other capital		
Reserves		
Monetary gold		
Special drawing rights		
Reserve position in IMF		
Foreign exchange assets		
Other claims		
Use of Fund credit		

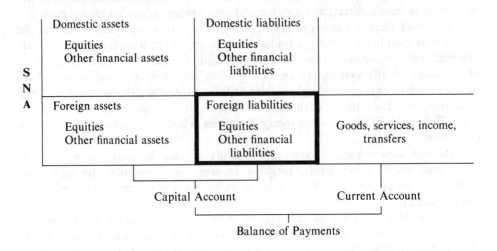

Figure 3. **Financial instruments in SNA and BOP**

Figure 3 illustrates the overlap of a national balance sheet, which records all financial assets and liabilities, and the balance-of-payments, which records all foreign transactions. The coverage of the capital account of the balance-of-payments coincides almost perfectly with the foreign sectoring of financial instruments in the SNA. The quadrant entitled "Foreign liabilities", of which the items in the core definition form a sub-set, covers all instruments which would fall under a broad concept of gross debt including equity-type liabilities.

NOTES AND REFERENCES

1. There are a few differences with respect to the treatment of financial leases and write-offs, but it is expected that these differences will be reconciled during the current revision of the SNA.

Chapter II

THE "CORE" DEFINITION OF EXTERNAL DEBT

1. THE PURPOSE OF THE "CORE" DEFINITION

The core definition represents an agreed view of the essential elements in the definition of external debt. Especially in the case of systems focusing on a particular sector, it provides criteria for the inclusion or exclusion of various types of financial instrument. It also provides a yardstick facilitating comparison of the practices of individual organisations.

At the same time, the core definition does not claim to be the unique definition of debt for all purposes. It may well have to be revised in due course in the light of further progress in statistical reporting, the evolution of financial markets or changes in the requirements of the users of the statistics. Nor is it applied in full detail by any of the four organisations, for reasons which will be clear from the chapters dealing with the individual reporting systems. However, its establishment has already led to changes in the practices of some of the organisations, sometimes in the composition of the actual debt totals recorded and sometimes in the presentation of data in such a way as to permit reconciliation of the totals with the core definition.

It also provides the starting-point for the considerable amount of work that remains to be done.

2. THE CORE DEFINITION AND ITS INTERPRETATION

2.1. Wording

The agreed core definition reads as follows:

– "Gross external debt is the amount, at any given time, of disbursed and outstanding contractual liabilities of residents of a country to non-residents to repay principal, with or without interest, or to pay interest, with or without principal."

19

This wording is one to which all the four organisations have agreed, but, like all compact definitions, it requires a certain degree of elaboration and commentary.

The first point to note is that it deals only with *gross debt*. There are good reasons for this choice: first, gross debt is the aggregate which is directly related to the problem of debt service, an essential element in the present situation; second, it is the obvious first step on the way to any more refined work on the aggregates involved. This concentration on gross debt is not intended to imply that "net" debt is not also a useful analytical concept[1], but it is one which involves an additional dimension of complexity in its definition, compilation and interpretation. The core definition has therefore been developed to deal with gross debt, leaving net debt to be tackled later.

The use of the term *contractual liabilities* is a crucial element in the definition, because it gives a precise criterion for deciding whether certain types of liability are included or not. It means, in the context of the definition, an obligation to make specified payments, including instances such as a financial obligation stemming from a court ruling, where there may be no contractual agreement. It excludes equity participations, which clearly do not meet this criterion.

The reference in the core definition to *principal and interest* implies rather narrower coverage than the broadest of the definitions suggested in Chapter I, namely, "all instruments that represent financial liabilities, irrespective of the type of payment or repayment involved". It still leaves certain "borderline cases", corresponding to items falling within categories 9 and 10 of Figure 1. These will be discussed in some detail in section 3.2. Some of them give rise to considerable difficulty.

The terms *principal* and *interest* make no distinction between payments in cash and in kind. The words *principal with or without interest* bring interest-free loans into the core definition, since these involve contractual repayment obligations; *interest with or without principal* does the same for loans of indefinite maturity, such as those involved in the recent expansion of "perpetual" bonds, since these have contractual interest payment obligations.

The words *disbursed and outstanding* draw an important distinction between that element of a loan which has been drawn down and is outstanding, which is included, and undisbursed amounts, which are excluded from the core definition even where a contractual agreement exists. While, for certain purposes, undisbursed loan balances are part of the contractual obligation and may be of considerable interest for evaluating a country's financial situation, they are a contingent – not an actual – repayment obligation on the borrower and therefore not part of the core definition. It is often useful to show aggregates that incorporate undisbursed loan amounts, but these should be carefully identified: for example, *Total debt, including undisbursed amounts*. *Disbursed and outstanding* also excludes arrangements such as frame agreements, under which specific loan contracts are to be concluded at some future date, until such time as any necessary further contracts have been concluded and the sums disbursed.

The fact that the definition makes no specific reference to the maturity of the debt is intended to convey that both short-term and long-term debt are included. For purposes of the core definition, "long-term" means over one year, "short-term" one year or less. This is the same treatment as in the BOP Manual, whereas in the SNA (1968) transactions of one year are counted as long-term. It should be noted that maturity may

20

be measured in terms of original maturity, extended maturity or residual maturity. However defined, a breakdown between the two is frequently provided in the published statistics (see Chapters IV to VII).

2.2. Interpretation of the Core Definition

Use of the core definition also involves a number of important questions of interpretation. These could only be explicitly built into the definition at the risk of overloading it, but they are nevertheless important for its application.

One essential point to note is that the definition should be taken in conjunction with the long-standing and authoritative body of definitions contained in the IMF Balance of Payments (BOP) Manual. Use of the BOP definitional system is of fundamental importance in deciding whether a contractual liability is external or domestic, in that existing BOP criteria clearly define the terms "resident" and "non-resident". It may be useful to quote in full the text defining the residence criterion in the Balance of Payments Manual (Fourth Edition)[2]:

"The residents of an economy comprise the general government, individuals, private nonprofit bodies serving individuals, and enterprises, all defined in terms of their relationship to the territory of that economy. Included with the territory of an economy are its territorial seas and those international waters beyond its territorial waters over which the economy has or claims to have exclusive jurisdiction; overseas territories and possessions may or may not be regarded as separate economies." (BOP Manual, paragraph 52).

The concept of residence for individuals is defined as follows:

"The concept of residence adopted for individuals is designed to encompass all persons who may be expected to consume goods and services, participate in production, or engage in other economic activities in the territory of an economy on other than a temporary basis. These are the persons whose general center of interest is considered to rest in a given economy." (BOP Manual, paragraph 59).

In the interpretation of the word "temporary", it has also been generally accepted that individuals living in a given economy for a year or more are residents of that economy.

The residence criterion has been chosen in preference to a number of other possibilities. One of these would have been to determine the external or domestic status of a transaction on the basis of the nationality of the transactors. A distinction based on nationality, however, would raise serious difficulties, particularly because of the large number of countries involved, either as host country or country of origin, in major migration movements. Furthermore, it would result in the classification of a transaction, say in London between an American-owned bank and a British bank, as a transaction to be registered as external by both the British and the American authorities. It would mean that, in many cases, the common-sense notion of an external transaction as being one between residents of different countries, i.e., one where a border is crossed, would not apply. The nationality criterion is nevertheless useful for specific purposes, for example in connection with the supervision of international banks or for monitoring the lending of different groups of banks to developing countries.

Another possible criterion would have been the currency of denomination of the debt instrument, domestic or foreign. This too, however, would have resulted in the recording of an external debt transaction, even though there had been no cross-border movement, in the case of foreign currency liabilities of one resident of a given economy to another. This approach also ignores the fact that the currency of denomination is of little significance in an external debt context where freely exchangeable currencies are involved, so that any service payment can easily be converted into any currency of the creditor's choice. In the case of countries with non-convertible currencies, however, or where there are foreign exchange regulations restricting the conversion from domestic to foreign currencies, the currency of denomination is relevant because of its importance for foreign exchange management.

Above all, the residence criterion – which is basic for macro-economic analysis – has the great advantage of being long-established in other statistical systems which overlap with debt measurement and with which it is desirable to preserve consistency. At the same time, it is a system which is familiar, in related contexts, to compilers and analysts.

The residence criterion means, under the core definition, that a contractual liability in foreign currency to a resident is not part of external debt, while a contractual liability in domestic currency to a non-resident is. Similarly, a contractual liability to a resident who is a non-national is not part of the external debt. There may be advantage, for analytical purposes, however, in treating these liabilities differently, for example in order to evaluate the status of the foreign exchange obligations of the economy concerned.

The residence criterion in a few cases gives results which might call for special treatment, or at least special presentation, in measuring external debt. The problems arise mainly in connection with   a) offshore banking units or centres, especially where the balances of these units or centres are large in relation to the host economy;   b) countries which sponsor "flag of convenience" or "brass plate" companies, but do not include these companies in their external sector;   c) countries' treatment of bank deposits by nationals living abroad (emigrants' deposits) in their measure of external debt;   d) countries' treatment of foreign currency deposits of residents; and   e) some accounts owned jointly by national and foreign donor governments, or to which both governments have access[3].

The problem of the offshore banking units or centres is both common to and important to the statistical systems of all the organisations discussed in this book, and is dealt with by them in the different ways described in the organisation chapters. In essence, the problem lies in the fact that the offshore banking units are not regarded in the same light by either all countries or all the systems used by the organisations. For example, some countries report them as non-resident, while others (and some systems) regard them as resident. One method of dealing with the problem is to ensure that the presentation of external debt for countries with offshore banking units identifies separately the liabilities of these units and usually shows simultaneously the corresponding asset position of the units. A similar problem arises for "flag of convenience" and "brass plate" companies, in that there is a conflict between the notion of the centre of economic interest, which for most of these nationals and "subsidiaries" would be the home country or the home country of the parent company, and the BOP twelve-month rule for residence. On this point the recommended treatment is that the positions of these categories of agent should be included in the core definition of debt. (See Appendix 1.)

As regards the countries where certain non-resident nationals (temporary emigrants, seamen, airline personnel) hold large deposits, it is recognised that these deposits will often not give rise to a subsequent outflow of foreign currency. Nevertheless, as long as the owner of the account is non-resident, such deposits clearly fall within the core definition of external debt.

3. THE RELATIONSHIP OF PARTICULAR TYPES OF CLAIM TO THE CORE DEFINITION

To avoid ambiguity, the Group has identified special types of liability which it considers as falling within the core definition and others which fall outside it.

As already stated in Chapter I, section 3, the financial instruments listed as items 2 to 8 in Figure 1 of that chapter are clearly to be regarded as external debt, even under a restrictive definition, whenever the liability they represent is to non-residents. It may be useful, before turning to certain special cases, to enumerate these items and to give a brief indication of their precise content.

Item 2: *Currency and transferable deposits*

Deposits payable on demand and holdings of notes and coin.

Item 3: *Other deposits*

Claims represented by evidence of deposit.

Item 4: *Bills and bonds, short-term*[4]

Bills and bonds of one year or less.

Item 5: *Bonds, long-term*

Bonds, debentures etc., the maturity of which is more than one year (including preferred shares, excepting participating preferred securities).

Item 6: *Short-term loans, not elsewhere classified (nec)*

All loans not classified elsewhere, the maturity of which is one year or less (including all loans repayable on demand). These include loans extended to business, government, households, etc. by banks, finance companies and others, including instalment loans, hire-purchase credit and loans to finance trade credit.

Item 7: *Long-term loans, (nec)*

All loans not classified elsewhere, the maturity of which is more than one year. The same examples as in item 6, with, in many cases, the important addition of mortgages.

Item 8: *Trade credit and advances*

Trade credit extended to enterprises, government and households; and advances for work which is in progress or to be undertaken.

3.1. Specific Inclusions

Certain specific types of instrument are not clearly identified in the listing of items 2 to 8, and their inclusion under the core definition requires comment.

The "Use of (International Monetary) Fund Credit" (UFC) is included in external debt, according to the core definition. UFC has not always been treated as debt, since it involves an exchange of domestic currencies against other currencies or SDRs[5]. However, the impact on a country of its UFC liabilities is similar to that of other external loans and the liabilities have the characteristics of the forms of external debt generally covered by the core definition. Some organisations have adopted the practice of showing a main total including use of fund credit and a narrower total excluding it[6].

Bridging loans, both bilateral and multilateral, are included in the core definition. In any maturity breakdown, they are classified as short-term debt, unless it is known that they have an actual maturity of over one year.

Loans repayable in the borrower's currency fall within the core definition, although presentational practices differ among the organisations. For example, the OECD has classified them in its statistics of resource flows to developing countries (the "DAC statistics") as "grant-like" flows whenever, as is the usual case, the donor country has expressed the intention in its original commitment not to repatriate the receipts but to hold them in the recipient economy. In its debt statistics, however, the OECD has decided to align itself on the core definition and include these amounts as external debt. In the World Bank's Debtor Reporting System, such flows are classified separately and are at present excluded from published debt statistics.

Arrears of principal and interest are included in the core definition. It is clear that arrears of principal remain part of external debt, just as payment on the due date would have reduced the debt. It is also clear that arrears of interest, when formally capitalised under an agreement to reorganise debt, should enter the data reported by debtor and creditor sources. The Group considered that there is no essential difference, for the purposes of compiling gross debt statistics, between formally capitalised arrears and interest arrears outstanding. Where known, both should be included in gross debt aggregates. This should be done by including all arrears of interest outstanding as an addition to the stock of short-term debt, as is the current BOP practice, until a change of status occurs as a result of their being paid off or rescheduled. (For the case where a creditor writes off or writes down a loan, see section 3.4.) In published figures, arrears

24

are included indistinguishably in short-term debt (currently in long-term debt in the World Bank's Debtor Reporting System in the case of arrears of principal on long-term debt).

As far as the recording of the reduction of arrears is concerned, a problem is caused by the multiplicity of accounting practices used to handle such cases. In debtor statements, arrears can be reduced through an actual payment or through refinancing, rescheduling, conversion or forgiveness. In creditor statements, they may also disappear from the record through write-off or specific provisioning. Actual payment clearly reduces the volume of outstanding debt; the question of reduction of arrears through various forms of debt reorganisation is more complex and is discussed in section 3.4.

Perpetual bonds and other securities (consols, etc.) which have no fixed repayment date are included in the definition by virtue of the specific reference to the contractual obligation to pay interest even without repaying principal.

3.1.1. *Inclusions Raising Special Definitional Problems*

A number of items clearly fall within the scope of the core definition but are themselves subject to differences as to possible definition and recording. They are therefore mentioned here in order to give a complete picture of the coverage of the core definition, but further work is needed, as mentioned in Chapter III, in order to improve compatibility between definitions and recording methods, both as between organisations and in the interests of consistency with other parts of the core definition coverage.

3.1.1.1. *Financial Leases*

In recent years, especially in the computer and aircraft sectors, it has become common practice for the users to lease equipment rather than purchase it outright. In many cases, under so-called "financial leasing", the transaction is for practical purposes analogous to a transfer of ownership with an associated contractual obligation to make regular payments, and so is a direct substitute for the contracting of a debt and requires to be included under the core definition. The difficulty resides in knowing exactly where to draw the line between financial leases, clearly directly comparable to debt transactions, and "operational" leases of a more conventional kind. This subject is dealt with in more detail in section 2.1.2.1 of Chapter III.

3.1.1.2. *Swap Arrangements*

The term "swap" is now used to describe a variety of financial arrangements that are very different in their relationship to debt, and hence in their relevance for debt statistics.

Official swaps between central banks are transactions which fall within the core definition of external debt. Technically, they are similar to the use of Fund credit. They involve an exchange of domestic currency for foreign currency, with an agreed future reversal of the transaction.

Currency and interest rate swaps involving transactions between debtors do not change the amount of debt, but alter the risk characteristic of their liabilities, enabling them to change the currency in which service payments have to be made or the basis on which interest is paid (usually from fixed-rate to floating-rate, or vice versa). Creditor-based debt statistics do not address these aspects, which may also be inadequately reported by debtors.

Asset swaps involving an exchange of claims between lenders alter the identity of the creditor, but do not otherwise affect debt statistics, unless one of the creditors is a resident of the debtor country.

In the case of the recent tendency on the part of certain developing countries to exchange debt against equity ("debt/equity swaps"), the result is clearly a reduction of debt under the terms of the core definition, although the amounts of cross-border liabilities, broadly defined, may not have changed.

Certain routine types of foreign exchange transaction are also called swaps, but the forward positions arising out of these transactions fall outside the scope of debt statistics and are not covered by the core definition.

3.1.2. Inclusions Raising Special Reporting Problems

In some cases, agreement on the inclusion of a type of liability in the core definition is accompanied by a recognition that serious practical reporting difficulties exist. Some of these, such as the reporting of arrears, have already been mentioned.

Another example is negotiable debt instruments. A bond denominated in domestic or foreign currency should clearly be recorded as external debt when the holder is a non-resident. The problem is the practical one of determining at all reliably the residence of the holder. The difficulty has been increased by the recent tendency for countries in a position to do so to buy back their own bonds originally issued on foreign capital markets. In the case of the bank-based reporting systems, however, and when the banks themselves are both the holders and the reporters, there can be a degree of certainty on this point.

It has been agreed in the Group that cross-border intra-company debt falls within the core definition, but this raises problems, especially as balance-of-payments statistics include this form of debt indistinguishably in direct investment. The adjustment on capital account raises no particular difficulty, providing the reporting is in sufficient detail, but there is no provision in the present system for the identification of the related interest payments in the balance-of-payments current account.

Another example is military debt. While there is no reason in principle to distinguish debt arising from military transactions from other debt, and it is therefore included in the core definition, there are often practical and political problems making it difficult to obtain the information.

Item 2, "currency and transferable deposits", clearly falls within the core definition, but whereas deposits are relatively easily captured by the normal reporting systems, this is not true of notes and coin held by non-residents.

3.2. Borderline Cases

The borderline cases, whose inclusion is subject to further consideration, are mainly those covered by items 9 and 10 of Figure 1, namely, "net equity of households on life insurance, pension funds" and "other accounts payable".

The first of these items, representing the reserves and other forms of saving held by insurance companies and pension funds in order to meet future risks, may be important when it comes to measuring "net debt". It is not at present to be regarded as substantial in the context of the indebtedness of developing countries.

The problem of the "accounts payable" is more difficult. These can indeed be in the nature of short-term contractual debt, since they include "accounts payable not included (elsewhere), for example, in respect of taxes, interest, dividends, rent, wages and salaries". But this is obviously a heterogeneous category, with the relevance to the core definition of external debt depending largely on the nature of the individual transaction, with little possibility of satisfactory generalisation, although a "broad" definition of debt would probably include them (meaning that external debt would be defined as items 2 to 8 plus items 9 and 10).

Other borderline cases involve types of claim which are not specifically covered in the SNA listing. These include, for example, barter credit and liabilities in the form of annuities.

3.3. Specific Exclusions

3.3.1. Equities

The most important general exclusions from the broad list of liabilities are the two forms of equity identified in Chapter I.

The SNA definition of corporate equities (item 11 in Figure 1) is "instruments and records acknowledging claims to the residual value, and residual income, of incorporated enterprises, after the claims of all creditors have been met". The definition goes on to state that "equity securities do not provide the right to a pre-determined income, or to a fixed sum on dissolution of the incorporated enterprise".

It is clear, therefore, that no contractual obligation of the kind specified in the core definition is involved.

The same is true of item 12, "Proprietors' net equity in enterprises".

3.3.2. Other Specific Exclusions

In a few cases where the core definition does not itself clearly indicate whether a category should be included or excluded, the Group has come down in favour of exclusion.

One such case is interest accruing but not yet due. Under standard accounting procedures, interest on most types of lending is subject to a continuous accrual process.

This is most evident in the case of bonds and other portfolio debt, where interest accrued since the previous interest date is normally calculated and included in the transaction price at the time of sale. By analogy, it might be considered that the accrued interest forms part of the value of the liability. However, interest is not contractually due until the actual date of payment, and for this reason is not included in accrued form in the core definition of debt. There is the additional point that its inclusion would distort the relationship between the stock of debt and future service payments.

For the same reasons, future interest not yet accrued is also excluded from the core definition.

Liabilities to the IMF arising from SDRs are the counterpart of foreign assets acquired when SDRs are issued, but the process by which SDRs are created resembles an unrequited transfer in that the holder acquires a financial asset without exchanging it for anything of economic value. In other words, the "liability" is contingent, and will have to be repaid only if the country withdraws from participation in the SDR account or if the SDR account is terminated. SDR liabilities are therefore excluded from the core definition. Although any use of SDR assets which brings a country's holdings below its cumulative allocation gives rise to an obligation to pay charges, this net use is not included in the external debt measure.

3.4. The Treatment of Debt Reorganisation

The increasing incidence of debt reorganisation in various forms in recent years has created new problems in the presentation of debt statistics. Many of these problems concern the timing and identification of financial flows – one of the principal subjects in the Group's future work – rather than the recording of the stock of debt, and are discussed more fully in Chapter III, section 2.5.

It is important in any discussion of the recording of debt to describe the way in which debt reorganisations affect debt statistics. Some arrangements have no impact on the outstanding amount of debt, but can affect the classification by creditor and debtor sector of the outstanding debt and certainly affect the timing of future debt service payments.

The techniques for implementing debt reorganisation are essentially three in number, each with several variants, and can be undertaken either to relieve a weak debtor or to enable a debtor to profit from changed financing possibilities. The three main techniques[7], more than one of which may be used in a particular case, are:

- *Rescheduling*, under which the debt contract is altered to rephase the schedule of interest and principal payments due to creditors;
- *Refinancing*, involving a new loan either *a)* to replace the original loan or loans or *b)* to cover some or all of the payments due on the original loan or loans;
- *Forgiveness*, in which a loan is extinguished, wholly or in part, by agreement between debtor and creditor.

In relation to the core definition, it will be seen that only debt forgiveness reduces the total amount of outstanding debt.

28

All these forms, other than debt forgiveness, may have a major effect on the sectoring of the debt, for example if the refinancing loan is made by an official agency to replace loans from the private sector. The maturity breakdown is clearly affected in a majority of cases.

There will also often be resectoring on the debtor side, especially where the reorganisation involves the assumption by the central bank or the government of debt previously owed by the private sector.

Apart from these forms of agreed debt reorganisation, there are certain unilateral actions which may affect the debt totals reported by either the creditor or debtor.

For example, a bank may undertake provisioning or write-offs of claims it regards as doubtful debts in the light of its own policies or supervisory requirements. This unilateral action does not affect the existence of the claims involved, but it can lead to asymmetry between creditor and debtor reporting systems, with the debtor continuing to report the whole liability, while the creditor reports only the residual value after provision or write-off. Provisioning may be undertaken either through the creation of a reserve on the liability side of the creditor's balance sheet or by deduction from the value of outstanding loans on the asset side. Adjustments on the asset side may lead to an understatement of actual claims on debtor countries. In reporting, it is desirable, in all cases where stated assets are reduced without a reduction in actual claims, that information be provided on the reductions in order to allow creditor data to be adjusted to show the full extent of the claims. This would avoid possible inconsistency between debtor- and creditor-based data – and continue to correspond to the core definition.

The equivalent unilateral action on the debtor side is repudiation, by which the debtor disclaims an obligation recorded by the creditor. Here too, unless special measures are taken, there will be asymmetry between the debtor reporting, which will no longer show the liability, and the creditor reporting, which will continue to record the obligation as a claim.

NOTES AND REFERENCES

1. Discussed in Chapter III, section 2.2.
2. This definition is also used in the SNA.
3. To avoid overburdening this section, the detailed arguments concerning the treatment of these problem cases are dealt with in a separate technical appendix (Appendix 1).
4. For a discussion of maturities, see the last paragraph of section 2.1 of this chapter.
5. The IMF Trust Fund was not classified as "Use of Fund Credit" because Trust Fund loans were direct loans financed by the sales of Fund gold in 1976-80, rather than a currency exchange from the Fund's ordinary resources. Repayments of these loans provided resources for loans under the new Structural Adjustment Facility, which, however, are classified in the Fund data as use of Fund credit. For a list of the main IMF facilities concerned, see Appendix 3.
6. For example, the OECD in its publication *Financing and External Debt of Developing Countries*.
7. It should be noted that the terminology of debt reorganisation differs, as do the methods of dealing with it, in the various reporting systems. The three terms are used here in a broad generic sense and the reader is referred to Chapters IV to VII for the definitions and methods applied by individual organisations.

Chapter III

OUTSTANDING ISSUES

1. GENERAL

While the establishment of the core definition of external debt and the improvement in the quality of published data represent substantial achievements, much remains to be done in refining concepts, achieving greater concordance among the reporting systems and improving the reliability of the data collected and published.

2. ISSUES REQUIRING FURTHER CONCEPTUAL WORK

2.1. Unresolved Core Definition Issues

As was pointed out in Chapter II, the core definition, like other statistical definitions, should not be regarded as having been fixed for all time. It may need clarification or occasional revision, taking into account: *a)* progress in reaching agreement on some of the still unresolved issues connected with it; *b)* improvements in reporting methods; and *c)* external circumstances, especially the emergence of new forms of debt and debt-related instruments.

The discussion in Chapter II of the application of the core definition referred to a number of unresolved issues. Some of these relate to items referred to in that chapter as "borderline cases"; others concern the precise definition and measurement of certain debt instruments which are accepted as falling within the general definition; a third set of issues relates to the new forms of debt instrument that are continually emerging.

2.1.1. The Borderline Cases

The Group will be taking up the "borderline cases", not only to try to identify particular sub-items of item 10 ("accounts payable") which should be included in the core definition, but also to decide on the appropriate treatment for item 9 ("Net equity of households on life insurance, pension funds") and for the other special items such as debt arising from barter trade and liabilities in the form of annuities.

31

2.1.2. Detailed Definition and Measurement Issues

2.1.2.1. Leasing

There is general agreement that leasing contracts do not, by definition, formally constitute debt transactions, since a lease does not create a liability to repay: the contractual payments (lease fees) are in the form of service payments, not interest and amortization. However, many leasing contracts are nevertheless directly comparable in their purposes and financial consequences to more conventional forms of debt instrument. There is general agreement among financial statisticians that at least in the extreme case of a lease arrangement which covers the full cost and carrying charges of the goods or equipment leased a change of ownership has effectively occurred. In these circumstances, the payments under the lease agreement take on the characteristics of debt service payments. Failure to take into account the economic and analytical similarity between the two types of transaction could lead to inconsistencies between countries and over time in the crucial question of the measurement of debt and debt service payments. On the other hand, too broad an interpretation of the debt content of leasing arrangements could have important practical consequences, notably for debt rescheduling negotiations.

The difficulty arises in deciding exactly how to distinguish between those leasing transactions which are analogous to debt transactions and those that are not. These two categories are usually referred to as financial (or finance) leases and operational (or operating) leases respectively.

One approach is to set a percentage threshold above which a lease is regarded as financial. In the Balance of Payments Manual, financial leases are defined, "as a rule of thumb", as arrangements where contractual payments exclusive of carrying charges cover at least 75 per cent of the cost of the goods (paragraph 217). In such cases the full equivalent of the market value of the goods (not the cumulative total of the expected lease payments) should be recorded as merchandise imports and the corresponding credit entry made in the capital account to record the credit extended to the nominal lessee [paragraph 363(c)] – implying the same balance-of-payments treatment as for a loan. The payments under the lease arrangement are recorded partly as interest payments and partly as amortization (paragraph 292). Payments under operational leases (i.e., where the 75 per cent figure is not reached) are recorded as service payments (paragraph 334).

Other organisations have considered that no lease covering less than the full value of the goods should be regarded as financial and therefore constituting a "full pay-out lease", but this seems to many analysts to be setting too high a threshold for practical purposes; the 75 per cent criterion avoids this pitfall, but is clearly arbitrary.

While it would be convenient to be able to define financial leases by reference to an arithmetic criterion of the kind applied by the IMF, it seems possible that other considerations will have to be taken into account. These include the existence of nominal purchase options, the intention of the parties to the agreement as to the ultimate ownership of the asset, the coverage of any guarantees granted in connection with the lease, etc.[1].

2.1.2.2. Debt Conversion

Two main forms of debt conversion are of direct relevance to the way in which debt is recorded: first, the exchange of a debt repayable in a foreign currency into local-currency debt; second, the recently-introduced practice on the part of some developing countries, especially those with relatively advanced economies and a high level of external debt, of encouraging the exchange of contractual debt liabilities against equity participation in local corporations[2].

In terms of the core definition, the first form is neutral as to external debt, if the new creditor is also a non-resident. Problems may arise, however, in identifying the residence of the new creditor.

The second form represents the substitution of equity investment, which lies outside the core definition, for debt falling within it. Whether this change in status is accurately reflected in the reported figures may, however, depend on the accounting and reporting practices both of the debtor and of the banks and financial institutions. The amounts involved in this form of swap are expected to increase over the next few years, and the implications for debt statistics will need to be kept under review.

2.1.2.3. Securitisation of International Lending

The "securitisation"[3] of international lending, as it affects the recording of debt, has three main aspects. First, it refers to the issue of securities by borrowers as a substitute for more direct forms of borrowing. Second, the term is also used in the narrower sense of the transformation of claims which are not easily marketable in their original form into forms which lend themselves more readily to financial trading techniques. Third, it is used to include the emergence of innovative financial instruments. The latter include various types of facility for the issuance of short-term or medium-term paper such as "note-issuance facilities" (NIFs), "revolving underwriting facilities" (RUFs), and standby credits and back-up facilities in general. All these aspects are readily accommodated in the core definition, the first two forms having no incidence on the existence of the debt, but merely its nature, while the third relates to external debt only to the extent that these facilities are actually drawn upon. However, these financial innovations may give rise to practical problems in reporting and compiling debt statistics. Even where strictly speaking undrawn amounts of standby credits and back-up facilities fall outside the core definition, it is important for debt analysis to have information on their amounts.

Securitisation in the sense of issuing securities rather than, for example, borrowing from international banks can add to the difficulty of ascertaining who is the ultimate lender, a problem already mentioned in earlier parts of this book, especially in connection with negotiable debt instruments.

Securitisation in the second sense could involve, for instance, the transformation of long-term loans from a single creditor to a single debtor into a multitude of smaller claims, changing hands at short notice. As in the first case, the problem for debt measurement is analogous to that of bonds, in that it becomes difficult and often impossible to identify the ultimate holder, who may even be the borrower himself if

33

market conditions make it attractive for him to buy in his own liability. It also has certain parallels with the problems raised by the swapping of debt.

Some of the new instruments covered by the third kind of securitisation have a different implication, namely that the instruments themselves are a contingent rather than an actual liability. In this respect, they are more analogous to the frame agreements mentioned in Chapter II as being excluded from the core definition. The main problem here is to obtain enough information to determine exactly when, in what form and to what extent the contingency becomes translated into actual borrowing.

One consequence of the spread of the new instruments, and of securitisation in general, has been to blur the traditional distinction between the international bank credit market and other sectors of the international capital market. This could distort the measurement of international banking flows, in at least three ways. First, some banking centres do not at present report all of their banks' holdings (or issues) of marketable instruments as part of the geographic analysis of their external positions, which results in an under-reporting of banking flows. Second, the sale of a marketable instrument by a bank to a non-bank results in a reduction in the bank's external claims, although no reduction has occurred in total debt (it will be recalled that the BIS derives all its statistics from the banks and that the IMF derives a considerable amount from the same source, while neither of the other two systems is especially geared to the recording of holdings of this type of asset by the non-bank sector). Third (with opposite effect), the development of these off-balance-sheet items has increased the extent to which banks may be called upon at certain moments to replace the original non-bank lenders, leading to a further reporting problem, in that international banking statistics might record an increase in banks' exposure to a country even though no additional debt had been incurred.

2.2. The Concept of Net Debt

The core definition is explicitly confined to gross debt, on the grounds that gross debt is an important concept in its own right, and is the essential first step towards the measurement of more complex aggregates in the debt field. One of these, referred to as "net debt", can be used to evaluate a country's external position or to assess the balance between its debt flow receipts and payments.

Many of the components needed for calculating "net debt" are overlooked in the existing reporting systems. The capital account of the IMF BOP records transactions in assets as well as liabilities, but without specifically indicating a total of "net debt", leaving the users to net out the figures they consider relevant for their own purposes; the OECD produces a figure, netting out estimated flight capital; in some of its series, the BIS quarterly reporting system covers both the banks' claims and liabilities vis-à-vis individual debtor countries and for certain purposes already nets out interbank positions within the reporting area and vis-à-vis non-reporting offshore banking centres.

The decision to focus on gross debt was strongly influenced by the consideration that it is far from clear exactly which assets should be used to offset the liabilities constituting gross external debt. For example, should these assets include all or part of the foreign exchange reserves, all or part of the bank assets, all or part of the non-bank

34

assets? Another difficulty is the fact that a single figure for "net debt" will in many cases mask important differences between the maturity structure, currency composition and risk features of the assets and the liabilities recorded. Moreover, allowance will have to be made for the role of some debtor countries as offshore banking centres, which means that the treatment will have to differ from country to country.

There is the further practical consideration that, while there is perfect symmetry in theory between claims and liabilities, this is not true of the reporting by the parties to a debt transaction, and still less of the reporting systems themselves, some of which are based largely on figures submitted by the creditors rather than the debtors.

It remains true that net debt is an important concept requiring further attention and needing to be taken up at an early stage.

2.3. Debt-Related Flows

Debt-related flows can conveniently be broken down into: a) flows leading to increases in the volume of gross debt, in other words, additional lending; b) flows leading to a decrease in the debt volume, e.g., repayments and debt conversions; and c) the interest paid on the debt. Repayments and interest together make up total debt service – the numerator in such indicators as the "debt service ratio".

2.3.1. Flows Affecting the Volume of Outstanding Debt

The problems involved in the recording of flows leading to changes in the volume of debt are more complex than would appear at first sight.

Some of these flows are themselves directly recorded (for example, in the OECD's statistics on financial flows to developing countries, in the OECD's Creditor Reporting System, the World Bank's Debtor Reporting System or the IMF's balance-of-payments reporting). This makes it possible to assess the consistency between the reporting of the actual flows and estimates based on differences in stocks. A key element in this process of reconciliation, and one in respect of which individual practices differ, is the choice of the exchange rate at which to value an individual stock or flow. This topic is discussed in more detail below.

A second major complication arises from the way debt reorganisations of different kinds are recorded. Here too practices vary considerably among organisations, as is also discussed below.

Another difficulty stems from the fact that short-term and long-term debt are not treated in the same manner in the various reporting systems. The reasons for this apparent inconsistency are essentially practical. Individual short-term debts can be contracted and liquidated within the period separating successive reporting dates for the stock of debt. This means that for short-term transactions any figure purporting to measure gross flows is difficult to interpret. For most purposes, therefore, the change in the amounts outstanding is normally used. By contrast, reporting of long-term transactions, especially those of an official or officially-guaranteed nature, is usually on the basis of gross flows, recording new disbursements and amortization payments separately.

2.3.2. Debt Service

The recording of debt service suffers from many of the same difficulties as that of debt-related capital flows, partly because amortization is common to both concepts. Here too, the short-term sector raises particular difficulties, with the added problem that interest payments are often indistinguishably included in a single figure for the amount due from the debtor.

2.4. Valuation Problems

The two main valuation problems relate to the valuation, especially the revaluation, of the assets and liabilities entering into the separate and aggregate balance sheets of the reporting entities, and the need to convert amounts originally expressed in different currencies into a single currency for the purpose of consolidation and comparison.

2.4.1. Valuation of Assets and Liabilities

This problem has already been mentioned in connection with the question of provisioning and write-offs affecting creditor balance sheets, but not the corresponding contractual obligations which are central to the core definition. Further asymmetries may arise with the development of markets for international debt liabilities at prices other than face value.

The organisations responsible for the reporting and compilation of debt statistics are attempting to provide the data necessary for reconciliation, but this is not as yet being done systematically, nor on a consistent basis.

2.4.2. The Currency Valuation Problem

The currency valuation problem takes on special importance at a time when the most widely-used currency of measurement is fluctuating strongly against the others, as in the case of the dollar in recent years. To give an idea of the importance of the problem, it has been estimated, on the basis of limited information concerning the currency composition of debt, that roughly half the large increase in the outstanding debt of the developing countries in 1985, as measured in US dollars, was due to the depreciation of the dollar against the other currencies, and that in 1986 an even larger share of the increase was due to this factor.

At one level, the problem raises familiar accounting difficulties concerning the relative valuation of stocks and flows when expressed in a common currency. If consistency between flow and stock figures is the aim, the choice is between recording both at exchange rates which are representative of the period of the flows but lead to end-period valuations which may differ from actual balance-sheet figures, and recording both at end-period rates which will usually be different from the actual value of the flows occurring during the period. A mix of the two approaches, which is often used in practice, leads to numerical inconsistencies between stock and flow figures.

The problem is analogous to the one involved in measuring assistance flows to developing countries. With total flows measured in US dollars, a change in the value of the dollar relative to other aid donor currencies alters the flow figure even when the amount of the individual currencies supplied has remained unchanged. A debtor's earning power in the currencies in which its external debt is denominated may also be unaffected by the changes in those currencies against the dollar, even though the dollar valuation of its debt may have changed considerably.

Practices at present vary somewhat among the organisations. The most frequent approach is to use end-period rates to calculate exchange-rate-adjusted changes in stocks and period-average rates to value flows, but there are technical differences as regards the length of the period or the computation of the average exchange rates for a period.

2.5. The Special Problem of Debt Reorganisation

The increasing incidence of debt reorganisations in recent years has created new problems in the presentation of debt statistics. In particular, there are problems related to timing and to the identification of actual financial flows. Present practices differ substantially, reflecting differences in the basic concerns and approaches underlying the individual reporting systems.

Timing problems arise from uncertainty about the implementation date of a rescheduling agreement and from differences in applying the agreement to service obligations falling due in different years. Such problems may lead to asymmetric reporting by debtors and creditors, and to the risk of double-counting.

One of the critical concerns of debt analysis, both for creditworthiness purposes and in support of economic policy evaluation, is to identify the level of financial flows available to a country. This information is typically derived from the pattern of past loan commitments and disbursements. The question of how the presentation of financial flow data in the case of debt reorganisations affects commitment and disbursement entries in published debt statistics is therefore of central importance.

It will be seen from Part II that there are divergencies between the organisations in their treatment of debt reorganisations. The Group is conscious of the further work required to improve consistency on this point.

3. IMPROVING CONCORDANCE OF DEBT REPORTING

The improvement of debt statistics requires greater consistency in the concepts, methods and presentation of those debt statistics already being collected and published. Debt measurement is not a hermetically closed subject and there are numerous intersections with statistical systems operating in other fields. Greater concordance with these other systems, in the view of the Group, is not simply a matter of conforming to the practices and definitions used elsewhere; these other systems should themselves take debt reporting considerations more into account. The fact that some of the Group's

37

member organisations, especially the IMF, play a major role in a number of these other systems should facilitate the task of achieving this type of convergence.

As far as concordance among the member organisations of the Group is concerned, the following issues remain outstanding.

First, there may be a need to modify the presentation of individual organisations' statistics so as to make it clear which data fall within the core definition and which do not, and which items falling outside the core definition are inextricably included in the recorded items. Group members are already making changes of this kind, but it is often necessary to move gradually in order not to upset and confuse regular users of the published data.

Second, members of the Group are in the process of identifying what additional information may be available, but not currently made public, that would bridge gaps between the existing presentations of debt (for example, separate reporting in the BOP of entries related to actual and imputed payments).

Third, a co-ordinated approach will be needed as regards the treatment of some of the unresolved problems mentioned earlier, especially those relating to the new forms of debt instrument.

Full agreement on definitions will remove a major cause of incomparability, but will not solve all the problems. Greater harmonization of estimation procedures used by the four organisations, already begun, will also help to reduce discrepancies. Nevertheless, differences in the data presented by the individual organisations will remain, if only because of differences in sources and collection methods. The establishment of the core definition is in itself a major step forward, but there is still more to be done.

NOTES AND REFERENCES

1. A starting-point for further discussion of this issue is provided by the considerable work done on accounting practices relating to leasing arrangements. In particular, the International Accounting Standards Committee in 1973 published International Accounting Standard 17, devoted entirely to leasing.

2. A third common form, but one which leaves the total debt and its currency distribution unaltered and which is therefore not relevant in this context, is the exchange of claims among banks.

3. For a comprehensive analysis of this and related questions, the reader is referred to the "Cross Report" ("Recent Innovations in International Banking", the report of a study group established by the central banks of the G-10 countries and chaired by Mr. Sam Y. Cross of the Federal Reserve Bank of New York, BIS, Basle, April 1986).

Part II

The chapters in this part of the book deal successively with the debt statistics of:

- The BIS (Chapter IV);
- The IMF (Chapter V);
- The OECD (Chapter VI);
- The World Bank (Chapter VII).

To facilitate comparison between the systems, the chapters are identically structured, to the extent possible. This means that readers will find the treatment of "undisbursed or contingent amounts", for example, in section 2.4.3 of each chapter.

Two synoptic tables, comparing various features of the different systems, will be found at the end of Part II. The summary nature of the information that can be contained in these tables means that they should be treated as a guide to, not a substitute for, the detailed description given in the organisation chapters themselves.

Chapter IV

THE BANK FOR INTERNATIONAL SETTLEMENTS' DEBT STATISTICS

1. ORIGINS OF DEBT STATISTICS ACTIVITIES AND METHODS USED

1.1. Membership and General Objectives

The Bank for International Settlements (BIS) is the world's oldest international financial institution, having been established in May 1930, following the Hague Conference in January of that year. The main role of the BIS is to promote co-operation among central banks. In this capacity it carries out four main functions: *a)* it acts as a "central banks' bank" in the sense that it holds and manages deposits from a large number of central banks throughout the world; *b)* it serves as a focal point for international monetary co-operation; *c)* it assists as Agent or Trustee in the execution of certain international financial agreements; and *d)* it carries out research and issues publications on monetary and economic subjects.

1.2. The BIS's Interest in Debt Statistics

1.2.1. Objectives Pursued

The BIS has been collecting statistical data on international banking since 1963. In general the prime objective of its reporting systems is to acquire information on international banking activities for its member central banks and the public in general. Obtaining information on individual countries' external indebtedness is, however, only one of the purposes served by collecting these data. They are also used, inter alia, to analyse the macro-implications of international banking flows, to monitor the international interbank market, to analyse the role of different national banking systems

41

in the international market, and to meet other interests of the central banks in the reporting countries in the workings of the international banking system. Moreover, to the extent that the BIS data do provide information on countries' external debt it is information on their external *banking* debt. For this reason, the figures, albeit timely, reliable and detailed, do not purport to provide a comprehensive picture of the total external debt of individual countries.

The BIS regularly publishes two creditor-based statistical series which contain information on countries' external debt: a quarterly series, information from which is also contained in the Bank's Annual Report; and a semi-annual series. The quarterly and semi-annual systems are similar in terms of collection methods, basic definitions and much of their general approach. Where they differ is in *a)* content, *b)* coverage and *c)* the degree of consolidation of the data obtained. The differences will be described in more detail later in this chapter, but it is important to note here that the quarterly system involves reporting by the banks in individual reporting countries on their unconsolidated business with non-residents, including the banks' own affiliates; in the semi-annual system, the reporting is partly on a worldwide consolidated balance-sheet basis, with claims and liabilities between different offices of the same bank being netted out, and partly on the same basis as in the quarterly reporting system.

Unless otherwise stated, the remainder of this chapter will refer to both reporting systems, but with special paragraphs under each heading, as necessary, describing those features which are specific to one or other of the systems.

1.2.2. *Use Made of Debt Information*

The information on countries' external banking debt contained in the statistics collected by the BIS is used by central banks to monitor the international debt situation, both collectively – for example, in its Euro-currency Standing Committee – and individually. Although some of the Bank's publications are in principle circulated only to banks and banking organisations, individual copies are usually freely available to other interested parties on request.

1.3. Collection Method

1.3.1. *Main Source*

The data for both the quarterly and the semi-annual reporting systems are obtained through regular reports from national monetary authorities on the activities of financial institutions (essentially deposit-taking banks) which carry out international banking business of any size. Most reporting countries provide data for all financial institutions that have foreign and domestic currency positions vis-à-vis non-residents exceeding a given minimum figure[1].

Some institutions specialising in the direct granting, or the refinancing, of export-related credits also report, while others (such as the United States Export-

Import Bank or the Banque Française du Commerce Extérieur) do not. Central banks located in reporting centres do not as a rule report to the BIS on their own international banking business, with two major exceptions[2]. In most countries contributing data to the quarterly reporting system the reporting banks account for well over 90 per cent, and in some cases for virtually 100 per cent, of the international assets and liabilities of financial institutions operating within their territories.

The quarterly system has a time-lag of three to four months between balance-sheet date and publication; the corresponding time-lag for the semi-annual system is five to six months.

Under the quarterly system, reports are received from authorities in eighteen industrialised countries and from six offshore banking centres (see Appendix 6); under the semi-annual system, data are provided by seventeen industrialised countries, although the consolidated nature of most of the figures means that the activities of a large number of banking offices outside the reporting area are also covered.

Under both systems, banks report directly to their national monetary authorities, usually the central bank, rather than to the BIS. The central banks then transmit the aggregated data, expressed in US dollars, to the BIS. The BIS then puts together the data received from individual reporting centres to arrive at totals for all reporting banks. While the main features and much of the detailed structure of each reporting system have been agreed between the BIS and the reporting monetary authorities, data provided by individual countries are to some extent less than fully consistent with one another owing to differences in national concepts and definitions. Nevertheless, opportunities for harmonizing different countries' data arise when domestic reporting systems are revised.

The quarterly system is based on the residence principle applied in balance-of-payments accounting. This means that only banking offices actually located within the reporting countries provide data, and they do so exclusively on their own (unconsolidated) business, including any positions vis-à-vis affiliates (branches, subsidiaries, joint ventures) located either in other reporting countries or outside the reporting area. To give an example, a German bank with its head office in Frankfurt would report, inter alia, on its own business and the business of all its affiliates in Germany with banks located elsewhere in the world, including business with its own overseas affiliates. Similarly, the Frankfurt branch of a New York bank would include positions vis-à-vis the US head office in its reporting.

The quarterly system provides data on cross-border positions in both local and foreign currency. In other words, it covers reporting banks' assets and liabilities vis-à-vis non-residents in any currency (including any unit of account such as the SDR or the ECU). However, it also includes statistics on reporting banks' assets and liabilities vis-à-vis residents in non-local currency.

The semi-annual system differs from the quarterly system in its content and coverage. The most important difference is that the semi-annual data are largely on a worldwide consolidated balance-sheet basis, which means that claims or credit lines between different offices of the same bank, wherever located, are netted out. As in the quarterly system, the compilation is based on reporting by financial institutions to national monetary authorities in the individual reporting countries. In contrast to the quarterly system, the data reported under the semi-annual system comprise only claims vis-à-vis countries outside the reporting area. The list of "vis-à-vis" countries therefore excludes the seventeen reporting countries and there are no data on liabilities. So far as reporting conventions are concerned, first, banks with head offices in the seventeen countries forming the principal reporting area provide worldwide consolidated data on their lending and undisbursed credit commitments to countries outside the reporting area. This also includes the local lending in foreign currency of affiliates located outside the reporting area. Second, banking offices in the reporting area whose head offices are located outside this area, or whose nationality cannot be identified, report on a territorial basis, as in the quarterly reporting system. These banking offices do not submit consolidated data but report their cross-border claims and undisbursed credit commitments vis-à-vis countries outside the reporting area (data which necessarily include any positions they may have vis-à-vis their own offices in outside-area countries).

Another feature of the semi-annual system is that, in general, the outside-area affiliates of banks with head offices in the reporting area also report their local assets and liabilities in local currency separately. The reason for including these data is that where the affiliates concerned have a local net asset position in local currency, it must be funded either from abroad or locally in foreign currency.

The same aggregation procedures are applied in the semi-annual as in the quarterly system.

1.3.2. Additional Sources

The data collected by the BIS focus on international bank activity. However, in order to provide a more comprehensive measure of an important part of external debt, the BIS co-operates with the OECD in aggregating the quarterly BIS figures on total bank claims with data on official or officially-guaranteed trade-related claims collected by the OECD. In many instances the resultant aggregates represent a very substantial proportion of the total indebtedness of individual countries and have the additional advantage of being reasonably timely.

The indebtedness figures so obtained are broken down into two sub-items: external bank claims and non-bank trade-related claims. External bank claims that are known to be trade-related credits benefiting from official insurance or guarantee are identified separately. No further breakdowns are provided. The data are pooled to eliminate double-counting and can be found in a semi-annual publication "Statistics on External Indebtedness: Bank and Trade-Related Non-Bank External Claims on Individual Borrowing Countries and Territories", issued jointly by the BIS and the OECD (see section on Publications at end of this chapter).

1.3.3. Confidentiality

All material other than that actually published remains confidential.

2. RELATIONSHIP TO THE CORE DEFINITION

2.1. General

The BIS contributed actively to the establishment of the core definition. As already indicated, however, its own statistical systems relate to banking and financial market activity and therefore do not seek to measure borrowing countries' total external debt. The relevance of the core definition for the BIS statistics is therefore not that of a checklist for filling in missing items.

It is also important to note that the BIS systems are exclusively concerned with stocks, which are however used to derive data on exchange-rate adjusted changes in stocks.

2.2. Core Items Excluded or Imperfectly Covered

As a minimum, on the liability side of the balance sheet, all reporting countries provide information on cross-border deposits and loans received by their banks from banks and non-banks abroad and, on the assets side (which is more relevant for analysing the gross external debt of developing countries), the external claims of their banks in the form of interbank deposits or credits extended to non-bank entities. Clearly, therefore, the main items falling within the core definition which are excluded from the BIS creditor reporting system are the cross-border claims of the non-bank sector.

As far as the statistical treatment of foreign-trade-related credits is concerned, almost all reporting countries include some information on this kind of credit on the claims side. Coverage varies considerably from country to country, however, depending both on the institutional arrangements under which the business is conducted and on the national classification rules used in determining whether a foreign-trade-related asset is treated as a claim on a resident or a non-resident (see 2.4.1 below). Unlike some of the other statistical systems dealt with in this report, the existence or absence of a guarantee has no effect in most cases on the statistical treatment of these claims; the same is true of the currency of denomination (local or foreign currency).

The reporting of foreign-trade-related credits in the BIS systems raises certain technical problems, which affect the coverage obtained. Fundamentally, there are two forms of foreign-trade-related credits: buyers' credits and suppliers' credits. A buyers' credit is one which a bank grants directly to a non-resident customer/importer. The reporting bank will as a rule classify such a credit as an external claim. A suppliers' credit, on the other hand, is a trade credit which a non-bank creditor, usually the exporter, originally grants to a non-resident importer. Such a credit may then find its way onto a bank's balance sheet. Depending on the practice followed by the reporting country concerned and on the way the bank acquired the suppliers' credit, statistical treatment would classify this credit either as a claim on the local exporter (not to be reported as an external claim) or as a claim on the non-resident importer (i.e., as an external claim). The obvious and most frequently used credit instrument in exporting is the trade bill. The decision whether such a bill should be considered as a local or external claim when acquired by a reporting bank depends essentially on whether it is classified according to the residence of the non-resident drawee/purchaser or that of the seller of the bill. Most reporting countries apply the first criterion (i.e., the residence of the non-resident drawee), while a small number of countries require banks to report suppliers' credits as an external claim only when they were acquired from a non-resident.

As far as international securities held by banks for their own account are concerned, a majority of reporting countries include as external assets short-term instruments, such as Treasury bills or certificates of deposit, and longer-term instruments in the form of notes, bonds, etc.

Items in course of collection and banks' holdings of foreign currency notes and coin are covered by about half the reporting countries.

Finally, since the information is mostly provided by banks on the basis of their own balance sheets, there may be some under-reporting of contractual debt, because of provisioning or write-offs, but practices vary from country to country.

2.3. Non-Core Items Collected or Published

About half the reporting countries also include banks' portfolio investments in foreign shares and equity participations, but do not identify them separately.

A small proportion of banks include holdings of gold bullion and banks' external business denominated in gold. Custody items are recorded only in exceptional cases.

2.4. Other Points Concerning the Relationship to the Core Definition

2.4.1. Residence

The quarterly system is constructed on a balance-of-payments or territorial basis. This means that only banks – both domestic and foreign-owned – located within reporting countries' boundaries (but not their foreign affiliates outside the reporting area) supply data. However, the tables containing figures on international activity by the nationality of the reporting banks, which are published from time to time as a separate feature in the quarterly reports, are constructed by aggregating the unconsolidated data in a different way, so that positions are shown according to the nationality of ownership of banking offices.

Under the semi-annual reporting system, banks with head offices in the reporting area report the international lending activities of all their offices at home and abroad on a worldwide consolidated basis, the positions between different offices of the same bank being netted out; banking offices in the reporting area whose head offices are located outside the area provide data on their claims on individual countries outside the reporting area on an unconsolidated basis only. In other words, the international lending of the head offices of these banks or of their outside-area affiliates is not covered by the statistics.

46

2.4.2. Maturity

Both short-term and long-term items are included, with a residual maturity breakdown available only in the semi-annual system.

2.4.3. Undisbursed or Contingent Amounts

The quarterly system excludes undisbursed commitments; the semi-annual system records reporting banks' legally binding credit commitments and credit guarantees arising from the underwriting of note issuance facilities and similar paper, but these commitments and guarantees are shown as a separate item, outside the debt totals.

2.4.4. Treatment of Certain Types of Instrument

2.4.4.1. Equity and Intra-Group Lending

As already mentioned, in the quarterly and semi-annual systems about half the reporting countries include the banks' portfolio investments in foreign shares and in most cases also participations.

2.4.4.2. Leasing

If the banks are themselves directly involved in a leasing transaction this will in general be included in the reported claims. In practice, however, many banks are engaged in such transactions through special subsidiaries, in which case, inclusion will also depend on institutional coverage, or on how the subsidiary is treated for banking consolidation purposes. The BIS itself has given no special instructions concerning the treatment of leases.

2.4.4.3. Loans Repayable in Local Currency

The reporting systems cover cross-border claims denominated in any currency and therefore include loans repayable in both local and foreign currency.

3. OTHER QUESTIONS REGARDING CONTENT

3.1. Methods of Currency Conversion

The data are reported in US dollars. The principle used for currency conversion is that non-dollar data are converted into US dollars at the rate ruling on the reference date, which for BIS statistics is the end of the quarter or half-year concerned.

The conversion is carried out either by the banks themselves or by the national monetary authorities. In countries where the banks report all their international business in dollar terms, they usually do so by first converting non-dollar positions at the exchange rates prevailing on the reference date for reporting. There are, however, some exceptions to this general practice, for example where there are options concerning the rate to be used or where officially designated exchange rates exist. In those countries where banks report all their international business in domestic currency, they do so by first applying closing middle market rates which the monetary authorities supply to them for each reference date. The monetary authorities in turn use closing middle market rates to convert the data thus received into US dollars. Finally, in those countries where banks report their international business in the individual currencies in which such assets and liabilities are actually denominated, the monetary authorities usually convert non-dollar data into US dollars at end-period exchange rates.

3.2. Treatment of Arrears

As in the core definition, arrears of principal are included by virtually all reporting centres in the data communicated to the BIS. In practice, the full amount of overdue loans continues to be shown as a claim on the borrower, at least until such time as the loan in question is repaid or partially or totally written off. It should be noted, moreover, that a number of the central banks collecting the banking data have no detailed information on the actual amount of "bad" loans which are not reported because they have been written off completely or which are reported net of specific provisions for expected losses. The time which must pass before a loan, or other asset, is formally considered overdue also differs from country to country.

The majority of countries include arrears of interest in the reported data.

3.3. Treatment of Debt Reorganisation

As in the case of the treatment of arrears the treatment of debt reorganisation depends on the accounting and provisioning practices of the individual banks and the subsequent reporting of the results. The BIS does not impose a particular approach. In practice, some banks in some countries report claims net of provisions, while most of the others record claims gross until they are officially written down or written off.

4. SECTORING

(As one major difference between the quarterly and semi-annual systems lies in the breakdowns they provide, this section of the chapter is in two parts, dealing first with the quarterly system and then with the semi-annual system.)

48

The Quarterly System (Q)

The quarterly reporting system provides for three overlapping breakdowns of the banks' external positions: a geographical breakdown, a currency breakdown and a sectoral breakdown between positions vis-à-vis non-banks and vis-à-vis banks. The currency breakdown and the bank/non-bank breakdown also extend to the reporting banks' foreign currency positions vis-à-vis residents. In addition, separate information in the form of an "of which" item, but without geographical breakdown, is provided on total positions vis-à-vis official monetary institutions.

4.1.(Q) Country Coverage

A full, or almost full, country-by-country breakdown of external assets and liabilities is supplied by all reporting countries except the United States. For banks in the United States the geographical breakdown is not complete: positions vis-à-vis most OPEC member countries and also a considerable number of the smaller developing countries are reported under residuals for the various geographical groupings.

4.2.(Q) Types of Debtor/Creditor

Statistics on reporting banks' external positions vis-à-vis non-banks are available, on a full country-by-country basis, from the eighteen industrialised reporting countries (again with the limitations concerning the incomplete geographical breakdown for data from the United States). The sectoral breakdown provided by three of the six offshore centres is incomplete.

Data on interbank claims are obtained as a residual by subtracting the positions vis-à-vis non-banks from the total. In some cases this approach may lead to distortions if a reporting centre's total assets include such items as securities and participations for which a sectoral breakdown may not be feasible. This means that the corresponding amounts to be allocated to "non-banks" are not known and not included in the non-bank figure. Consequently, the residual items obtained through the subtraction of the non-bank figures may somewhat overstate the share of the interbank market proper.

Moreover, difficulties may arise at the individual bank level in correctly identifying claims on non-banks where the exact nature of the foreign counterparties is not known.

Banks' asset and liability positions vis-à-vis foreign official monetary institutions are indistinguishably included in the totals for the vis-à-vis countries in question by all industrial reporting countries.

4.3.(Q)   Types of Claim

Given that the quarterly system provides considerable and simultaneous detail on the bank/non-bank, currency and country-by-country breakdowns of claims, no disaggregation by type of instrument is provided.

4.4.(Q)   Currency Breakdown

In the quarterly system, the reporting banks' external assets and liabilities are broken down into positions in domestic (i.e., local) currency, in all foreign currencies taken together and in ECUs. For total external positions, this breakdown is given for banks in all industrial reporting countries. With the exception of the United States, banks in the industrial reporting countries also provide a breakdown of their external foreign currency positions into major individual currencies and ECUs. The BIS uses more detailed information on the geographical allocation of positions in different currencies to calculate exchange-rate-adjusted changes in stocks (see section 5.1. below).

4.5.(Q)   Maturity Breakdown

Unlike the semi-annual system, the quarterly system provides no maturity breakdown.

The Semi-Annual System (SA)

The semi-annual system is in some respects less comprehensive than the quarterly system, insofar as it focuses only on the international asset positions of banks in the seventeen reporting countries[3]; moreover, it provides no currency breakdown. On the other hand, the analytical conception of the semi-annual system is in some respects more complex and more detailed, providing, for instance, two separate breakdowns of asset positions vis-à-vis each borrowing country – a maturity breakdown and a sectoral one.

4.1.(SA)   Country Coverage

The semi-annual system is a mixed scheme containing certain elements of a more limited territorial reporting system along with the features of a worldwide consolidated reporting of banks' business. To speak in this context of a geographically defined "reporting area" is therefore not quite correct. If the BIS nonetheless uses this term, it is largely for reasons of convenience, in order to indicate which countries participate in the system and submit data. However, worldwide consolidated balance-sheet reporting means that the activities of a great number of banking offices located outside the reporting area are also covered.

In contrast to the quarterly system, the data in the semi-annual system relate exclusively to positions vis-à-vis countries outside the principal reporting area. For this reason, the list of "vis-à-vis" countries does not include the seventeen reporting countries.

Full details of claims on individual countries outside the reporting area are provided for all the breakdowns. Instances of countries providing an incomplete geographical breakdown are negligible.

4.2.(SA)   Types of Debtor/Creditor

The individual items in this breakdown are: *i)* claims on banks; *ii)* claims on the public sector; and *iii)* claims on the non-bank private sector of borrowing countries. There is a separate unallocated item for claims which either cannot be assigned to a particular sector or are reported by countries not yet providing a sectoral breakdown (Denmark, Finland, Luxembourg and Sweden). The definitions used by individual reporting countries for this sectoral breakdown are not uniform.

4.3.(SA)   Types of Claim

There is no breakdown by type of instrument but undisbursed credit commitments are reported separately.

4.4.(SA)   Currency Breakdown

There is no currency breakdown of external claims in the semi-annual system.

4.5.(SA)   Maturity Breakdown

The maturity breakdown of banks' claims under the semi-annual system is on the basis of residual maturities. Three maturity bands are shown: up to and including one year, over one year up to and including two years, and over two years. There is also a separate entry for unclassified claims. In the case of roll-over credits the residual maturity is as a rule calculated on the basis of the latest date on which repayment is due to be made by the borrower.

With minor exceptions, all reporting countries provide a full maturity breakdown.

51

5. SPECIAL FEATURES

5.1. Data for Calculating "Net Debt" and Flows

A feature of the BIS quarterly reporting system is that the treatment of assets and liabilities is virtually symmetrical and on a gross basis. Material for the calculation of net debt is therefore available.

The BIS does not collect *flow* data, but in the quarterly system estimates are made of exchange-rate-adjusted changes in stocks. This is because movements of the US dollar against the other currencies mean that differences between BIS quarterly stock data for different reference dates will contain two distinct elements: changes in positions resulting from actual movements of funds and valuation changes resulting from exchange rate changes. In the semi-annual system, estimates of exchange-rate-adjusted changes are made only for total claims on particular countries and groups of countries.

In the quarterly system, most reporting countries supply reasonably complete currency breakdowns of their banks' positions, and this enables the BIS to calculate exchange-rate-adjusted changes in stocks at constant (end-of-quarter) exchange rates. These country-by-country estimates of capital flows net of valuation effects were first published for the first quarter of 1984.

5.2. Data on Debt Service

The BIS systems, being based exclusively on stock data, contain no information on debt service.

5.3. Debt Service Projections

No debt service projections are collected or published.

NOTES AND REFERENCES

1. In the semi-annual system the cut-off points below which banks in some reporting countries are not required to report data are higher than in the quarterly system, meaning that fewer institutions report.

2. United Kingdom reporting includes the Banking Department of the Bank of England; United States reporting includes the Federal Reserve Bank of New York, which is in charge of the international operations carried out by the Federal Reserve System.

3. See Appendix 6. When Norway joins the system, as is planned, the semi-annual reporting system will cover all those industrial countries which report under the quarterly system.

PUBLICATIONS

A. Regular Publications Containing Debt Statistics

   1. International Banking and Financial Market Developments

      – Frequency, date of publication: quarterly

      Obtainable from:

      – Monetary and Economic Department
         Bank for International Settlements
         CH 4002 Basle

End-of-period stock data shown for the most recent quarters and years; exchange-rate-adjusted changes in stocks shown for the latest nine quarters.

   2. Maturity Distribution of International Bank Lending

      – Frequency, date of publication: half-yearly

      Obtainable from:

      – Monetary and Economic Department
         Bank for International Settlements
         CH 4002 Basle

Data shown for latest reporting date (and for earlier periods when data are revised).

   3. Statistics on External Indebtedness: Bank and Trade-Related Non-Bank External Claims on Individual Borrowing Countries and Territories

      – Frequency, date of publication: half-yearly

      Obtainable from:

      – Monetary and Economic Department
         Bank for International Settlements
         CH 4002 Basle

and   – OECD (see Chapter VI, section on publications) also on diskette

Data shown for latest three end-half-years.

B. Other Publications containing Debt Statistics

4. The Nationality Structure of the International Banking Market

- Frequency, date of publication: now usually published as a special feature of the BIS quarterly reports (see publication A.1)

Obtainable from:

- Monetary and Economic Department
  Bank for International Settlements
  CH 4002 Basle

Data shown for two preceding years.

5. International Banking Statistics, 1973-1983

- Date of publication: April 1984

Obtainable from:

- Monetary and Economic Department
  Bank for International Settlements
  CH 4002 Basle

Ten-year series.

BANK FOR INTERNATIONAL SETTLEMENTS
MONETARY AND ECONOMIC DEPARTMENT
BASLE

SEMI-ANNUAL INTERNATIONAL BANKING STATISTICS
POSITIONS OF ALL REPORTING BANKS ON COUNTRIES
OUTSIDE THE REPORTING AREA
(IN MILLIONS OF US DOLLARS)
GRAND TOTAL
END-JUNE 1987

POSITIONS VIS-A-VIS	TOTAL (1)	CROSS-BORDER CLAIMS IN ALL CURRENCIES AND LOCAL CLAIMS IN NON-LOCAL CURRENCIES										LOCAL CURR POSITIONS OF REPORTING BANKS' FOREIGN AFFILIATES WITH LOCAL RESIDENTS		MEMORANDUM ITEM FROM BIS QUARTERLY REPORTING-SYSTEM
		DISTRIBUTION BY MATURITY				DISTRIBUTION BY SECTORS				BANKS WITH HEAD OFFICES OUTSIDE THE COUNTRY (10)	UNDISBURSED CREDIT COMMITMENTS (11)	LOCAL CURRENCY CLAIMS ON LOCAL RESIDENTS (12)	LOCAL CURRENCY LIABILITIES TO LOCAL RESIDENTS (13)	CROSS-BORDER LIABILITIES OF QUARTERLY REPORTING BANKS (14)
		UP TO AND INCLUDING ONE YEAR (2)	OVER ONE YEAR UP TO TWO YEARS (3)	OVER TWO YEARS (4)	UNALLOCATED (5)	BANKS (6)	PUBLIC SECTOR (7)	NON-BANK PRIVATE SECTOR (8)	UNALLOCATED (9)					
DEVELOPED COUNTRIES OUTSIDE THE REPORTING AREA														
ANDORRA	201	189		11	1	143		57	1	23	4			2,403
CYPRUS	1,331	608	144	557	22	138	243	881	69	30	76	2	55	1,815
GIBRALTAR	150	104	6	29	11	37	49	70	24	20	18	26		685
GREECE	14,539	4,677	1,369	7,662	831	3,272	5,608	5,036	623	239	1,240	812	746	7,195
ICELAND	1,514	512	176	884	64	320	705	324	165	8	323	8	25	334
LIECHTENSTEIN	2,001	1,664	8	146	5	42		1,876	83		107			4,554
MALTA	94	75		8	5	25	18	45	6		46			1,233
MONACO	481	330	18	129	25	293		170	18	197	14	39	51	2,089
NORWAY	20,407	11,989	848	6,119	1,451	8,876	1,445	5,858	4,228	242	3,943	195	139	8,107
PORTUGAL	10,386	3,156	902	5,981	337	1,476	5,069	3,458	383	99	1,322	700	474	6,166
TURKEY	9,134	4,808	885	2,832	609	2,742	4,760	1,991	271	90	2,357	140	111	3,445
VATICAN	10	10							6					122
YUGOSLAVIA	9,587	2,993	1,070	5,472	52	4,125	3,760	1,295	407	82	496		6	1,530
AUSTRALIA	36,488	17,125	1,935	14,857	2,561	11,645	5,899	18,315	629	2,442	15,381	20,914	14,481	10,048
NEW ZEALAND	12,758	3,900	1,157	6,737	964	1,738	5,900	4,740	380	222	1,937	3,087	3,638	3,359
SOUTH AFRICA	15,863	10,717	1,320	3,533	283	7,130	3,202	5,188	343	172	1,569	197	758	3,035
RESIDUAL	53				53				53		27	744		1,660
TOTAL	134,967	62,857	9,860	54,947	7,293	42,003	34,918	50,388	7,648	3,845	31,110	26,864	20,485	58,446
EASTERN EUROPE														
ALBANIA	13	6		4	3	11	2							29
BULGARIA	4,661	1,894	607	2,072	78	2,651	1,772		228	19	966	8		1,591
CZECHOSLOVAKIA	3,648	2,161	364	1,087	36	1,756	1,513		379	17	792			1,270
GERMAN DEM.REP.	12,988	4,932	1,820	6,064	172	7,126	5,233		629	16	1,931	32		7,907
HUNGARY	11,073	3,494	694	6,423	462	5,063	5,428		582	34	1,523	199	155	1,931
POLAND	10,866		1,575	6,270	141				532	122	212	10		1,662
ROMANIA	2,468			1,076					148					2,257
SOVIET UNION	29,076	11,879	2,434	14,247	516	14,312	13,153		1,611	116	2,738	56	28	12,656
RESIDUAL	255				255				255	15	93			84
TOTAL	75,048	27,993	7,929	37,441	1,685	38,360	32,324		4,364	355	8,575	307	183	28,401
OPEC COUNTRIES OF WHICH:														
A) MIDDLE EAST														
IRAN	991	886	33	50	22	455	213	268	55	4	149			5,340
IRAQ	7,714	4,686	1,193	1,702	133	3,117	2,692	1,748	157	72	964	7		1,586
KUWAIT	5,791	5,542	47	125	77	4,525	158	1,069	39	221	345	7	48	14,586
LIBYA	509	488				384		113	12		83			6,479
OMAN	1,366	387	139	800	40	138	923	163	43	18	463	181	177	2,491
QATAR	555	464	9	49	33	267	62	203	43	38	196	515	445	1,379
SAUDI ARABIA	5,371	4,394	112	750	115	1,755	62	3,103	451	15	1,829	1,891	1,715	49,437
UNITED ARAB EMIRATES	4,025	3,225	112	573	115	1,807	401	899	918	235	740	5	20	25,560
RESIDUAL	1,035	960		11	62	923	2	48	62	572	183			14,752
SUB-TOTAL	27,357	21,032	1,647	4,060	618	13,371	4,496	7,711	1,779	1,150	4,952	2,600	2,405	123,410
B) OTHER														
ALGERIA	13,128	3,505	2,059	7,286	278	3,469	3,930	5,575	154	4	2,007	53	803	1,869
BRUNEI	61	51	9			44	5	8	4		26	26	8	648
ECUADOR	5,146	1,896	447	2,749	54	936	3,792	371	47	20	648	110	102	2,126
GABON	1,230	414	185	631		40	360	836	4		101	138	60	245
INDONESIA	16,832	6,602	1,561	8,631	238	1,424	8,574	6,770	73	163	754	565	406	5,304
NIGERIA	10,082	5,436		4,455	134	1,609	4,574	3,544	355	228	693	82		2,931
TRINIDAD/TOBAGO	985	253	97	581	54	35	725	218	7	76	117	143	56	1,531
VENEZUELA	25,644	7,760	1,199	16,139	535	3,618	15,525	6,383	107	48	1,620	351	386	16,615
RESIDUAL	33				44				44		12			1,189
SUB-TOTAL	73,141	25,917	7,003	38,878	1,343	11,175	37,171	23,996	799	575	8,874	1,577	1,403	31,510
TOTAL	100,498	46,949	8,650	42,938	1,961	24,546	41,667	31,707	2,578	1,725	13,826	4,177	3,808	154,920

Source: *Maturity Distribution of International Lending.*

TABLE 4 a
EXTERNAL POSITIONS OF ALL REPORTING BANKS VIS-A-VIS INDIVIDUAL COUNTRIES [1]
(in millions of US dollars)
vis-a-vis all sectors

VIS-A-VIS COUNTRIES	Amounts outstanding							
	1985 Dec.	1986 March	1986 June	1986 Sept.	1986 Dec.I	1986 Dec.II	1987 March.	1987 June
Reporting area: European countries	Assets							
Austria.........U	24,292	24,229	27,111	30,292	33,628	33,628	35,404	35,572
Belg-Luxembourg.U	129,226	136,522	142,378	156,042	169,315	169,315	177,676	184,174
(of w.in B.fr.)..	5,672	5,862	6,782	7,442	7,813	7,813	9,006	9,564
Denmark.........U	28,326	30,186	32,653	33,783	34,150	34,150	35,670	37,720
Finland.........U	13,083	13,601	13,869	14,968	14,783	14,783	16,226	17,528
France..........U	114,955	115,719	121,313	127,985	136,012	136,012	140,833	146,975
(of w.in Fr.fr.).	3,227	3,159	4,760	4,176	5,322	5,322	6,910	7,874
Germany, Fed.R..U	88,797	97,341	97,384	106,115	106,595	106,595	117,179	117,257
(of w.in DM).....	57,729	64,248	64,495	69,079	70,991	70,991	81,640	81,350
Ireland..........U	10,461	12,043	13,056	13,356	13,899	13,899	14,726	15,547
Italy...........U	76,339	73,920	80,430	79,123	94,795	94,795	98,640	100,257
(of w.in Lit.)...	1,824	2,212	4,280	4,107	6,591	6,591	8,726	8,075
Netherlands.....U	35,438	37,592	41,888	46,487	52,266	52,266	56,571	60,519
(of w.in Fl.)...	4,324	4,695	5,687	6,637	7,611	7,611	8,135	8,475
Norway..........U	14,031	14,133	15,633	16,484	16,813	16,813	17,500	19,188
Spain...........U	21,991	22,494	21,572	22,139	21,269	21,269	22,102	23,454
Sweden.........U	20,769	21,472	21,694	23,242	23,703	23,703	26,570	28,063
Switzerland.....U	43,900	44,580	47,523	50,984	60,320	60,320	62,829	62,215
(of w.in Sw.fr.).	9,622	8,378	10,442	12,060	13,313	13,313	14,487	15,214
United Kingdom..U	288,860	296,911	311,647	356,355	371,728	371,728	380,492	397,828
(of w.in £)......	16,021	17,753	19,289	19,223	22,673	22,673	25,745	26,109
Sub-total......	910,488	940,743	988,151	1077,355	1149,276	1149,276	1202,418	1246,297
Other industrial countries								
Canada.........U	46,901	50,602	53,313	53,912	55,602	55,602	57,872	56,123
Japan..........U	167,935	191,438	210,711	262,963	332,272	332,272	377,233	431,397
(of w.in Yen)...	27,039	25,243	30,370	41,010	46,169	46,169	59,694	67,661
United States....	359,390	378,481	392,715	429,611	466,297	466,297	474,175	501,061
(of w.in Dollar).	329,494	340,851	349,876	380,352	415,500	415,500	413,445	438,521
Sub-total......	574,226	620,521	656,739	746,486	854,171	854,171	909,280	988,581
Other reporting countries								
Bahamas.........U	93,658	93,346	96,986	102,959	102,366	102,366	96,921	99,292
Bahrain.........U	13,449	12,555	12,094	12,443	12,716	12,716	11,373	12,771
Cayman Islands.?U	81,146	80,329	90,313	96,994	107,367	107,367	107,089	110,028
Hong Kong.......U	77,857	81,803	88,590	105,595	120,001	120,001	142,854	157,038
Neth.Antilles...U	11,042	10,023	10,851	10,543	10,914	10,914	11,388	11,505
Singapore.......U	71,971	75,060	82,872	94,267	103,339	103,339	109,583	118,066
Sub-total......	349,123	353,116	381,706	422,801	456,703	456,703	479,208	508,700
Total report.area.	1833,837	1914,380	2026,596	2246,642	2460,150	2460,150	2590,906	2743,578
Reporting area: European countries	Liabilities							
Austria.........U	16,384	18,305	19,620	22,307	24,695	24,688	26,931	27,873
Belg-Luxembourg.U	112,509	120,653	125,841	142,048	156,024	156,024	167,631	175,576
(of w.in B.fr.)..	5,616	6,439	6,675	7,186	8,082	8,082	8,970	9,049
Denmark.........U	13,091	12,630	13,385	13,758	13,788	13,788	15,383	16,727
Finland.........U	4,713	4,545	4,400	5,029	5,488	5,488	5,746	6,828
France..........U	89,194	90,776	91,096	94,706	107,590	107,580	114,799	126,690
(of w.in Fr.fr.).	2,181	3,197	3,236	3,063	4,008	4,008	6,871	7,295
Germany, Fed.R..U	73,209	89,899	100,569	121,067	141,522	140,878	161,279	172,833
(of w.in DM).....	41,726	55,048	63,819	77,744	94,730	94,550	110,726	116,181
Ireland..........	4,344	4,542	5,068	5,626	5,996	5,996	5,849	6,210
Italy...........U	51,531	44,892	48,342	48,504	60,510	60,478	59,582	60,729
(of w.in Lit.)...	541	791	877	1,110	1,173	1,173	1,691	1,641
Netherlands.....U	59,553	64,373	69,223	71,166	74,729	74,728	80,187	84,449
(of w.in Fl.)...	6,849	7,098	7,867	7,631	8,610	8,610	9,165	8,950
Norway..........U	7,370	7,262	7,185	6,643	6,906	6,906	7,062	8,107
Spain...........U	22,132	22,850	23,750	27,420	27,292	27,292	29,062	32,818
Sweden.........U	5,724	6,908	6,783	7,970	7,070	7,070	9,254	11,429
Switzerland.....U	220,447	223,344	233,312	246,247	254,782	253,922	273,771	279,530
(of w.in Sw.fr.).	33,269	37,474	40,585	48,647	50,456	50,424	57,416	56,702
United Kingdom..U	350,721	366,226	391,166	432,262	452,896	452,721	475,759	503,284
(of w.in £)......	14,810	16,259	18,368	20,353	23,257	23,256	28,146	28,737
Sub-total......	1030,922	1077,205	1139,740	1244,753	1339,288	1337,559	1432,295	1513,083
Other industrial countries								
Canada.........U	37,901	44,401	45,505	47,533	47,802	47,802	48,945	46,363
Japan..........U	94,311	109,820	114,788	149,391	193,576	193,545	231,200	251,442
(of w.in Yen)...	12,963	18,941	25,693	37,117	37,428	37,397	47,081	51,340
United States....	442,512	450,582	470,361	499,572	534,217	534,149	527,398	566,875
(of w.in Dollar).	413,882	414,712	431,889	455,048	486,145	486,077	468,203	503,655
Sub-total......	574,724	604,803	630,654	696,496	775,595	775,496	807,543	864,680
Other reporting countries								
Bahamas.........U	99,361	99,370	104,139	113,046	111,946	111,945	102,905	109,784
Bahrain..........	18,189	17,051	15,209	17,839	19,150	19,150	16,572	18,674
Cayman Islands.?U	85,561	85,901	90,587	107,373	119,824	119,817	115,950	115,647
Hong Kong.......U	82,293	88,264	94,042	110,473	130,751	130,750	151,032	157,474
Neth.Antilles...U	21,138	21,309	22,322	24,637	24,925	24,921	27,231	28,412
Singapore.......U	70,245	73,498	78,830	88,610	101,267	101,267	106,162	112,493
Sub-total......	376,787	385,393	405,129	461,978	507,863	507,850	519,852	542,493
Total report.area.	1982,433	2067,401	2175,523	2403,227	2622,746	2620,905	2759,690	2920,256

Source: *International Banking and Financial Market Developments.*

Estimated exchange rate adjusted changes

Assets

1985 Q2	1985 Q3	1985 Q4	1986 Q1	1986 Q2	1986 Q3	1986 Q4	1987 Q1	1987 Q2	VIS-A-VIS COUNTRIES
									Reporting area: European countries
-288	768	2,054	-1,046	1,898	1,672	2,839	16	438	Austria U
4,692	407	3,961	2,831	1,337	7,724	10,991	548	7,755	Belg-Luxembourg U
169	-293	-80	-155	588	174	89	562	698	(of w.in B.fr.)
678	2,135	3,597	898	1,481	-245	-95	3	2,265	Denmark U
282	41	-34	86	-123	685	-331	808	1,376	Finland U
-2,420	1,184	1,896	-2,117	2,703	3,104	6,685	-403	6,892	France U
-58	-535	-465	-261	1,548	-864	1,038	1,196	1,066	(of w.in Fr.fr.)
-280	2,537	4,475	3,853	-4,649	1,717	-2,483	3,929	1,304	Germany,Fed.R. U
-285	2,707	1,864	2,938	-3,228	-1,093	-931	5,312	817	(of w.in DM) U
239	-718	376	1,189	619	-71	344	98	904	Ireland
-569	-3,336	7,154	-4,574	4,651	-4,037	14,526	-60	2,452	Italy U
910	-1,476	-46	276	1,965	-526	2,349	1,807	-391	(of w.in Lit.)
-1,231	900	2,484	969	3,193	2,973	5,160	1,970	4,282	Netherlands U
-32	-223	353	108	728	474	694	-50	422	(of w.in Fl.)
915	794	76	-162	1,231	517	206	207	1,751	Norway U
-1,513	-1,852	-2,262	-139	-1,526	-45	-973	17	1,451	Spain U
309	-558	499	209	-248	962	265	2,023	1,610	Sweden U
3,018	1,539	7,078	-713	1,637	1,648	8,783	95	-258	Switzerland[2] U
435	261	2,191	-1,921	1,393	615	1,144	135	859	(of w.in Sw.fr.)
-3,510	6,540	20,877	1,721	8,021	37,869	14,113	-3,736	18,715	United Kingdom U
-873	-882	408	1,279	1,012	974	3,063	1,084	314	(of w. in £)
322	10,381	52,231	3,005	20,225	54,473	60,030	5,515	50,937	Sub-total
									Other industrial countries
-2,192	-1,272	-1,184	3,038	2,044	10	1,678	1,300	-1,651	Canada U
-2,642	14,006	16,718	18,124	14,133	47,251	70,386	35,484	54,993	Japan U
3,096	-1,598	8,083	-4,944	2,718	8,601	6,815	9,016	8,333	(of w.in Yen)
10,625	6,214	25,278	16,832	11,647	34,521	36,957	3,782	27,320	United States
8,440	4,262	22,161	11,357	9,025	30,476	35,148	-2,055	25,076	(of w.in Dollar)
5,791	18,948	40,812	37,994	27,824	81,782	109,021	40,566	80,662	Sub-total
									other reporting countries
1,192	-8,337	4,459	-548	3,404	5,754	-666	-5,831	2,431	Bahamas U
-871	-1,175	-936	-1,052	-592	204	238	-1,560	1,423	Bahrain U
-1,157	777	3,595	-1,348	9,418	5,824	10,263	-1,844	3,113	Cayman Islands [3] U
-288	5,938	3,194	2,893	5,645	15,677	14,630	20,279	14,482	Hong Kong U
-305	-1,066	1,201	-1,176	693	-486	279	221	151	Neth.Antilles U
-845	4,488	1,684	1,775	6,190	9,856	9,357	3,644	8,762	Singapore U
-2,274	625	13,197	544	24,758	36,829	34,101	14,909	30,362	Sub-total
3,839	29,954	106,240	41,543	72,807	173,084	203,152	60,990	161,961	Total report.area

Liabilities

1985 Q2	1985 Q3	1985 Q4	1986 Q1	1986 Q2	1986 Q3	1986 Q4	1987 Q1	1987 Q2	VIS-A-VIS COUNTRIES
									Reporting area: European countries
-248	1,117	453	1,335	722	1,792	2,111	1,103	1,112	Austria U
4,371	2,698	1,879	4,095	1,429	11,540	12,292	4,448	9,057	Belg-Luxembourg U
84	36	-92	483	-128	34	624	235	220	(of w.in B.fr.)
1,072	696	2,171	-875	392	-66	-119	1,066	1,399	Denmark U
-18	65	13	-272	-240	543	424	124	1,099	Finland U
-1,763	-888	5,885	-1,062	-2,342	652	11,933	2,826	12,509	France U
198	114	268	886	-16	-363	868	2,569	526	(of w.in Fr.fr.)
1,456	1,512	13,730	13,220	6,739	13,969	17,109	12,086	13,156	Germany,Fed.R. U
1,017	921	9,832	10,731	5,794	8,307	13,785	9,069	6,953	(of w.in DM) U
82	11	329	55	406	629	297	-508	373	Ireland
329	-113	9,319	-8,163	2,175	-1,416	11,413	-3,245	1,532	Italy U
67	-177	-109	217	49	161	27	461	-	(of w.in Lit.)
-625	16	-597	2,625	2,659	-877	2,424	1,703	4,783	Netherlands U
-2	-986	316	-168	373	-893	658	-95	-120	(of w.in Fl.)
246	139	461	-337	-310	-809	213	-93	1,081	Norway U
-316	171	-1,716	170	375	3,064	-351	851	3,887	Spain U
-487	190	-918	1,027	-287	988	-964	1,923	2,207	Sweden U
5,033	3,654	7,043	-3,596	3,440	4,920	6,275	10,026	7,165	Switzerland[2] U
237	1,129	550	1,859	109	4,157	1,369	3,058	-186	(of w.in Sw.fr.)
-164	10,604	17,605	7,499	17,049	33,313	19,266	9,597	28,950	United Kingdom U
-361	560	706	1,029	1,630	2,976	2,498	2,851	535	(of w. in £)
8,968	19,872	55,657	15,721	32,207	68,242	82,323	41,907	88,310	Sub-total
									Other industrial countries
-4,519	573	1,959	6,215	787	1,703	186	640	-2,532	Canada U
-3,839	13,067	9,275	13,056	2,050	31,590	45,363	31,694	20,683	Japan U
916	1,106	5,197	4,469	4,943	9,759	1,755	6,031	4,546	(of w.in Yen)
3,386	3,372	21,442	6,209	17,724	27,370	34,583	-10,391	39,898	United States
328	124	23,524	830	17,177	23,159	31,097	-17,874	35,452	(of w.in Dollar)
-4,972	17,012	32,676	25,480	20,561	60,663	80,132	21,943	58,049	Sub-total
									other reporting countries
-3,519	-5,786	6,352	-271	4,506	8,644	-1,172	-9,569	6,932	Bahamas U
-1,265	-869	1,074	-1,267	-1,966	2,528	1,279	-2,798	2,117	Bahrain U
1,299	-869	5,733	-53	4,153	16,105	12,545	-5,267	-193	Cayman Islands [3] U
435	6,194	4,812	4,772	4,564	15,269	20,526	17,559	6,760	Hong Kong U
121	774	1,984	-52	772	1,957	86	1,747	1,287	Neth.Antilles U
-2,346	4,652	4,908	1,929	3,912	8,477	12,980	2,478	6,591	Singapore U
-5,275	4,096	24,863	5,058	15,941	52,980	46,244	4,150	23,494	Sub-total
-1,279	40,980	113,196	46,259	68,709	181,885	208,699	68,000	169,853	Total report.area

TABLE I (continued)

Breakdown by borrower of bank and trade-related non-bank short

and long-term external claims of the reporting countries

(in millions of US dollars)

Borrowing country or territory (1) Jun. 87	External bank claims		Non-bank trade-related credits (3) (c)	Total (a)+(c) (d)
	Total (a)	of which: identified guaranteed claims (2) (b)		
46. Finland.........	17,605	135	277	17,882
47. Gabon...........	1,407	597	507	1,915
48. Gambia..........	49	43	32	81
49. German Dem.Rep(6)	12,502	1,543	1,760	14,262
50. Ghana...........	421	104	73	494
51. Gibraltar.......	247	1	10	257
52. Greece..........	14,348	637	1,600	15,948
53. Grenada.........	12	1	7	19
54. Guatemala.......	477	156	193	670
55. Guiana, French...	-	-	1	1
56. Guinea..........	203	51	147	350
57. Guinea-Bissau....	16	1	17	33
58. Guyana..........	66	3	36	102
59. Haiti...........	33	6	37	70
60. Honduras........	325	87	231	556
61. Hong Kong.....(4)	9,663	1,927	984	10,647
62. Hungary.........	10,853	266	375	11,228
63. Iceland.........	1,481	37	54	1,535
64. India..........	8,330	629	1,829	10,159
65. Indonesia.......	18,172	3,171	5,112	23,284
66. Iran...........	1,296	107	2,331	3,627
67. Iraq...........	8,435	2,933	4,086	12,521
68. Israel.........	5,699	1,104	10,017	15,716
69. Ivory Coast.....	3,478	559	623	4,101
70. Jamaica........	540	150	245	785
71. Jordan.........	1,639	252	890	2,528
72. Kampuchea.......	-	-	7	7
73. Kenya..........	1,163	360	488	1,651
74. Kiribati.......	-	-	-	-
75. Korea, Dem.P.Rep.	658	-	417	1,075
76. Korea, Rep......	29,889	2,025	5,704	35,592
77. Kuwait.........	7,867	18	1,563	9,431
78. Laos...........	21	-	6	27
79. Lebanon......(4)	1,120	54	136	1,256
80. Liberia.....(4,5)	9,982	368	200	10,183
81. Libya.........	655	4	1,053	1,708
82. Macao.........	1,095	-	1	1,096
83. Madagascar.....	235	56	151	386
84. Malawi........	84	14	37	121
85. Malaysia.......	11,588	753	1,471	13,059
86. Maldives.......	15	1	2	17
87. Mali..........	53	12	49	102
88. Malta.........	104	-	40	144
89. Mauritania.....	115	51	47	162
90. Mauritius......	98	16	25	123
91. Mexico........	76,029	3,513	4,680	80,708
92. Mongolia.......	-	-	1	1
93. Morocco.......	5,461	1,648	1,846	7,306
94. Mozambique.....	350	92	295	645
95. Namibia.......	3	-	-	3
96. Nauru.........	64	-	-	64
97. Nepal.........	85	69	12	97
98. Neth.Antilles (4)	7,191	321	62	7,253
99. New Zealand....	12,130	179	500	12,630
100. Nicaragua......	578	43	152	731
Pays ou territoire emprunteur (1) Jun. 87	Créances bancaires extérieures		Crédits non bancaires liés à des opérations commerciales (3) (c)	Total (a)+(c) (d)
	Total (a)	dont: montant identifié de créances garanties (2) (b)		

Ventilation par emprunteur des créances extérieures à court et à long terme des pays

déclarants, liées à des opérations bancaires et à des opérations commerciales non bancaires

(en millions de dollars des Etats-Unis)

TABLEAU I (suite)

Source: *Statistics on External Indebtedness.*

Chapter V

THE INTERNATIONAL MONETARY FUND'S DEBT STATISTICS

1. ORIGINS OF DEBT STATISTICAL ACTIVITIES AND METHODS USED

1.1. Membership and General Objectives

The International Monetary Fund is an intergovernmental monetary and financial organisation comprising 151 member countries (on 15th October 1987). Its policies, activities and relations with member countries are laid down in its Articles of Agreement, Article I. The primary purposes of the organisation are: to promote international co-operation among members through consultation and collaboration on international monetary issues; to facilitate the balanced growth of international trade and, therefore, contribute to high levels of employment and real income and the development of productive capacity; to promote exchange stability and orderly exchange arrangements; to foster a multilateral system of payments and transfers for current transactions and seek the elimination of exchange restrictions; to make financial resources available, on a temporary basis, to permit them to correct payments imbalances; and to seek reduction of both the duration and magnitude of payments imbalances.

The Fund has three main functions. First, it administers a code of conduct with respect to exchange rate policies, payments related to current account transactions, and convertibility of currencies to ensure effective operation of the international monetary system. Second, it provides members with financial resources enabling them to observe the code of conduct while correcting or avoiding payments imbalances. Finally, it provides a forum in which members can consult with each other and collaborate on international monetary matters[1].

To enable the Fund to fulfil these functions, member countries are required to provide it with information on their exchange rate and other economic and financial policies. The Fund staff collects information on members' balance of payments, reserves, external debt and other economic and financial variables during regular consultations between the Fund and its members pursuant to Article IV of the Articles of Agreement, and members regularly provide data to the Fund's Bureau of Statistics concerning various economic areas. For members which are undergoing balance-of-payments difficulties the Fund can provide financial resources under a number of policies and facilities[2] depending on the cause of the imbalance and the time needed for adjustment. Under these arrangements, Fund resources are used to support appropriate policies intended to correct the causes of the imbalances.

1.2. The IMF's Interest in Debt Statistics

1.2.1. Objectives Pursued

To fulfil its broad mandate in international financial affairs, the Fund has from its inception collected a wide range of financial information. The importance for the Fund of accurate statistical information was recognised in the Articles of Agreement which state that "The Fund may require members to furnish it with such information as it deems necessary for its activities" and that "It shall act as a center for the collection and exchange of information on monetary and financial problems" (Article VIII, section 5). The collection of financial data has been focused on three main areas of concern – balance of payments, government finance, and money and banking – and comprehensive statistical methodologies have been developed in these areas. The heightened problems related to external debt that have developed in recent years, as well as the Fund's own role in the alleviation of these problems, have placed emphasis on the production of additional and more detailed data concerning external debt.

Comprehensive statistics on external debt have been collected by the Fund on a country-specific basis for many years for use in consultation discussions with members, although no integrated methodology or set of definitions was specifically developed for this compilation of debt data. These country data are usually compiled and presented in a manner which facilitates discussions with national authorities and are not published. Also, the Fund's Bureau of Statistics has focused its attention on compiling and publishing data consistent with the statistical methodologies in the three areas mentioned above, all of which provide sub-sets of debt stock or debt-related flow data which aid in assessing countries' external positions. The data collected during consultations and by the Bureau are generally complementary.

Balance-of-payments statistics, which contain comprehensive coverage of current debt service payments and of capital account transactions, include all debt-related flows; the capital account further includes operations in financial instruments which lie outside the core concept of debt. In addition to capital flows, the Fund also collects and publishes stock data for capital account categories for 34 countries. Government finance statistics include information on both external and domestic debt of various levels of government. Money and banking statistics contain data on external liabilities of different classes of financial institutions including monetary authorities, deposit money banks, and other financial institutions. A data base has been developed on international banking statistics, which provides a picture of the external debt of a country that is intermediated by banks either in the country itself or by non-resident banks. This is achieved by combining the information provided by money and banking statistics with data furnished by major international banking centres.

These sets of data do not provide comprehensive statistics on total external debt but they do identify many of the major components of that debt. The Fund's Bureau of Statistics is currently working towards producing a more comprehensive picture of a country's external debt by combining the substantial amount of data already collected with additional information from debtor and creditor sources.

1.2.2. Use Made of Debt Information

The analytical uses of the Fund's external debt data fall into three categories: i) the analysis of economic developments of individual member countries; ii) the analysis of global economic developments relevant to Fund policies; and iii) economic research into areas of interest to the Fund. These uses are both internal, with a direct impact on the analysis underlying the Fund's own policies, and external, through numerous publications and through collaboration with other organisations.

In the Fund's country analysis, data on external debt and debt-related flows, including debt service payments and financing transactions, are an important element in evaluating the external position of a country. Emphasis is placed both on analysing recent economic developments in a country and projecting the impact of current and alternative policies on a country in the medium term. Accumulated debt, particularly in the heavily indebted countries, will have a major impact on the policy options available to a country and therefore accurate and comprehensive information on the debt stock, its maturity structure, the terms under which it was incurred, and a number of other factors are critical to a clear understanding of the current economic situation of a country and policy analysis. Complete data on debt rescheduling and the other forms of debt reorganisation which are available to a country are also necessary to evaluate a country's options. When countries have a programme supported by Fund resources, the incurring of new debt is a major concern as adequate capital flows must be maintained to meet growth and balance-of-payments objectives, but these flows must not exceed the country's ability to service the resulting debt. To meet this concern Fund programmes often contain quantitative targets or performance criteria on the contracting of new external financing.

A major project in which the Fund analyses and projects global economic and financial trends is the *World Economic Outlook* (WEO). The WEO provides recent historical data and short- and medium-term forecasts for global external debt broken down by regions and various analytical groupings of countries. This publication uses debt data from all available sources and the resulting figures represent the Fund's best estimate of gross external debt. Both historical data and forecasts are presented according to several analytical categories, not only for debt outstanding but also for debt service, debt service ratios, use of Fund credit[3] and international reserves.

Much of the work on debt, especially that part of it leading to publications, naturally falls into the category of research. A considerable amount of material is made available to the public in the Fund's World Economic and Financial Surveys and the

Occasional Paper series; particularly relevant to the assessment of external debt is *International Capital Markets: Recent Developments and Prospects*. Further, many of the Fund's economic research papers are published in the IMF Staff Papers.

The *International Capital Markets* (ICM) papers assess the recent developments in international lending through banks and bond markets and use the data calculated from the *International Banking Statistics* (IBS) stock figures to analyse geographic patterns of capital flows through these markets. Papers concerning external debt restructuring and export credit policies are produced every year and a half. Papers related to the external financial positions of member countries are produced on an intermittent basis.

1.3. Collection Method

1.3.1. Main Sources

As was discussed in the previous sections, collection of data on external debt within the Fund follows two separate paths – collection of comprehensive data on a country-specific basis for use in consultations and negotiations with countries and collection of data by the Fund's Bureau of Statistics for publication.

The data collected by the Fund's area departments for individual country debt analysis come from a number of sources within the country and from international sources. These data are as comprehensive as possible but their coverage and classification are geared to the circumstances of the country and particular needs of analysis. Such data are not published but are used to prepare global debt analyses such as those presented in the World Economic Outlook.

The Fund's Bureau of Statistics does not collect comprehensive data on external debt but does collect data in certain areas which provide important debt components. The four major areas of data collection which are relevant to external debt are balance-of-payments statistics (BOP), government finance statistics (GFS), money and banking statistics (MBS), and international banking statistics (IBS). For the first three areas, data are reported to the Bureau of Statistics by a network of correspondents in 137 countries.

In each of these areas the Fund has developed detailed methodologies for the compilation and classification of data (see below). These methodologies have been developed within the Fund and have been reviewed by national compilers and analysts. They are available to national correspondents to assist them in data compilation and are revised periodically. The data sent to the Fund by country correspondents comply as closely as basic sources will permit with the methodologies. The Fund further aids countries in implementing methodologies through an extensive programme of technical assistance in statistical areas through statistics courses at the IMF Institute and through country missions.

The Fund's international banking statistics are compiled from information on external assets and liabilities of banks which are reported in the money and banking statistics as well as from 31 international banking centres. The latter report on the detailed geographic distribution of foreign assets and liabilities, generally distinguishing between positions with banks and non-banks. The Fund and the BIS receive the same information from 25 countries; the Fund, however, receives geographically distributed data from six countries which are not in the BIS reporting system. The Fund's method of compiling IBS statistics also differs in some respects from that employed by the BIS (see Section 2.2 below and Chapter IV on the BIS).

With respect to statistics on use of Fund credit and IMF Trust Fund operations, the Fund compiles the data from the accounts of the Fund's Treasurer's Department.

1.3.2. *Additional Sources and Use of Estimation*

With respect to data compiled and published by the Bureau, estimations are seldom used for specific country observations. Estimates are only published when small components of a total are not available but are known from past performance to be relatively stable. Such estimates are clearly marked in Bureau statistical publications. The principle underlying this policy is that users of data should be presented with the most timely and accurate hard data available and can then make their own estimates of missing components or periods.

This policy applies to the publication of data on specific countries. However, estimates are frequently used for data on world and regional totals. It would cause considerable delays to publish such totals only for periods for which all country components were available. To provide totals for current periods, a number of estimating techniques are used, including extrapolation or carry-forward from latest observations, interpolation for periods between actual observations and specific estimates by Bureau economists. These techniques generate estimates for countries which are used to calculate totals which are published but the country estimates themselves are generally not published.

1.3.3. *Confidentiality*

Apart from some of the data collected by Fund staff in the course of their missions, most of the information on individual countries is not regarded as confidential.

In the IBS, disaggregated figures received from individual banking centres are confidential, but they can be combined to show the positions of all banking centres vis-à-vis banks or non-banks in a given country.

2. RELATIONSHIP TO THE CORE DEFINITION

2.1. General

The Fund, as discussed above, does not compile for publication comprehensive data which correspond to all elements included in the core definition. However, for those elements for which data are collected, there is a very high degree of correspondence with the core definition. Strong efforts are made to keep the Fund's statistical methodologies internally consistent. For example, in all statistics published by the Bureau, the residence criterion is used to distinguish external from domestic transactions. The components of debt statistics which are published usually relate to disbursed amounts and the instruments included in "debt" closely correspond to the core definition's coverage except for the balance-of-payments data which use the broader instrument coverage of the BOP capital accounts.

Balance-of-payments data are the most comprehensive in terms of coverage collected by the Bureau. The Fund's *BOP Manual*[4] provided the starting-point for the Working Group's efforts to arrive at a core definition because   *a)* it has provided, for many years, a relatively unambiguous basis for distinguishing external operations from domestic, i.e., the residence criterion, and   *b)* the capital account of the BOP provides an exhaustive framework for financial instrument analysis. The Group adopted the residence criterion as part of the core definition and identified a sub-set of capital account instruments to be included in the core. All BOP data are therefore consistent with the core definition in terms of residence but the degree of detail of the capital account makes it somewhat difficult to isolate the specific types of instrument falling within the core.

As discussed in Chapter I, the concept of financial liabilities used in the BOP capital account is broader than that embodied in the core definition, primarily owing to the inclusion of equity-type liabilities in BOP statistics. However, the detailed presentation of capital-account transactions, which classifies operations under direct investment, portfolio investment, other long- and short-term capital and reserves, provides sufficient elaboration to allow a close approximation of those instruments that fall within the core concept. Flow data are published for 132 countries, while stock data on financial assets and liabilities, according to the same capital-account classification scheme as for the flow data are published for 34 countries. The detail provided permits exclusion of the major non-core items such as equities (see Section 2.4.4.1).

Balance-of-payments stock and flow data deal with arrears and debt reorganisation in the manner described in Appendix 4. The impact of these changes is not separately identified but is included with other transactions in the appropriate categories. In the future, the Bureau will be requesting its BOP compilers to supply separate information on arrears and debt reorganisation to provide a specific source of data for these transactions and to facilitate reconciliation between BOP and external debt data.

The *Government Finance Statistics Yearbook* (GFSY) contains detailed annual data on the operations of government, including revenue, expenditures and financing transactions. Data are presented for central and, where available, other levels of government. In addition to tables on flow transactions, stock data on domestic and external debt are classified according to both type of instrument and type of debt holder. The methodology for defining and classifying debt statistics is provided by the *Manual on Government Finance Statistics* (GFS Manual), which defines debt as "the outstanding stock of recognised direct liabilities of the government to the rest of the economy and the world generated by government operations in the past and scheduled to be extinguished by government operations in the future or to continue as perpetual debt" (GFS Manual, p. 324). It encompasses debt resulting from assumption of the debt of

64

others for policy purposes or because of guarantees. The instruments included in government debt are bonds, bills, loans, advances and other government contractual obligations, which correspond to the coverage of instruments of the core definition. The distinction between domestic and external debt is made on the basis of residence of the debt holder. Separate information, however, is collected when available for domestic debt repayable in foreign exchange and foreign debt repayable in national currency.

Money and banking statistics which cover the domestic and external balances of a broad range of financial institutions are presented on a monthly basis in *International Financial Statistics* (IFS). For most countries stock data are published in local currency for the monetary authorities and deposit money banks and, where available, for other financial institutions and insurance companies. Foreign assets and liabilities are distinguished from domestic balances on the basis of residence to the extent that the underlying data permit. Foreign liabilities of the monetary authorities generally include short-term obligations to non-resident banks and to other monetary authorities, use of Fund credit and Trust Fund loans. For some countries long-term foreign liabilities are shown separately and this category includes long-term bonds, bonds issued abroad and other obligations to non-residents with a maturity of more than one year.

The liabilities of deposit money banks (DMBs) include, in addition to those of ordinary commercial banks, any time deposits placed with the Treasury or other government bodies, including the postal cheque system. The "Foreign Liabilities" of DMBs comprise obligations due to non-residents irrespective of the instruments involved and would include demand, time and savings deposits and short- and long-term securities issued by banks.

Other Financial Institutions include those that accept time and savings deposits and issue bonds and carry out many of the functions of deposit money banks apart from accepting transferable deposits. The group most commonly includes savings banks, finance companies, development banks and offshore banking units. The foreign liabilities of these institutions are generally of the same nature as those of deposit money banks.

The financial institutions section of the IFS country pages presents as full a picture as data availability permits of the foreign liabilities of a country's financial sector. With minor exceptions, the instruments included correspond closely to those covered by the core definition and residence is used to distinguish foreign from domestic balances. The foreign liability positions of deposit banks, other than monetary authorities, are presented in US dollars in a world table.

The international liquidity section of the IFS country pages provides a summary in US dollars of the external position of a country's financial institutions. Data are presented for monetary authorities, deposit money banks and, where available, other financial institutions and offshore banking units. Where positions vis-à-vis non-resident non-banks are important, they are shown separately as "of which" items.

The Fund reports its financial arrangements with all member countries in a series of world tables in IFS and separately on the IFS country pages. On the country page, the "Fund Position" section presents total liabilities to the Fund in the form of use of Fund credit with details of outstanding purchases under the various Fund policies and facilities. Liabilities to the IMF Trust Fund are shown separately. Data in the "Fund Position" section are denominated in SDRs.

The Fund's International Banking Statistics (IBS) are published in the IFS in three sets of world tables which combine data from money and banking statistics with data provided by 31 major international banking centres. The reported data cover both asset and liability positions. From the external debt perspective, the three liability tables are relevant. These show:

1. Liabilities of deposit banks in a country to deposit banks in the rest of the world (Table 8yad)[5];

2. Liabilities of deposit banks in a country to non-banks in the rest of the world (Table 7ydd)[5];

3. Liabilities of non-banks in a country to deposit banks in the rest of the world (Table 7yrd)[5].

The IBS tables on bank liabilities to banks and non-banks abroad (8yad and 7ydd) are derived from the money and banking statistics, which are primarily directly reported data of countries. The figures on domestic non-banks' liabilities to banks abroad (7yrd) are derived from the reports of creditor banks in 31 international banking centres. The sum of these data for a given country is an estimate of its stock of external debt that passes through domestic and foreign banks. For many countries the IBS data will comprise a very important element of the total external debt. In addition, the IBS data are obtained from banks' balance-sheet records and these are normally available on a much more timely basis than non-banks' debt sources.

In principle, the debt positions that are not captured by the IBS are those of domestic non-banks vis-à-vis foreign non-banks. This includes inter-government positions and supplier credits, and therefore the amount of debt left uncovered can be quite important in many countries. Other data that are not included in the Fund's IBS are positions of domestic monetary authorities vis-à-vis foreign monetary authorities. The main reason for excluding positions among monetary authorities is that these often reflect special transactions, e.g., swaps that are made at non-market rates and do not reflect the conditions in the international capital markets. However, positions of monetary authorities with deposit banks are included because they are made at market rates and are included in the data received from the international banking centres.

The IBS stock data are used to calculate flow data, using available information on the currency composition of the international banks' external positions. The calculation method is explained in Section 3.1. The flow data are used for internal analysis and for the International Capital Markets papers.

The IBS data correspond closely in most respects with the elements of the core definition. Both the money and banking data and the data from the international banking centres from which IBS are derived distinguish foreign from domestic balances on the basis of residence. The bulk of the financial instruments involved – deposits, loans, advances, securities of various maturities – are within the core concept.

2.2. Core Items Excluded or Imperfectly Covered

With the exception of balance-of-payments statistics, the Fund's debt compilation systems relate to specific classes of financial instruments. The coverage of debt for those areas is as comprehensive as possible and, as described above, corresponds closely to the core definition. The balance-of-payments statistics cover the whole economy with the capital account transactions including all operations in financial assets and liabilities including those which fall outside the core definition such as equities.

The reports from some of the international banking centres might diverge from the core definition. In a number of countries, when a loan or security has become non-performing, the value of that claim is reduced or eliminated from the balance sheet of the bank concerned even though the claim on the debtor still exists (see Chapter II, Section 3.5, for a discussion of provisioning and write-offs). This will result in an understatement of the actual claims on the country which has the non-performing debt and in the period when the adjustment is made it will appear, other things being equal, that the debtor country has made a repayment. Such provisioning can lead to asymmetry in reporting of debt between creditor and debtor sources. As information on provisioning vis-à-vis particular countries is not generally available, the IBS cannot be adjusted to exclude the impact. Provisioning by major industrial countries' banks against their holdings of developing-country debt has been quite substantial in some cases, so understatement of debt from this source can be quite large. This difficulty only affects the data on non-bank liabilities to non-resident banks, as the money and banking data on which the other IBS tables are based comprise reporting by the debtor which does not reflect provisioning by creditors.

2.3. Non-Core Items Collected or Published

As mentioned above, the balance-of-payments statistics cover the whole economy with the capital account including all operations in financial assets and liabilities. Further, some of the major international banking centres include equity holdings in their reports on claims on other countries. As these are not reported separately and as a given country's debt to foreign banks is measured as the total of reported claims on that country, the debt to banks might include some element of equity-type liabilities where they exist. This problem also affects only the table on the liabilities of non-banks in a country to banks in the rest of the world, as this is the only table compiled from the reports of the international banking centres in the Fund's IBS.

2.4. Other Points Concerning Relationship to Core Definition

2.4.1. Residence

One of the crucial points in the "core" definition and in the relationship of any particular debt statistics system to that "core" is the definition of residence. As far as the Fund is concerned, the standards used, as in the core definition itself, are those set out in the *Balance of Payments Manual* (Fourth Edition), in which the residents of an economy are defined as "general government, individuals, private non-profit bodies serving individuals, all defined in terms of their relationship to the territory of that economy". (The section of the BOP Manual dealing with this point is reproduced in full in Appendix 2.) Lists of what should be classified under central, state and local government, non-financial public enterprises, and public financial institutions are regularly published in the Fund's *Government Finance Statistics Yearbook* (GFSY)[6].

Practical questions about residence arise most often concerning individuals, particularly when they are located abroad but retain substantial interest in the country, i.e., emigrant workers. According to the core definition, and assuming that they have been abroad for more than one year, their accounts in their home country should form part of the country's foreign debt. However, since their funds are usually spent domestically, the Fund prefers separate reporting on these banking liabilities.

Another important question is the treatment of the offshore banking units (OBUs). These OBUs are generally limited to transacting with non-residents under special licences or regulations. However, some of them may conduct limited transactions with domestic residents, although they would not normally take deposits from them. The standards used in the IFS and the United Nations' *System of National Accounts* (SNA) suggest that the OBUs should be classified as part of the financial system in which they reside, but most countries do not in fact include them in their domestic monetary statistics because their accounts add nothing to domestic liquidity, however important their transactions may be for the country's international liquidity. OBUs are therefore identified separately in the "International Liquidity" section.

2.4.2. Maturity

The Fund's statistics included both short-term and long-term debt data. Maturity analyses are only published for some of the time series.

2.4.3. Undisbursed or Contingent Amounts

The Fund's published statistics are consistent with the core definition's provision that external debt statistics should be recorded on the basis of amounts disbursed and outstanding. Money and banking statistics and international banking statistics include only outstanding liabilities and exclude off-balance-sheet contingent liabilities such as letters of credit, guarantees, undrawn loans, and unactivated loan or note facilities. The balance-of-payments system is based on change of ownership of financial instruments and therefore includes only actual liabilities and disbursements; entering into contingent liability commitments does not in and of itself change the ownership of a financial asset or liability. The *Manual on Government Finance Statistics* recommends that all contingent government liabilities should be excluded from government debt statistics.

2.4.4. Treatment of Certain Types of Instrument

2.4.4.1. Equity and Intra-Group Lending

The Fund's balance-of-payments statistics treat intra-company financing[7] as part of direct investment in the capital account, irrespective of the financial instrument involved in the transaction. However, the direct investment category is sub-divided by instrument, and equity and debt financing can be distinguished if the full details are provided by compilers[8]. The Fund's money and banking statistics specifically exclude equity-type liabilities from foreign liabilities. The IBS, however, may include some amount of equities as a number of reporting countries include equities among their financial claims on other countries.

2.4.4.2. Leasing

According to the BOP methodology, a lease arrangement expected to cover at least 75 per cent of the cost of the goods, together with the carrying charges, is a financial lease, i.e., this is presumptive evidence of a financing arrangement which is equivalent to a change of ownership. (For further details, see Section 2.1.2.1 of Chapter III).

2.4.4.3. Loans Repayable in Local Currency

Loans repayable in local currency are generally included in the external debt measure of the Fund. However, there are some special problems with respect to the classification of counterpart funds. In a number of instances, donor governments provide assistance to developing countries in the form of commodities which are sold in the local market. The local currency balances that are generated by these sales are often deposited with the central bank under the joint control of the donor and recipient governments, frequently with substantial restrictions on how they may be spent. These deposits present some problems with respect to classification as external debt or restricted domestic deposits. The BOP statistics treat the original transfer of the goods as a loan, unless there is clear evidence that the transaction is in fact an unrequited transfer. It is normal practice in money and banking statistics to treat the balances with the central bank as neither a foreign liability to the donor government nor a domestic deposit of the recipient government as long as there is joint control. The balances are, where important, classified separately. The GFS do not record the deposits when they are generated, but record withdrawn funds as grants or loans at the time of withdrawal, depending on whether the transaction must be repaid.

2.4.4.4. Military

Fund statistics include debt resulting from transactions of a military nature, just as the broader BOP statistics include the transactions themselves. It should be noted, however, that since data on government debt are provided by the governments themselves and it is known that some governments prefer not to report debt of this kind, there may be some omissions in the data.

3. OTHER QUESTIONS REGARDING CONTENT

3.1. Method of Currency Conversion

Economic and financial data that are reported to the Fund by member countries are normally expressed in the reporting countries' currencies. To convert the national-currency data into a common currency or SDRs, the end-of-period exchange rates are used for stock data and period-average exchange rates for flow or transaction data. The use of period-average exchange rates for the flow data implies that the transactions are assumed to be spread evenly over the period.

The exchange rate adjustment technique applied in estimating flow data of the Fund's international banking statistics, which are reported in US dollars, involves the following steps: *a)* deposit banks' external positions are converted to the original currencies using data on the currency composition of these positions at end-of-period exchange rates; *b)* changes in the positions over the period are calculated, in the original currencies; *c)* the changes are then converted back into US dollars using period-average exchange rates; and *d)* the changes expressed in US dollars are aggregated across the original currencies.

Both end-of-period and period-average exchange rates are reported to the Fund by member countries and are published in IFS.

3.2. Treatment of Arrears

Both amortization and interest arrears are included in the external debt measure of the Fund.

The balance-of-payments treatment of arrears is described in detail in Appendix 4.

3.3. Treatment of Debt Reorganisation

In Fund terminology, debt refinancing describes a rollover of maturity of debt obligations or the conversion of existing or future debt service payments into a new medium-term loan, while debt rescheduling describes the formal deferment of debt service payments with new maturities applying to the deferred amounts. Debt forgiveness refers to an annulment of the obligation.

The balance-of-payments treatment of debt reorganisation is described in detail in Appendix 4.

4. SECTORING

For a full picture of the various statistical breakdowns normally presented in the various publications, the reader is referred to the specimen tables in the final section of this chapter and, for some aspects, to the synoptic tables at the end of Part II. The following is a summary of the main dimensions of the breakdowns available in the case of the Fund.

4.1. Country Coverage[9]

The basic distinction adopted by the Fund is between industrial and developing countries. The further breakdown normally used is into area sub-groups for Africa[10], Asia, Europe, Middle East[10] and Western Hemisphere. Memorandum items are shown for the Oil-Exporting Countries and Non-Oil Developing Countries in all the world tables. The World tables on international banking statistics further show aggregate data for "major offshore banking centres" defined with reference to seven developing countries (the Bahamas, Bahrain, the Cayman Islands, Hong Kong, the Netherlands Antilles, Panama and Singapore) where the banking system, acting as financial entrepot, acquires substantial external accounts, beyond those associated with economic activity in the country concerned. The country composition of "World" is all countries for which the series is available in the Fund's files; as data are not available for all series for all countries, the country coverage of some areas, mainly Africa and Asia, differs from series to series.

The analytical groupings used in the *World Economic Outlook* go beyond the above breakdown for developing countries and group countries according to *a)* their predominant export; *b)* financial criteria; and *c)* other criteria of economic relevance. See the specimen tables at the end of the chapter and Appendix 7 for the groupings used in the recent World Economic Outlook and International Capital Markets papers.

4.2. Types of Debtor/Creditor

The Fund's *Balance of Payments Manual* has a different degree of debtor sectorisation among the different categories of the capital accounts. The most detailed sectorisation is in "other capital", which includes all capital transactions that are not covered in direct investment, portfolio investment, or reserves. The Manual recommends a sub-division of the "other capital" into three broad types of domestic debtor: *a)* official sector, which includes the central government, the state and local governments, and the central bank; *b)* deposit money banks, which include all public and private monetary institutions except the central bank; and *c)* other sectors, which include all other public and private sectors not covered above.

In addition to the BOP Manual's broad coverage of the domestic debtor types, the Manual on Government Financial Statistics sub-divides the public sector into central government, state and local governments, and public enterprises, while the IFS sectorises the financial system of a country into four categories: monetary authorities, the deposit money banks, other banking institutions (which include offshore banking units), and other financial institutions.

On the creditor side, the sectoral distribution is less detailed than on the debtor side. The bank/non-bank disaggregation is available in the IFS, as well as data on the IMF. The *World Economic Outlook* provides aggregate debt information about official creditors, financial institutions, and other private creditors.

4.3. Types of Claim

See specimen tables at end of chapter.

5. SPECIAL FEATURES

5.1. Data for Calculating "Net Debt" and Flows

In addition to the "net foreign asset" items in the monetary and financial survey section of the IFS country pages, the Fund also collects and publishes detailed figures on gross assets, which can be offset against gross external debt liabilities to obtain estimates of various concepts of "net" debt.

As far as flows are concerned, the IMF balance-of-payments statistics are the most important comprehensive source available. For more specialised data, the IBS stock data are the source for estimating detailed flow statistics on lending and deposit-taking by banks, analysed in the *International Capital Markets* series. (See Section 2.1.)

The *GFS Manual* also provides a framework for reconciling changes in external debt during periods with net borrowing flows which are recorded on a cash basis by providing memorandum items for discounts and premia on new issues and redemptions, addition of accrued interest to debt, non-cash debt transactions and revaluation in national currency.

5.2. Data on Debt Service

The balance-of-payments statistics include all debt-service payments. To get a full picture, it is necessary to deal with both the current and the capital account. However, the details might not be available for all countries, i.e., the debt service payments are included in the aggregates but not necessarily identified separately.

5.3. Debt Service Projections

The WEO series includes short- and medium-term forecasts of global external debt and debt service payments, generally from information obtained from country authorities in consultation discussions.

NOTES AND REFERENCES

1. For further details see *The Role and Function of the International Monetary Fund*, Washington DC, 1981.

2. See Appendix 3.

3. Use of Fund credit is the sum of members' outstanding purchases and the Fund's net operational receipts and expenditures in that currency that increase the adjusted Fund holdings above quota. It measures the amounts that a member is obligated to repurchase.

4. *Balance of Payments Manual,* Fourth Edition, (1977); *A Manual on Government Finance Statistics* (1986); and *A Guide to Money and Banking Statistics in IFS* (1984 – draft not available to the public).

5. The tables have the following titles in IFS:
   1. Cross-Border Interbank Liabilities by Residence of Borrowing Bank;
   2. Cross-Border Bank Deposits of Non-banks by Residence of Borrowing Bank;
   3. Cross-Border Bank Credit to Non-banks by Residence of Borrower.

6. While strict application of the residence criterion is a feature of all the Fund's reporting systems, additional information is given in the GFSY distinguishing, when data permit, domestic debt repayable in foreign exchange and foreign debt repayable in national currency.

7. Short-term capital flows between affiliated monetary institutions are not included under direct investment because they reflect the regular business activities of those institutions more than direct investments (*BOP Manual*, p. 417).

8. Only a few countries provide such details at present.

9. The term "country", as used in the Fund's statistical publications, does not in all cases refer to a territorial entity which is a state as understood by international law and practice; the term also covers some territorial entities that are not states but for which statistical data are maintained and provided internationally on a separate and independent basis.

10. Note that Egypt and the Libyan Arab Jamahiriya are classified as part of the Middle East, not Africa.

PUBLICATIONS

A. Regular Publications Containing Debt Statistics

1. Balance of Payments Statistics

- Frequency, date of publication: monthly (20th of month) plus two-part yearbook (December)

Obtainable from:

- International Monetary Fund
  Washington, D.C. 20431, USA

- Price $46.00 for twelve monthly issues and yearbook (university libraries, faculty and students, $23) $15 for yearbook only

- Also available in tape form: ($1 750 a year to single users, $750 to universities, $7 500 to time-sharers)

Data shown for last available eight years (on annual basis) and on a quarterly basis for the last available five quarters.
Principal series available on tapes back to 1965 (annual data) and 1970 (quarterly data).

2. Government Finance Statistics Yearbook

- Frequency, date of publication: annual (December)

Obtainable from:

- International Monetary Fund
  Washington, D.C. 20431, USA

- $24.00 per copy
  (university libraries, faculty and students, $12)

- Also available in tape form:
  ($1 750 a year to single users, $750 to universities, $7 500 to time-sharers)

Data shown for last available ten years. Principal series available on tapes back to 1965 (annual data), 1970 (quarterly data).

74

3. *International Financial Statistics (IFS)*

 - Frequency, date of publication: monthly (1st of month) and annual (September) and two supplements

Obtainable from:

 - International Monetary Fund
   Washington, D.C. 20431, USA

 - Price single copy, $12 for monthly issue, $25 for yearbook, $12 for each supplement annual subscription, $120 (university libraries, faculty and students, $60) subscribers outside US, special airspeed arrangements for surcharge of $100

 - Also available in tape form: ($1 750 a year to single users, $750 to universities, $7 500 to time-sharers)

Principal series shown for last available seven years (annual), four years (quarterly) and seven months (monthly).
Principal series available on tapes as follows:

Series IFS-A: back to 1948 (annual) (most series)
1957 (quarterly)
1976 (monthly)
Series IFS-B: back to 1948 (annual) (most series)
1957 (quarterly)
1957 (monthly)

4. *International Capital Markets: Developments and Prospects*

 - Frequency, date of publication: periodical

Obtainable from:

 - External Relations Department
   International Monetary Fund
   Washington, D.C. 20431, USA

 - Price $15 (university libraries, faculty and students, $11)

5. *World Economic Outlook*

 - Frequency, date of publication: periodical

Obtainable from:

 - External Relations Department
   International Monetary Fund
   Washington, D.C. 20431, USA

 - Price $15 (university libraries, faculty and students, $11)

United States

Table 3. DETAILED PRESENTATION: STOCK DATA, 1979–86, END OF PERIOD

(In billions of SDRs)

	Code	1979	1980	1981	1982	1983	1984	1985	1986
CAPITAL ACCOUNT (net)	. . V 4	**69.95**	**83.32**	**121.57**	**124.08**	**85.59**	**3.69**	**−101.17**	**−216.16**
CAPITAL, EXCLUDING RESERVES (net)	9 . . V 4	55.56	62.34	95.73	93.29	53.35	−31.95	−140.48	−255.82
Direct investment abroad (net)	3 L . V 4	142.61	168.87	196.18	188.33	197.91	215.75	209.16	212.47
45. Equity capital (net)	3 A 1 V 4	...	...	...	...	...	...	...	...
46. Reinvestment of earnings (net)	3 B 1 V 4	...	...	...	...	...	...	...	...
47. Other long-term capital (net)	3 D 1 V 4	...	...	...	...	...	...	...	...
48. Short-term capital (net)	3 D 2 V 4	...	...	...	...	...	...	...	...
Direct investment in United States (net)	3 Y . V 4	**−41.34**	**−65.12**	**−93.40**	**−113.03**	**−130.91**	**−167.90**	**−168.08**	**−171.13**
49. Equity capital (net)	3 M 1 V 4	...	...	...	...	...	...	...	...
50. Reinvestment of earnings (net)	3 N 1 V 4	...	...	...	...	...	...	...	...
51. Other long-term capital (net)	3 P 1 V 4	...	...	...	...	...	...	...	...
52. Short-term capital (net)	3 P 2 V 4	...	...	...	...	...	...	...	...
Portfolio investment (net)	6 . 1 V 4	**−63.76**	**−80.22**	**−99.28**	**−125.21**	**−143.01**	**−181.86**	**−244.38**	**−310.93**
Public Sector Bonds (net)	6 M 1 V 4	−62.40	−71.23	−89.23	−109.34	−114.51	−142.89	−158.98	−165.03
53. Assets	6 A 1 V 4	...	...	...	...	...	...	...	...
54. Liabilities constituting foreign authorities' reserves	6 T 1 V 4	52.30	59.65	75.84	94.12	95.87	100.24	97.29	98.51
U.S. Treasury marketable bonds and notes	6 T 1 V X	27.85	31.72	45.38	63.02	65.07	71.14	71.87	76.68
U.S. Treasury nonmarketable bonds and notes	6 T 1 V Y	13.20	11.49	10.13	7.93	6.92	5.92	3.23	1.06
Other securities	6 T 1 V P	11.24	16.45	20.33	23.16	23.87	23.19	22.20	20.77
55. Other liabilities	6 Q 1 V 4	10.10	11.58	13.39	15.22	18.64	42.64	61.69	66.51
U.S. Treasury marketable securities held by International financial institutions	6 Q 1 V X	4.12	3.60	4.77	4.22	4.95	10.37	...	...
Other	6 Q 1 V Y	1.70	3.30	5.75	9.80	13.70	32.28	28.81	...
Security issues in foreign currencies	6 Q 1 V V	4.28	4.68	2.88	1.21	—	—	—	...
Other Bonds (net)	6 N 1 V 4	24.06	26.61	30.18	36.26	38.57	29.64	−8.66	−50.63
56. Assets	6 B 1 V 4	31.86	34.10	39.37	51.41	55.09	63.06	66.45	65.53
57. Liabilities constituting foreign authorities' reserves	6 U 1 V 4	...	...	...	...	...	...	...	...
58. Other liabilities	6 R 1 V 4	7.80	7.49	9.18	15.15	16.52	33.42	75.11	116.16
Corporate Equities (net)	6 P 1 V 4	−25.42	−35.60	−40.23	−52.13	−67.06	−68.61	−76.74	−95.25
59. Assets	6 D 1 V 4	11.26	15.03	15.09	17.02	24.98	27.86	36.27	41.61
60. Liabilities constituting foreign authorities' reserves	6 V 1 V 4	...	...	...	...	...	...	...	...
61. Other liabilities	6 S 1 V 4	36.68	50.63	55.32	69.15	92.04	96.47	113.01	136.89
Other long-term capital of resident official sector (net)	4 . 1 V 4	**33.20**	**38.14**	**46.54**	**53.70**	**60.71**	**69.41**	**63.87**	**58.22**
62/63. Loans extended	4 C 1 V 4	39.56	44.81	52.85	60.21	74.31	84.54	78.12	72.43
64. Other assets	4 K 1 V 4	3.31	3.82	4.89	5.86	...	...	...	...
65. Liabilities constituting foreign authorities' reserves	4 W 1 V 4	—	—	—	—	—	—	—	—
66/67. Other loans received	4 P 1 V 4	—	—	—	—	—	—	—	—
68. Other liabilities	4 S 1 V 4	9.68	10.48	11.19	12.37	13.60	15.13	14.25	14.20
Other long-term capital of deposit money banks (net)	5 . 1 V 4	**16.03**	**18.90**	**32.82**	**49.17**	**64.53**	**78.78**	**61.07**	**58.45**
69/70. Loans extended	5 C 1 V 4	...	...	...	...	...	...	...	...
71. Other assets	5 K 1 V 4	16.03	18.90	32.82	49.17	64.53	78.78	61.07	58.45
72. Liabilities constituting foreign authorities' reserves denominated in national currency	5 U 1 V 4	...	...	...	...	...	...	...	...
73. Liabilities constituting foreign authorities' reserves denominated in foreign currency	5 V 1 V 4	...	...	...	...	...	...	...	...
74/75. Other loans received	5 P 1 V 4	...	...	...	...	...	...	...	...
76. Other liabilities	5 S 1 V 4	...	...	...	...	...	...	...	...
Other long-term capital of other sectors (net)	8 . 1 V 4	**.55**	...	...	...	...	...	...	...
77/78. Loans extended	8 C 1 V 4	...	...	...	...	...	...	...	...
79. Other assets	8 K 1 V 4	4.17	...	...	...	...	...	...	...
80. Liabilities constituting foreign authorities' reserves	8 W 1 V 4	...	...	...	...	...	...	...	...
81/82. Other loans received	8 P 1 V 4	...	...	...	...	...	...	...	...
83. Other liabilities	8 S 1 V 4	3.62	...	...	...	...	...	...	...

Source: *Balance of Payments Yearbook.*

Korea
542

Billions of Won: Year Ending December 31

TABLE G. OUTSTANDING DEBT
BY TYPE OF DEBT INSTRUMENT
CONSOLIDATED CENTRAL GOVERNMENT

(at End of Period)

		1978	1979	1980	1981	1982	1983	1984	1985	1986	1987P
I	Total Debt (same as F.I)	2,980	3,530	5,328	7,346	9,343	10,715	11,614	12,751	13,125	....
II	Domestic Debt (same as F.II)........	861	1,183	1,511	2,851	4,020	4,743	5,241	5,422	5,759	....
1	Long-term Bonds	570	901	1,097	2,010	2,809	3,140	2,800	2,462	2,536	....
	of which: Extrabudg. Accts...........	539	876	1,076	1,871	2,323	2,829	2,618	2,411	2,536	....
3	Long-term Loans n.e.c.	291	256	414	841	1,211	1,603	2,441	2,960	3,223	....
	of which: Extrabudg. Accts...........	209	194	255	393	759	1,105	1,931	2,423	2,406	....
4	Short-term Loans & Advances	—	26	—	—	—	—	—	—	—	....
	of which: Extrabudg. Accts...........	—	26	—	—	—	—	—	—	—	....
III	Foreign Debt (same as F.III)	2,119	2,347	3,817	4,495	5,323	5,972	6,373	7,329	7,366	....
8	Long-term Loans n.e.c.	2,119	2,347	3,817	4,495	5,323	5,972	6,373	7,329	7,366	....

OTHER LEVELS OF GOVERNMENT

TABLE St.
STATE, REGION OR PROVINCE GOVTS.

A. REVENUE AND GRANTS

		1978	1979	1980	1981	1982	1983	1984	1985	1986	1987P
I	Total Revenue & Grants(II + VII).....	1,212	....	....	....	....	....	....	....	....	....
II	Total Revenue (III + VI)	567	....	....	....	....	....	....	....	....	....
III	Current Revenue (IV + V)	524	....	....	....	....	....	....	....	....	....
IV	Tax Revenue (1 - 7)	330	....	....	....	....	....	....	....	....	....
1	Tax on Inc., Profits,Cap.Gains........	33	....	....	....	....	....	....	....	....	....
4	Taxes on Property	245	....	....	....	....	....	....	....	....	....
5	Dom. Taxes on Goods & Serv.........	44	....	....	....	....	....	....	....	....	....
3,6,7	Other Taxes.....................................	8	....	....	....	....	....	....	....	....	....
V	Nontax Revenue (8 - 13)	194	....	....	....	....	....	....	....	....	....
8,9	Prop.Inc.&Op.Sur.of Dept.Ent.	10	....	....	....	....	....	....	....	....	....
10,11	Fees, Sales, Fines	155	....	....	....	....	....	....	....	....	....
13	Other Nontax Revenue	29	....	....	....	....	....	....	....	....	....
VI	Capital Revenue	43	....	....	....	....	....	....	....	....	....
VII	Grants...	645	....	....	....	....	....	....	....	....	....
18	From Other Levels of Nat. Govt.....	645	....	....	....	....	....	....	....	....	....

B. EXPENDITURE BY FUNCTION

		1978	1979	1980	1981	1982	1983	1984	1985	1986	1987P
I	Total Expenditure (C.II)	1,169	....	....	....	....	....	....	....	....	....
1	General Public Services	120	....	....	....	....	....	....	....	....	....
2	Defense	5	....	....	....	....	....	....	....	....	....
3	Public Order and Safety..................	8	....	....	....	....	....	....	....	....	....
4	Education	585	....	....	....	....	....	....	....	....	....
5	Health	38	....	....	....	....	....	....	....	....	....
6	Social Security and Welfare............	37	....	....	....	....	....	....	....	....	....
7	Housing & Commun. Amenities	64	....	....	....	....	....	....	....	....	....
10	Agricult.,Forestry,Fish.,Hunt.	96	....	....	....	....	....	....	....	....	....
11	Nonfuel Mining, Mfg. & Const.	2	....	....	....	....	....	....	....	....	....
12	Transport. & Communication	211	....	....	....	....	....	....	....	....	....
13	Other Economic Services	1	....	....	....	....	....	....	....	....	....
14	Other	2	....	....	....	....	....	....	....	....	....

C. EXPENDITURE AND LENDING MINUS
REPAYMENTS BY ECONOMIC TYPE

		1978	1979	1980	1981	1982	1983	1984	1985	1986	1987P
I	Tot.Exp.& Lend-Repay.(II + V)........	1,170	....	....	....	....	....	....	....	....	....
II	Total Expenditure (III + IV)..............	1,169	....	....	....	....	....	....	....	....	....
III	Current Expenditure (1 - 3)	860	....	....	....	....	....	....	....	....	....
1	Expenditure on Goods & Serv.........	366	....	....	....	....	....	....	....	....	....
1.1 - 3	Wages & Salar.& Empr.Contrib.	280	....	....	....	....	....	....	....	....	....
1.4	Other Purch.of Goods & Serv.	87	....	....	....	....	....	....	....	....	....
2	Interest Payments...........................	2	....	....	....	....	....	....	....	....	....
3	Subsidies & Other Curr. Transf......	492	....	....	....	....	....	....	....	....	....
3.3	Transf.to Oth.Lev. of Nat.Govt.	446	....	....	....	....	....	....	....	....	....
IV	Capital Expenditure (4 - 7)	308	....	....	....	....	....	....	....	....	....
4,5,6	Stocks, Land, Cap. Assets..............	301	....	....	....	....	....	....	....	....	....
7	Capital Transfers.............................	7	....	....	....	....	....	....	....	....	....
V	Total Lending Minus Repay.............	2	....	....	....	....	....	....	....	....	....
S.14	DEFICIT/SURPLUS (A.I-C.I)	41	....	....	....	....	....	....	....	....	....

TABLE L.
LOCAL GOVERNMENTS

A. REVENUE AND GRANTS

		1978	1979	1980	1981	1982	1983	1984	1985	1986	1987P
I	Total Revenue & Grants(II + VII).....	835	....	....	....	....	....	....	....	....	....
II	Total Revenue (III + VI)	175	....	....	....	....	....	....	....	....	....
III	Current Revenue (IV + V)	144	....	....	....	....	....	....	....	....	....
IV	Tax Revenue (1 - 7)	116	....	....	....	....	....	....	....	....	....
1	Tax on Inc., Profits,Cap.Gains........	63	....	....	....	....	....	....	....	....	....
1.1	Individual.......................................	44	....	....	....	....	....	....	....	....	....
4	Taxes on Property	33	....	....	....	....	....	....	....	....	....
5	Dom. Taxes on Goods & Serv.........	16	....	....	....	....	....	....	....	....	....
3,6,7	Other Taxes.....................................	4	....	....	....	....	....	....	....	....	....

Source: Government Finance Statistics Yearbook 1986.

77

Cross-Border Interbank Liabilities by Residence of Borrowing Bank

8ya*d*

Billions of US Dollars:

		1981	1982	1983	1984	1985 III	1985 IV	1986 I	1986 II	1986 III	1986 IV	1987 I	1987 II	1987 July	1987 Aug	1987 III
World	001	1,762.3	1,859.0	1,923.9	2,011.5	2,207.5	2,351.6	2,436.6	2,545.0	2,781.3	2,998.6	3,160.0	3,326.9	....	....	....
Internatl. Monetary Inst.(BIS)	096	27.66	29.00	32.50	32.55	34.91	41.92	39.31	39.39	37.40	36.23	44.83	44.22	43.41	42.69	48.23
USSR & Other Nonmembers n.i.e.	910	29.27	25.05	24.91	24.59	31.20	33.72	34.45	38.58	41.31	42.25	42.72	43.58	....	....	....
All Countries	010	1,705.4	1,805.0	1,866.4	1,954.4	2,141.4	2,275.9	2,362.8	2,467.0	2,702.5	2,920.1	3,072.4	3,239.1			
Industrial Countries	110	1,156.4	1,216.5	1,258.5	1,325.5	1,482.6	1,593.6	1,666.8	1,742.9	1,935.5	2,112.9	2,245.4	2,373.0			
United States	111	162.45	209.01	246.95	270.67	286.57	307.42	315.91	324.18	366.70	396.41	392.16	405.47	407.63	417.05	....
Canada	156	37.93	38.75	36.29	34.55	35.45	34.30	34.51	35.55	33.83	36.53	35.85	33.74			
Australia	193	.33	.32	.36	1.15	.09	.42	.39								
Japan	158	97.96	97.51	104.29	123.47	151.92	173.10	198.83	214.48	263.50	339.13	396.22	446.67			
New Zealand	196	1.17	1.28	1.21	1.09	1.23	1.06	1.12	1.55	1.82	3.57	4.06				
Austria	122	18.91	19.82	20.35	20.73	25.03	28.34	29.02	31.78	34.76	37.73	39.32	41.05	41.14	43.26	42.39
Belgium-Luxembourg	126	156.42	148.65	143.47	145.93	172.88	185.44	193.09	199.99	215.76	231.12	241.49	254.46			
Denmark	128	....	5.39	6.75	7.88	10.41	13.42	13.92	16.73	14.88	14.47	16.43	17.71			
Finland	172	4.92	6.80	7.56	9.45	11.47	12.82	14.03	15.97	18.54	20.53	22.88	26.12	26.54	54.62	56.56
France	132	123.00	129.52	128.06	128.65											
Germany	134	50.73	49.35	41.97	40.76	46.75	53.85	58.17	59.78	70.00	71.82	74.63	76.82	75.58	77.21	....
Iceland	176	.25	.26	.34	.37	.42	.44	.40	.40	.42	.44	.48	.50	.53	.56	.57
Ireland	178	....	13.05	3.01	3.05	3.22	3.41	4.44	4.89	4.79	5.34	5.69	6.24			
Italy	136	50.01	46.46	50.39	....											
Netherlands	138	51.11	47.64	42.00	37.69	42.50	46.34	48.34	53.22	56.07	57.86	65.32	66.92	65.54	66.03	
Norway	142	2.77	3.24	3.25	4.03	6.44	6.41	7.07	7.53	8.49	7.71					
Spain	184	....	13.83	12.02	12.58	11.59	10.86	11.18	11.34	12.62	13.23	14.20	15.49	16.69	16.47	
Sweden	144	13.87	14.88	15.88	15.66	19.43	19.20	23.69	23.80	25.79	27.15	32.03	34.95			
Switzerland	146	37.34	131.59	29.57	128.66	34.52	39.49	40.99	45.13	49.38	52.04	58.45	62.58			
United Kingdom	112	325.02	349.19	364.75	385.54	429.04	452.09	467.58	478.54	531.27	547.80	576.27	595.85			
Developing Countries	200	548.99	588.45	607.96	628.84	658.83	682.29	696.04	724.10	767.01	807.23	827.01	866.05	....	....	....
of which: Major Offshore Bkg.Ctrs.	016	348.13	372.51	379.79	395.02	420.34	433.88	443.77	465.49	502.96	534.54	547.04	584.50			
Africa	605	12.43	13.66	14.75	14.84	16.42	17.02	17.13	17.05	17.47	18.32	18.22	18.69			
Algeria	612	1.37	1.11	1.06	1.45	2.91	2.95	3.46	3.54	4.12	4.41	....	....			
Benin	638	.09	.11	.15	.15	.16	.17	.16	.14	.13	.13	.17	.19			
Botswana	616	.01	—	.01	.01	.02	.01	.01	.03	.03	.03	.02	.02	.02	.02	
Burkina Faso	748	.02	.02	.02	.01	.01	.02	.01	.01	.02	.02	.02	.01			
Burundi	618	.01	.01	.01	.01	.01	.01	.01	.01	.01	.01	.01	.01	.01		
Cameroon	622	.19	.32	.22	.17	.22	.26	.22	.28	.29	.34	.30	.37			
Cape Verde	624	—														
Central African Rep.	626	—	—	—	—	—	—	—	.01	—	.01	—	.01			
Chad	628	.01	.01	—	.01	.01	.01	—	.01	.01	.01	.01	.01			
Comoros	632	—														
Congo	634	.08	.08	.09	.10	.12	.14	.17	.16	.16	.17	.07	.09			
Côte d'Ivoire	662	.38	.31	.32	.14	.17	.19	.21	.27	.33	.26	.20	.37			
Equatorial Guinea	642	—		—		—		—								
Ethiopia	644	.07	.07	.06	.05	.06	.06	.05	.07	.06	.07	.07	.07			
Gabon	646	.12	.11	.05	.03	.10	.11	.12	.12	.12	.14	.15	.19			
Gambia, The	648	.02	.02	.01	.01	.02	.02	.01	.01	.03	.01	.01	.01	.01		
Ghana	652	.16	.13	.15	.24	.32	.37	.44	.40	.56	.85	.51				
Kenya	664	.02	.03	.02	.02	.01	.01	.02	.02	.01	.01	.01				
Lesotho	666	—	—	.02		—		—								
Liberia	668	.07	.06	.06	.04	.04	.05	.04	.04	.04	.03	.04				
Madagascar*	674	.18	.12	.13	.16	.15	.16	.15	.16	.14	.14	.14				
Malawi	676	.02	.02	.03	.03	.04	.03	.03	.04	.05	.04	.03	.04	.04		
Mali	678	....	....			.04	.04	.05	.05	.06	.06	.07	.06			
Mauritania	682	.19	.19	.17	.19	.17	.14	.17	.19	.19	.16					
Mauritius	684	—		.01	.01	.01	.01	—	—	—	—	—		.01		
Morocco	686	.73	.53	.55	.47											
Niger	692	.04	.09	.06	.04	.03	.05	.05	.04	.05	.04	.03				
Nigeria	694	.86	.74	.63	.25	.31	....	.39	.30	.25	.27	.17				
Rwanda	714	.02	.01	.02	.02	.02	.02	.02	.02	.02	.01	.02	.02	.03		
Senegal	722	.32	.36	.31	.29	.36	.46	.46	.48	.48	.38	.40	.43			
Seychelles	718													.01	—	
Sierra Leone	724	.15	.16	.20	.21	.21	.21	.22	.09	.16	.15	.16	.19	.21		
Somalia	726	.06	.07	.08	.09	.08	.09	.09	.09	.10	.12	.12	.18			
South Africa*	199	4.89	5.94	7.32	8.27	8.01	8.33	7.62	7.42	6.98	7.38	7.37	7.48			
Sudan	732	.96	.89	.68	.56											
Swaziland	734	.01	.01	.02	.01	.01	—	.01	.01	—	.01		.01	.01	.01	.02
Tanzania	738	.05	.07													
Togo	742	.06	.05	.04	.04	.05	.06	.06	.06	.06	.08	.06	.06			
Tunisia	744	.31	.32	.34	.38	.06	.03	.07	.19	.14	.03					
Uganda	746	.04	.03	.01	.01	.02	.01	.01	.02	.01	.01					
Zaire	636	.07	.42	.40	.30	.25	.25	.31	.33	.39	.39	.41	.23			
Zambia	754	.64	1.00	.71	.54	.62	.60	.39	.37	.36	.41	.64				
Zimbabwe	698	.18	.25	.35	.11	.11	.07	.05	.08	.09	.07	.07				
Asia	505	134.53	156.69	171.06	195.48	220.97	233.00	243.94	256.81	289.03	318.18	349.43	371.06			
Afghanistan	512	....	....													
Bangladesh	513	.27	.28	.20	.18	.19	.19	.21	.19	.16	.17	.13	.13			
Burma	518	....	....		—	.04	.06	.05	.04	.02	.02	.03				
China, People's Rep.	924	3.87	2.91	3.34	3.65	5.72	6.63	7.14	8.20	8.45	8.39	8.70	9.30	8.76		
Fiji	819	.01	.01	.01	.01	.04	.04	.07	.06	.06	.11	.19	.04	.02	.03	
Hong Kong	532	45.37	54.12	59.63	65.94	78.27	83.33	87.38	93.39	110.39	125.78	148.30	161.27			
India	534	....	....													
Indonesia	536	.62	.90	.92	.67	.48	.49	.67	.33	.33	.30	.35	.39			

Source: *International Financial Statistics.*

78

Cross-Border Bank Credit to Nonbanks by Residence of Borrower

7yr d   *(7yrd 900) Billions of US Dollars:*

	1981	1982	1983	1984	1985 III	1985 IV	1986 I	1986 II	1986 III	1986 IV	1987 I	1987 II	1987 July	1987 Aug	1987 III
World ... 001	673.0	734.3	761.2	763.6	828.9	882.7	914.9	952.4	988.0	1,014.4	1,068.9	1,088.3	....	....	....
Nonmonetary Internatl. Orgs. ... 096	2.90	3.77	6.02	6.92	7.59	11.01	10.75	11.59	12.05	15.83	15.71	17.44	....	....	....
USSR & Other Nonmembers n.i.e. 910	7.86	7.34	6.56	6.17	6.69	7.48	7.53	7.93	8.27	9.13	9.80	10.13	....	....	....
All Countries ... 010	662.2	723.2	748.6	750.5	814.6	864.3	896.6	932.9	967.7	989.4	1,043.3	1,060.7	....	....	....
Industrial Countries ... 110	244.4	282.1	286.2	279.9	311.0	346.0	365.8	383.7	406.4	415.0	447.4	465.9	....	....	....
United States ... 111	41.32	57.32	58.02	68.26	83.94	93.47	103.79	110.47	116.66	119.25	125.12	131.06	....	....	....
Canada ... 156	9.07	11.17	10.61	11.01	12.18	13.71	14.92	16.84	17.04	16.66	18.30	19.55	....	....	....
Australia ... 193	8.75	14.11	17.44	19.73	20.65	22.26	22.36	22.20	23.18	23.97	25.28	24.65	....	....	....
Japan ... 158	12.86	9.55	11.28	8.52	8.05	10.25	10.18	13.69	16.40	16.26	21.39	29.96	....	....	....
New Zealand ... 196	2.85	3.83	4.46	5.06	6.04	6.80	7.30	7.54	8.57	8.99	10.17	10.44	....	....	....
Austria ... 122	3.11	3.39	3.59	3.36	3.98	4.17	4.45	4.86	5.24	5.69	5.78	5.76	....	....	....
Belgium-Luxembourg ... 126	....	12.46	12.02	11.84	12.01	11.89	12.14	12.33	12.88	12.90	14.41	14.47	....	....	....
Denmark ... 128	11.22	12.17	12.44	10.33	12.72	15.62	16.83	17.60	18.66	18.59	19.54	20.01	....	....	....
Finland ... 172	4.25	4.55	4.38	4.66	5.22	5.62	6.20	6.19	6.16	6.13	6.56	6.26	....	....	....
France ... 132	11.29	15.02	16.37	17.06	18.15	19.56	19.35	19.28	19.66	19.76	20.54	19.49	....	....	....
Germany ... 134	43.16	44.98	40.73	35.14	40.81	43.14	46.29	47.37	50.71	48.97	54.31	54.05	....	....	....
Iceland ... 176	.61	.63	.71	.73	.76	.94	.87	.86	.89	.98	1.08	1.01	....	....	....
Ireland ... 178	4.26	5.56	5.50	5.26	5.90	7.39	8.48	8.71	9.11	9.52	10.45	10.77	....	....	....
Italy ... 136	22.78	22.14	22.72	19.64	20.17	22.73	23.87	24.81	23.72	24.66	26.73	25.72	....	....	....
Netherlands ... 138	5.65	6.81	6.75	7.34	8.15	9.39	10.19	10.55	10.87	13.23	14.21	17.69	....	....	....
Norway ... 142	7.48	8.36	7.28	6.71	6.79	7.45	7.04	7.65	7.79	8.63	8.45	8.26	....	....	....
Spain ... 184	15.34	16.16	16.44	15.43	13.82	13.95	14.00	12.76	12.50	11.25	11.62	11.02	....	....	....
Sweden ... 144	9.03	10.29	10.58	6.96	7.59	9.30	8.98	8.53	8.95	10.15	9.47	9.01	....	....	....
Switzerland ... 146	8.55	8.64	7.71	7.31	7.93	9.39	9.92	10.39	10.98	12.35	15.58	17.36	....	....	....
United Kingdom ... 112	12.24	13.76	15.98	13.83	14.40	16.71	16.93	18.60	23.96	24.35	25.25	26.07	....	....	....
Industrial not specified ... 189	.92	1.26	1.23	1.73	1.80	2.21	1.70	2.52	2.48	2.70	3.17	3.33	....	....	....
Developing Countries ... 200	315.89	348.75	369.34	366.85	387.38	398.59	402.84	406.40	413.49	415.35	426.28	426.20	....	....	....
of which:Major Offshore Bkg.Ctrs. 016	25.19	30.85	31.56	32.73	40.05	44.67	46.86	47.27	50.52	51.94	55.04	56.08	....	....	....
Africa ... 605	45.73	50.07	50.82	46.90	50.49	52.28	52.83	53.83	55.18	54.66	55.69	55.14	....	....	....
Algeria ... 612	7.48	6.99	6.67	5.90	6.95	7.50	7.83	8.05	8.29	8.24	8.57	8.13	....	....	....
Angola ... 614	.32	.37	.39	.49	.64	.70	.70	.70	.70	.75	.78	.73	....	....	....
Benin ... 638	.10	.19	.18	.16	.15	.18	.17	.16	.17	.15	.17	.14	....	....	....
Botswana ... 616	.03	.05	.05	.02	.02	.02	.02	.02	.02	.02	.03	.03	....	....	....
Burkina Faso ... 748	.02	.03	.04	.03	.03	.03	.03	.03	.03	.03	.03	.03	....	....	....
Burundi ... 618	—	.01	.03	.03	.03	.04	.03	.04	.04	.03	.03	.03	....	....	....
Cameroon ... 622	.82	.73	.81	.79	.81	.86	.84	.85	.81	.97	1.07	1.07	....	....	....
Cape Verde ... 624	—	—	—	—	.01	.01	.01	.01	.01	.01	.01	.01	....	....	....
Central African Rep. ... 626	.01	.01	.01	.01	.01	.01	.01	.01	.01	.01	.02	.02	....	....	....
Chad ... 628	.02	.01	.01	—	—	—	—	—	—	—	....	....	....	....	....
Comoros ... 632	—	—	—	—	—	—	—	—	—	—	....	....	....	....	....

Cross-Border Bank Deposits of Nonbanks by Residence of Borrowing Bank

7yd d   *Billions of US Dollars:*

	1981	1982	1983	1984	1985 III	1985 IV	1986 I	1986 II	1986 III	1986 IV	1987 I	1987 II	1987 July	1987 Aug	1987 III
World ... 001	....	....	....	....	....	....	....	....	....	....	....	....	....	....	....
Nonmonetary Internatl. Orgs. ... 096	....	....	....	....	....	....	....	....	....	....	....	....	....	....	....
USSR & Other Nonmembers n.i.e. 910	....	....	....	....	....	....	....	....	....	....	....	....	....	....	....
All Countries ... 010	559.8	618.2	678.5	698.7	768.4	806.9	832.7	870.3	916.5	951.6	986.8	1,015.3	....	....	....
Industrial Countries ... 110	382.7	428.0	461.7	481.6	540.3	561.0	583.3	618.3	651.9	675.3	706.9	737.7	....	....	....
United States ... 111	27.47	45.55	58.83	67.45	73.73	73.84	73.23	74.56	77.54	80.59	76.00	77.85	77.15	78.97	....
Canada ... 156	23.11	18.99	25.00	27.04	27.98	30.34	33.21	31.26	30.86	32.38	32.21	32.15	....	....	....
Australia ... 193	.40	.41	.29	1.12	2.29	2.50	3.40	....	....	....	....	....	....	....	....
Japan ... 158	2.44	2.49	2.36	3.58	5.35	6.20	4.55	5.87	6.86	6.86	4.86	5.63	....	....	....
New Zealand ... 196	....	....	....	....	....	....	....	....	....	....	....	....	....	....	....
Austria ... 122	6.66	6.32	6.04	7.48	8.81	9.71	10.30	11.13	12.20	13.19	13.42	13.24	13.29	13.50	13.55
Belgium-Luxembourg ... 126	32.86	31.88	30.71	33.18	42.22	44.28	51.12	55.66	60.45	65.28	73.70	77.62	....	....	....
Denmark ... 128	....	.54	.41	.41	.65	1.44	1.51	2.06	1.99	1.93	2.41	2.66	....	....	....
Finland ... 172	....	....	....	....	....	....	....	....	....	....	....	....	....	....	....
France ... 132	21.57	28.10	30.67	36.59	....	....	....	....	....	....	....	....	....	....	....
Germany ... 134	16.07	15.34	15.95	17.47	17.82	21.92	21.53	24.05	26.79	29.47	33.02	34.44	33.92	34.93	....
Iceland ... 176	....	....	....	....	....	....	....	....	....	....	....	....	....	....	....
Ireland ... 178	....	12.67	2.66	2.60	3.33	3.57	3.67	3.78	3.67	3.75	3.95	3.87	....	....	....
Italy ... 136	1.37	1.67	1.82	....	....	....	....	....	....	....	....	....	....	....	....
Netherlands ... 138	14.18	15.21	14.35	15.44	18.51	19.44	20.31	22.18	24.59	25.83	28.74	29.71	29.64	28.88	....
Norway ... 142	3.63	3.44	3.49	3.47	4.25	4.90	5.19	5.60	6.59	7.94	....	....	....	....	....
Spain ... 184	....	7.51	9.38	10.41	11.42	11.78	12.01	12.53	13.26	13.46	14.17	14.24	14.20	14.65	....
Sweden ... 144	1.91	.68	1.31	1.30	3.11	2.40	3.28	3.55	4.47	2.09	5.06	4.21	....	....	....
Switzerland ... 146	97.46	109.61	107.91	105.93	121.96	124.31	127.69	132.46	139.57	141.68	147.33	155.15	....	....	....
United Kingdom ... 112	123.40	137.61	150.53	146.09	154.75	157.87	167.52	181.37	187.66	192.70	203.72	217.43	....	....	....
Industrial not specified ... 189	....	....	....	....	....	....	....	....	....	....	....	....	....	....	....
Developing Countries ... 200	177.01	190.21	216.80	217.03	228.09	245.84	249.38	251.95	264.63	276.30	279.93	277.66	....	....	....
of which:Major Offshore Bkg.Ctrs. 016	124.90	136.69	158.98	158.78	163.17	178.50	179.22	180.75	193.24	203.40	207.63	204.78	....	....	....
Africa ... 605	1.96	1.83	1.93	2.39	2.94	3.19	3.31	3.35	3.78	3.90	4.06	4.08	....	....	....
Algeria ... 612	1.06	.90	1.02	1.53	1.99	2.14	2.25	2.33	2.70	2.79	....	....	....	....	....
Angola ... 614	....	....	....	....	....	....	....	....	....	....	....	....	....	....	....
Benin ... 638	....	....	....	....	....	....	....	....	....	....	....	....	....	....	....
Botswana ... 616	—	—	—	—	—	—	.01	—	.01	—	.01	.01	.01	.01	....
Burkina Faso ... 748	.03	.03	.03	.02	.03	.03	.04	.02	.02	.02	.03	.03	....	....	....
Burundi ... 618	—	—	—	.01	—	.01	—	—	.01	.01	.01	.01	.01	....	....
Cameroon ... 622	....	....	....	....	....	....	....	....	....	....	....	....	....	....	....
Cape Verde ... 624	....	....	....	....	....	....	....	....	....	....	....	....	....	....	....
Central African Rep. ... 626	....	....	....	....	....	....	....	....	....	....	....	....	....	....	....
Chad ... 628	....	....	....	....	....	....	....	....	....	....	....	....	....	....	....

Source: International Financial Statistics.

	1986 I	1986 II	1986 III	1986 IV	1987 I	1987 II	1987 III	Mar	Apr	May	June	July	Aug	Sept	Oct	Line
Exchange Rates																
End of Period																
	23.448	24.234	24.812	25.112	26.420	26.143	26.361	26.420	26.757	26.331	26.143	25.902	26.448	26.361	27.380	Market Rate ... aa
End of Period (ae) Period Average (rf)																
	20.600	20.580	20.448	20.530	20.550	20.456	20.600	20.550	20.484	20.466	20.456	20.440	20.453	20.600	20.725	Market Rate ... ae
	20.095	20.519	20.465	20.464	20.517	20.478	20.496	20.563	20.505	20.473	20.456	20.450	20.439	20.601	20.706	Market Rate ... rf
Fund Position																
End of Period																
	440	440	440	440	440	440	440	440	440	440	440	440	440	440	440	Quota ... 2f.s
	5	2	2	5	10	12	3	10	11	—	12	12	3	3	11	SDRs ... 1b.s
	31	31	39	39	39	39	39	39	39	39	39	39	39	39	39	Reserve Position in the Fund ... 1c.s
	922	859	802	959	923	924	867	923	956	940	924	921	914	867	867	Use of Fund Credit: Gen. Dept. ... 2e.s
	189	165	141	342	318	295	271	318	318	318	295	295	295	271	271	incl.: Comp. Financing Facility ... 2dus
	—	—	—	—	—	—	—	—	—	—	—	—	—	—	—	Oil Facility ... 2dzs
	302	295	283	273	266	277	265	266	278	272	277	277	271	265	265	Credit Tranche: Ordinary ... 2ees
	181	160	139	115	98	77	56	98	95	89	77	74	74	56	56	Credit Tranche: SFF ... 2dds
	202	202	202	204	216	263	263	216	239	239	263	263	263	263	263	Credit Tranche: EAR ... 2dhs
	50	37	37	25	25	13	13	25	25	22	13	13	13	13	13	Extended Facility: Ordinary ... 2kxs
	94	91	79	76	64	61	49	64	61	61	61	49	49	49	46	Trust Fund Loans Outstanding ... 2ets
International Liquidity																
End of Period																
	744	1,055	1,098	1,728	1,668	1,445	1,101	1,668	1,674	1,468	1,445	1,455	1,501	1,101	941	Total Reserves minus Gold ... 1l.d
	6	2	2	6	13	16	4	13	15	—	16	15	4	4	14	SDRs ... 1b.d
	36	37	47	47	50	50	50	50	51	50	50	49	50	50	51	Reserve Position in the Fund ... 1c.d
	703	1,016	1,049	1,675	1,605	1,380	1,048	1,605	1,608	1,418	1,380	1,391	1,447	1,048	876	Foreign Exchange ... 1d.d
	1,725	1,892	2,077	2,259	2,485	2,672	2,875	2,485	2,521	2,590	2,672	2,762	2,811	2,875	2,910	Gold (Million Fine Troy Ounces) ... 1ad
	586	645	719	799	888	976	1,071	888	907	939	976	1,017	1,042	1,071	1,089	Gold (National Valuation) ... 1and
	2,818	2,816	1,888	1,815	1,821	1,484	....	1,821	1,677	1,494	1,484	1,475	1,474	....		Monetary Auth: Other Liabilities ... 4..d
	1,455	1,633	1,693	1,813	1,849	1,908	1,903	1,849	1,812	1,839	1,908	1,837	1,828	1,903		Commercial Banks: Assets ... 7a.d
	149	145	132	142	137	192	172	137	157	172	192	194	202	172		of which: Claims on Nonbanks ... 7add
	3,514	3,499	3,253	2,623	2,637	2,746	2,707	2,637	2,650	2,658	2,746	2,734	2,662	2,707		Commercial Banks: Liabilities ... 7b.d
	2,788	2,603	2,371	1,841	1,854	1,902	1,897	1,854	1,856	1,875	1,902	1,862	1,855	1,897		of which: Liab. to Nonbanks ... 7bdd
	1,111	1,112	4	5	3	3	....	3	4	3	3	4	4	....		Develop. & Sav. Bks: Liabilities ... 7f.d
	1,111	1,112	4	5	3	3	....	3	4	3	3	4	4	....		of which: Liab. to Nonbanks ... 7fdd
	579	546	446	441	436	415	....	436	440	481	415	400	414	....		OBU: Foreign Assets ... 7k.d
	261	238	179	145	150	144	....	150	144	144	144	144	160	....		of which: Claims on Nonbanks ... 7kdd
	3,678	3,458	3,456	3,473	3,448	3,381	....	3,448	3,389	3,403	3,381	3,358	3,369	....		OBU: Foreign Liabilities ... 7md.d
	14	9	9	5	8	9	....	8	9	8	9	12	12	....		of which: Liab. to Nonbanks ... 7mdd
	991	1,356	1,450	1,940	1,823	1,365	....	1,823	1,512	1,398	1,365	1,290	1,351	....		US Liabilities to Philippines ... 9a.d
	2,353	2,410	2,166	2,220	2,300	2,126	....	2,300	2,140	2,082	2,126	2,227	2,164	....		US Claims on Philippines ... 9b.d
Monetary Authorities																
End of Period																
	26.30	33.66	35.95	51.42	52.03	49.28	....	52.03	52.40	48.82	49.28	50.30	51.74	....		Foreign Assets ... 11
	38.55	30.53	30.05	55.73	47.22	42.49	....	47.22	46.82	46.04	42.49	42.07	42.02	....		Claims on Government ... 12a
	4.58	4.77	5.01	4.09	4.03	4.29	....	4.03	3.98	4.01	4.29	4.29	4.32	....		Claims on Official Entities ... 12b
	28.94	23.22	22.17	11.04	13.30	13.96	....	13.30	13.68	13.54	13.96	13.98	13.82	....		Claims on Commercial Banks ... 12e
	29.07	28.99	28.58	9.51	9.21	9.13	....	9.21	9.19	9.17	9.13	9.12	9.11	....		Claims on Other Financial Inst ... 12f
	42.75	40.61	42.49	52.29	50.80	51.57	....	50.80	47.24	51.17	51.57	50.15	47.85	....		Reserve Money ... 14
	25.85	21.89	21.46	29.31	26.52	27.36	....	26.52	28.58	28.77	27.36	27.59	27.60	....		of which: Currency Outside Bks. ... 14a
	.63	.58	.34	.34	.34	.34	....	.34	.34	.34	.34	.34	.34	....		Bonds ... 16a
	81.86	80.95	60.46	63.25	63.49	56.08	....	63.49	61.54	56.91	56.08	55.27	55.63	....		Foreign Liabilities ... 16c
	4.02	14.07	13.80	16.41	26.32	40.12	....	26.32	37.13	37.28	40.12	50.62	57.10	....		Government Deposits ... 16d
	-1.83	-15.06	4.66	-.60	-15.15	-28.96	....	-15.15	-20.18	-.51	-28.96	-36.62	-39.90	....		Other Items (Net) ... 17r
Commercial Banks																
End of Period																
	14.60	16.16	18.05	20.67	21.58	21.66	....	21.58	16.51	19.25	21.66	20.37	18.21	....		Reserves ... 20
	10.08	7.91	7.10	4.81	1.23	1.02	....	1.23	.94	.93	1.02	.50	.48	....		Central Bank Bonds ... 20c
	29.98	33.60	34.61	37.22	38.00	39.04	....	38.00	37.13	37.63	39.04	37.55	37.40	....		Foreign Assets ... 21
	12.82	13.96	13.03	18.86	16.32	18.31	....	16.32	19.08	17.67	18.31	20.98	21.95	....		Claims on Government ... 22a
	23.76	23.74	23.92	16.12	20.23	16.21	....	20.23	17.36	14.45	16.21	12.22	12.02	....		Claims on Official Entities ... 22b
	116.80	114.28	112.04	89.21	96.11	100.52	....	96.11	99.48	100.82	100.52	103.97	105.38	....		Claims on Private Sector ... 22d
	12.26	12.06	12.00	13.35	14.07	14.70	....	14.07	13.66	13.42	14.70	14.30	14.77	....		Demand Deposits ... 24
	84.62	86.31	88.73	93.86	95.40	94.42	....	95.40	89.95	90.74	94.42	93.49	94.83	....		Time and Savings Deposits ... 25
	7.95	7.70	7.51	4.88	5.18	3.46	....	5.18	3.34	3.75	3.46	3.35	3.09	....		Bonds ... 26a
	3.05	3.16	3.08	2.98	3.36	2.69	....	3.36	2.98	2.72	2.69	2.36	2.27	....		Import Deposits ... 26b
	72.38	72.01	66.53	53.89	54.19	56.18	....	54.19	54.28	54.40	56.18	55.89	54.44	....		Foreign Liabilities ... 26c
	7.31	10.69	12.89	10.26	7.29	8.79	....	7.29	7.82	8.39	8.79	9.88	10.40	....		Government Deposits ... 26d
	27.16	22.45	21.10	9.89	11.46	14.95	....	11.46	12.31	14.62	14.95	14.82	14.77	....		Credit from Central Bank ... 26g
	21.20	23.61	24.05	27.84	28.35	27.18	....	28.35	28.63	26.74	27.18	27.62	27.83	....		Capital Accounts ... 27a
	-27.89	-28.33	-27.14	-30.02	-25.83	-25.59	....	-25.83	-22.48	-24.04	-25.59	-26.10	-26.96	....		Other Items (Net) ... 27r
Monetary Survey																
End of Period																
	-97.96	-85.70	-56.43	-28.46	-27.64	-23.95	....	-27.64	-26.29	-24.86	-23.95	-23.30	-20.94	....		Foreign Assets (Net) ... 31n
	214.24	191.50	185.92	166.84	159.50	142.05	....	159.50	150.97	146.49	142.05	132.15	127.31	....		Domestic Credit ... 32
	40.04	19.73	16.38	47.92	29.92	11.89	....	29.92	20.95	18.04	11.89	2.55	-3.52	....		Claims on Government (Net) ... 32an
	28.34	28.50	28.92	20.21	24.26	20.50	....	24.26	21.35	18.46	20.50	16.51	16.34	....		Claims on Official Entities ... 32b
	116.80	114.28	112.04	89.21	96.11	100.52	....	96.11	99.48	100.82	100.52	103.97	105.38	....		Claims on Private Sector ... 32d
	29.07	28.99	28.58	9.51	9.21	9.13	....	9.21	9.19	9.17	9.13	9.12	9.11	....		Claims on Other Financial Inst. ... 32f
	38.11	33.94	33.46	42.66	40.60	42.06	....	40.60	42.24	42.19	42.06	41.89	42.38	....		Money ... 34
	84.62	86.31	88.73	93.86	95.40	94.42	....	95.40	89.95	90.74	94.42	93.49	94.83	....		Quasi-Money ... 35
	8.58	8.28	7.84	5.21	5.52	3.80	....	5.52	3.68	4.09	3.80	3.69	3.43	....		Bonds ... 36a
	-15.02	-22.73	-.54	-3.45	-9.66	-22.17	....	-9.66	-11.19	8.21	-22.17	-30.22	-34.26	....		Other Items (Net) ... 37r
	38.34	33.84	34.82	38.36	40.84	41.94	....	40.84	41.82	41.90	41.94	43.23	43.87	....		*Money, Seasonally Adjusted* ... 34..b
	....	....	....	....	....	....	....	....	....	....	....	....	....	....		*Bank Debits (Monthly Averages)* ... 39d
Development and Savings Banks																
End of Period																
	6.05	7.02	3.97	2.78	3.64	5.48	....	3.64	4.74	4.99	5.48	6.07	....			Claims on Government ... 42a
	55.22	55.46	14.79	15.63	14.73	14.45	....	14.73	15.06	14.75	14.45	14.31	....			Claims on Private Sector ... 42d
	14.29	15.87	13.45	13.32	13.54	13.51	....	13.54	13.40	13.52	13.51	13.61	....			Time and Savings Deposits ... 45
	5.83	5.50	1.56	1.45	1.40	1.30	....	1.40	1.40	1.40	1.30	1.28	....			Bonds ... 46a
	22.90	22.89	.07	.09	.07	.07	....	.07	.07	.07	.07	.08	....			Foreign Liabilities ... 46c
	6.50	5.24	7.40	6.50	6.65	7.03	....	6.65	6.86	6.94	7.03	6.80	....			Capital Accounts ... 47a
	11.75	12.97	-3.71	-2.96	-3.29	-1.97	....	-3.29	-1.93	-2.19	-1.97	-1.40	....			Other Items (Net) ... 47r

Source: International Financial Statistics.

Table 4. Bank Lending to Developing Countries, 1983–First Half 1987[1,2]

(In billions of U.S. dollars; or in percent)

	1983	1984	1985	1986	1986 First half	1987 First half
Developing countries	**34.3**	**14.8**	**7.7**	**−1.4**	**−6.8**	**3.4**
Growth rate	*7*	*3*	*1*	*—*	*−1*	*1*
Africa	5.4	−0.3	1.3	−1.9	−1.7	−1.1
Of which:						
Algeria	*0.2*	*0.1*	*1.9*	*0.9*	*0.5*	*−0.6*
Côte d'Ivoire	*−0.1*	*−0.3*	*—*	*—*	*—*	*—*
Morocco	*0.3*	*0.1*	*0.1*	*—*	*0.1*	*0.1*
Nigeria	*1.3*	*−0.4*	*−0.7*	*−0.3*	*−0.2*	*−0.3*
South Africa	*3.0*	*−1.4*	*−0.3*	*−2.1*	*−1.2*	*−0.2*
Asia	9.0	8.1	6.3	4.8	−1.5	4.0
Of which:						
China	*0.8*	*1.3*	*4.8*	*0.7*	*−0.9*	*2.0*
India	*0.9*	*0.1*	*1.7*	*0.3*	*0.1*	*0.8*
Indonesia	*2.7*	*0.7*	*—*	*0.6*	*−0.1*	*0.7*
Korea	*2.0*	*3.5*	*2.2*	*−2.4*	*−0.1*	*−3.6*
Malaysia	*1.9*	*1.4*	*−1.4*	*−0.5*	*−0.7*	*−0.6*
Philippines	*−1.3*	*0.1*	*−0.5*	*−0.1*	*−0.3*	*0.4*
Europe	1.3	2.2	1.8	−0.5	0.6	0.2
Of which:						
Greece	*1.3*	*1.8*	*1.6*	*0.4*	*0.1*	*−0.1*
Hungary	*0.9*	*0.2*	*2.1*	*2.0*	*1.4*	*0.9*
Turkey	*0.5*	*0.9*	*0.5*	*1.5*	*1.6*	*0.6*
Yugoslavia	*—*	*0.2*	*0.2*	*−0.9*	*−0.8*	*−0.6*
Middle East	3.6	−0.9	−2.3	−2.4	−1.4	0.2
Of which:						
Egypt	*−0.7*	*0.6*	*−0.3*	*−0.1*	*—*	*−0.5*
Israel	*−0.3*	*−0.6*	*−0.8*	*−1.2*	*−0.7*	*−0.2*
Western Hemisphere	15.0	5.7	0.6	−1.5	−2.9	0.1
Of which:						
Argentina	*2.3*	*−0.2*	*0.5*	*1.2*	*1.2*	*−0.2*
Brazil	*5.2*	*5.2*	*−2.9*	*—*	*—*	*1.5*
Chile	*0.3*	*1.2*	*0.2*	*−0.4*	*−0.3*	*−0.7*
Colombia	*0.6*	*0.1*	*—*	*0.4*	*−0.4*	*−0.2*
Ecuador	*0.2*	*−0.1*	*0.2*	*0.3*	*—*	*0.2*
Mexico	*2.8*	*1.3*	*1.4*	*−0.6*	*−1.0*	*−0.2*
Venezuela	*−1.2*	*−2.2*	*0.5*	*−1.1*	*−0.1*	*−0.3*
Memorandum items						
Fifteen heavily indebted countries	11.3	5.1	−1.2	−1.5	−1.9	−0.3
Countries experiencing debt-servicing problems	8.3	3.3	−0.5	−8.9	−6.4	0.3
Gross concerted lending disbursements[3]	13.1	10.4	5.4	3.1	1.6	3.5
Total, BIS-based	26.4	11.6	14.4	−2.9	−8.8	5.1
Growth rate	*7*	*2*	*3*	*−1*	*−2*	*1*
Gross bond issues	3.1	5.3	9.6	5.4	3.3	2.1

Sources: Bank for International Settlements (BIS); Organization for Economic Cooperation and Development; International Monetary Fund, *International Financial Statistics*; and Fund staff estimates.

[1] IMF-based data on cross-border lending by banks are derived from the Fund's international banking statistics (IBS) (cross-border interbank accounts by residence of borrowing bank plus international bank credits to nonbanks by residence of borrower), excluding changes attributed to exchange rate movements. BIS-based data are derived from quarterly statistics contained in the BIS's *International Banking and Financial Market Developments*; the figures shown are adjusted for the effects of exchange rate movements. Differences between the IMF data and the BIS data are mainly accounted for by the different coverages. The BIS data are derived from geographical analyses provided by banks in the BIS reporting area. The IMF data derive cross-border interbank positions from the regular money and banking data supplied by member countries, while the IMF analysis of transactions with nonbanks is based on data from geographical breakdowns provided by the BIS reporting countries and additional banking centers. Neither the IBS series nor the BIS series are fully comparable over time because of expansion of coverage.

[2] Excluding the seven offshore centers (The Bahamas, Bahrain, the Cayman Islands, Hong Kong, the Netherlands Antilles, Panama, and Singapore).

[3] Excluding bridge loans.

Source: International Capital Markets.

Table A47. Developing Countries—by Region: External Debt, by Class of Creditor, End of Year, 1979–88[1]

(In billions of U.S. dollars)

	1979	1980	1981	1982	1983	1984	1985	1986	1987	1988
Developing countries										
Total debt	533.9	634.1	748.0	848.5	900.0	949.0	1,018.8	1,113.5	1,210.9	1,247.8
Short-term	108.7	145.1	179.8	204.4	188.0	192.0	173.6	170.1	183.1	191.0
Long-term	425.2	489.0	568.3	644.1	712.1	757.1	845.3	943.4	1,027.8	1,056.8
Unguaranteed[2]	78.9	93.1	116.1	133.4	129.7	128.3	130.2	132.5	129.9	125.1
Guaranteed[2]	346.3	395.9	452.2	510.7	582.3	628.8	715.0	810.9	897.9	931.7
To official creditors	168.7	192.3	216.6	245.8	272.1	298.2	340.5	400.3	460.6	490.8
To financial institutions	140.2	163.3	190.2	214.1	258.3	276.2	317.3	344.4	368.8	372.2
To other private creditors	37.4	40.3	45.4	50.8	52.0	54.4	57.2	66.2	68.5	68.7
By region										
Africa										
Total debt	86.1	98.4	109.1	122.3	130.8	132.9	143.2	161.3	179.0	185.0
Short-term	11.1	15.2	19.2	24.7	26.8	25.9	22.1	19.1	19.5	19.9
Long-term	75.0	83.2	89.8	97.5	104.0	107.0	121.1	142.3	159.5	165.2
To official creditors	30.5	35.8	41.3	46.8	53.3	58.0	68.1	83.3	99.3	106.5
To financial institutions[3]	27.3	29.4	30.5	31.4	31.6	30.8	33.2	38.4	40.1	38.5
To other private creditors[4]	17.2	18.1	18.1	19.3	19.1	18.3	19.8	20.6	20.2	20.1
Asia										
Total debt	113.6	136.8	158.7	183.9	204.4	218.9	246.5	268.8	293.0	304.6
Short-term	21.6	29.2	36.1	40.8	42.4	44.7	47.6	39.4	44.1	46.4
Long-term	92.1	107.6	122.6	143.1	162.0	174.2	199.0	229.4	249.0	258.2
To official creditors	52.9	59.6	65.1	73.7	80.5	85.6	98.8	116.5	133.1	142.8
To financial institutions[3]	15.3	20.4	24.3	30.2	36.5	38.9	45.0	51.7	54.8	56.1
To other private creditors[4]	23.9	27.6	33.2	39.2	44.9	49.8	55.1	61.2	61.1	59.3
Europe										
Total debt	81.0	93.6	102.0	106.8	107.4	111.9	127.3	145.3	154.0	156.8
Short-term	15.8	17.2	16.7	15.3	14.5	15.8	17.5	19.8	20.9	22.7
Long-term	65.2	76.4	85.3	91.5	92.9	96.1	109.8	125.5	133.1	134.0
To official creditors	27.8	31.8	37.3	42.2	43.5	45.9	52.1	62.2	67.7	68.3
To financial institutions[3]	21.7	25.6	29.0	29.3	29.8	32.6	39.9	46.2	48.6	48.9
To other private creditors[4]	15.8	19.0	18.9	20.0	19.6	17.6	17.8	17.1	16.8	16.8
Middle East										
Total debt	65.2	74.1	90.5	102.8	113.2	123.0	130.6	146.7	163.9	168.2
Short-term	24.7	27.7	35.8	42.2	46.9	48.0	48.5	51.9	55.0	54.7
Long-term	40.5	46.4	54.7	60.6	66.2	75.0	82.1	94.8	108.9	113.5
To official creditors	29.8	33.4	36.8	41.7	44.7	50.6	56.2	65.8	77.0	82.0
To financial institutions[3]	3.9	4.3	5.0	5.7	7.7	8.7	10.0	11.5	12.9	13.1
To other private creditors[4]	6.8	8.7	12.8	13.2	13.9	15.7	15.9	17.5	18.9	18.3
Western Hemisphere										
Total debt	187.9	231.2	287.8	332.8	344.3	362.3	371.2	391.4	421.0	433.3
Short-term	35.6	55.7	72.0	81.4	57.4	57.5	37.9	39.9	43.6	47.3
Long-term	152.4	175.5	215.9	251.4	286.9	304.8	333.3	351.4	377.3	386.0
To official creditors	27.7	31.8	36.1	41.2	50.1	58.2	65.3	72.6	83.5	91.2
To financial institutions[3]	71.9	83.7	101.4	117.5	152.6	165.2	189.2	196.7	212.4	215.5
To other private creditors[4]	52.8	60.0	78.4	92.6	84.2	81.3	78.8	82.2	81.4	79.3

[1] Excludes debt owed to the Fund.
[2] By an official agency of the debtor country.
[3] Covers only public and publicly guaranteed debt.
[4] Includes all unguaranteed debt on the presumption that this is owed mainly to private creditors.

Source: World Economic Outlook.

Chapter VI

THE OECD'S DEBT STATISTICS

1. ORIGINS OF DEBT STATISTICAL ACTIVITIES AND METHODS USED

1.1. Membership and General Objectives

The Organisation for Economic Co-operation and Development is an inter-governmental organisation consisting of the main industrial countries in Western Europe, North America and the Pacific region[1].

The three basic aims of the Organisation, as set out in Article 1 of the 1961 Convention setting up the OECD[2], are:

- To achieve the highest sustainable economic growth and employment and a rising standard of living in Member countries, while maintaining financial stability, and thus contribute to the development of the world economy;
- To contribute to sound expansion in Member as well as non-Member countries in the process of economic development;
- To contribute to the expansion of world trade on a multilateral, non-discriminatory basis in accordance with international obligations.

1.2. The OECD's Interest in Debt Statistics

1.2.1. Objectives Pursued

The OECD's debt statistical reporting systems form part of a complex designed to monitor economic developments in general and to prepare analyses related to the specific interests of individual OECD committees.

These cover such topics as the formulation of development co-operation policy, the analysis of resource flows and the relationship between trade, its financing and indebtedness with respect to individual countries or groups of countries (including, in addition to the developing countries, other non-OECD countries, in particular the members of the Council for Mutual Economic Assistance (CMEA), trade policy, creditworthiness and risk analysis, competition and developments in capital markets. Debt is a focus of concern not only as a constraint on economic growth and social progress in the developing countries but also because of its ramifications for the functioning of the international financial system and the impact of debt-related phenomena on trade flows.

The part of the OECD Secretariat which is most active in the collection and publication of information on external debt is the Development Co-operation Directorate (DCD), but analysis of pertinent segments of the data base is also performed in several other Directorates (see Section 1.2.2). Since 1960, when the inter-donor Development Assistance Group, later to become the OECD's Development Assistance Committee (DAC)[3], was created, detailed statistics on the flow of official development assistance and other capital to the developing countries have been collected by the DCD and these are the basic material for most published statistics on aid and aid-related flows. The collection of external debt figures, originally an outgrowth of these "DAC" statistics, is now a separate but related part of the data collection on international resource transfers and is no longer limited to developing countries.

1.2.2. Use Made of Debt Information

The DCD's use of the debt statistics mainly concerns the economic situation of the developing countries which are the principal recipients of the aid and other financial flows from the Member countries of the Development Assistance Committee, for which the Directorate acts as Secretariat.

Other Committees of the OECD, however, are also vitally concerned in the debt problem and participate actively in the OECD's work on the subject.

In the work falling under the authority of the Economic Policy Committee, OECD debt statistics are used in particular by Working Party III and in the preparation of global balance-of-payments projections.

In the case of the Trade Committee, debt problems are discussed at meetings of the Group on Export Credits and Export Credit Guarantees. The figures are also used in the preparation of studies concerning particular groups of countries, for example the producers of certain commodities.

The Committee on Financial Markets uses the data in its work on international financial markets, as well as at its regular meetings on East-West financial relations.

1.3. Collection Method

1.3.1. Main Source

The main instrument for the collection of debt statistics is the Creditor Reporting System (CRS)[4]. This system was originally sponsored and designed jointly by the OECD and the World Bank in 1967, with the OECD's Development Co-operation Directorate taking responsibility for the operation of the system. The CRS shares many essential features with the World Bank's Debtor Reporting System (DRS), the two systems being designed to be as complementary as possible. In particular, their coverage is in principle identical as regards debt owed by public borrowers or private sector borrowers with public sector guarantees to OECD countries reporting in the CRS, so that CRS figures not only provide a cross-check for common reporting pairings, but can also be used directly as supplementary information for debtor countries which do not report to the World Bank's DRS.

The CRS was established with the aim of supplying "a regular flow of data on indebtedness and capital flows". Within this general objective, it has become, over the years, a major source of information not only on the categories of indebtedness it covers (the notable exclusion being unguaranteed bank claims – see Section 1.3.2), but also on the terms and conditions of external (especially official) lending, as well as the sectoral and geographic distribution of flows to the developing countries. In 1980, coverage was expanded to include flows to, and the indebtedness of, all other countries (the "extended" CRS), using the same reporting forms and norms.

Under the Creditor Reporting System and its extension, the 18 Members of the Development Assistance Committee[5], together with three OECD members which are not members of the Committee[6], provide data on official development assistance [ODA[7]], on officially-supported lending (which includes both official lending and officially-guaranteed private ending) and on the corresponding debt. The reporters are official aid agencies (or in some cases an agency responsible for co-ordinating the statistical reporting of several aid agencies), export guarantee agencies, and, in specific instances, official bodies which have undertaken direct lending to a borrowing country, for example in connection with debt reschedulings.

A distinctive feature of the CRS is that it obtains detailed information on individual transactions, which means that it lends itself to an extremely wide range of analyses. The aggregated information derived from the CRS is supplemented by, and can be checked against, the aggregated information provided in other systems, including those of the other organisations described in this report – especially the World Bank and the BIS – as well as the "DAC" reporting system on flows to developing countries. It is worth noting that the consistency of definitions and overall approach with the reporting of annual aggregates to the DAC means that many of the reporters have themselves integrated the two systems in their own bookkeeping.

The system involves reporting on a number of different forms (reproduced in Appendix 8).

One series of forms (Forms 1B, 1C) provides details of each official-sector loan or credit with a maturity exceeding 1 year and each officially insured or guaranteed export credit with a maturity exceeding five years. These reports are in principle provided continuously to the OECD throughout the year within two months of the commitment date (Forms 1C within one month).

A second form (Form 2), compiled annually, provides the following information for official sector loans (mostly ODA lending) to developing countries: a) commitments; b) disbursements; c) amortization; d) interest payments; e) undisbursed debt; f) disbursed debt outstanding at the end of each calendar year; g) arrears of principal; h) arrears of interest. Form 2, together with Form 3A described below, provides a full record of official sector lending (largely government-to-government development lending).

A third (semi-annual) set of forms provides reporting on new and outstanding officially-guaranteed or officially-insured private export credits (Form 3) and on official financing support for exports (sometimes referred to as direct official export credits) (Form 3A). Form 3 is compiled by agencies that insure or guarantee export credits extended by exporters (supplier credits) or financial institutions (financial trade credit, also referred to as buyer credits). Form 3A is compiled by the official agencies of the 6 DAC countries extending direct official export credits. Each form shows for each borrowing country: *a)* new transactions guaranteed during the half-year; *b)* payments made by the borrower; *c)* the resultant balances outstanding; *d)* arrears of principal and interest; *e)* projected service payments. A Form 3B is being introduced to cover also insured or guaranteed export credits with an original maturity of less than one year (this reporting already takes place on a voluntary basis and the results are incorporated in the material on total outstanding debt on export credit account).

The DAC reporting system provides aggregated information on flows of *a)* gross and net official development lending; *b)* gross and net official export credits; *c)* gross and net private export credits; *d)* debt reorganisation; *e)* interest receipts on official flows. This information is used to extend or corroborate the detailed reporting in the CRS, while, in the opposite direction, the CRS figures can be used to supplement those provided in the DAC system.

It will be seen from comparison with Section 1.3.1 of Chapter VII that the reporting framework provided by these various CRS forms resembles very closely that used in the World Bank's Debtor Reporting System, although the coverage of the guaranteed claims reported on differs, in that the CRS records guarantees by agencies in the lending country, and the DRS records credits guaranteed by agencies in the debtor country.

1.3.2. *Additional Sources and Use of Estimation*

The OECD's aggregated data on external debt draw on several additional sources.

From the BIS

The debt stock figures on export credits merged with the BIS figures on bank claims and adjusted to eliminate double-counting are published jointly by the OECD and the BIS in the *OECD/BIS Survey* (see section on Publications at end of chapter). The results are also the nucleus of the OECD's comprehensive stock data, which further include the following non-CRS materials:

From the World Bank and IMF

– Lending by multilateral organisations, including regional development banks;

- Use of Fund credit;
- Supplementary information on bank claims.

From the World Bank (Debtor Reporting System)

- Privately-extended export credits taken up by public sector entities, or guaranteed by the public sector in borrowing countries, but not officially guaranteed in the lending country;
- (For a number of countries) Private sector borrowing not covered by a guarantee in either the borrowing country or the lending country;
- Claims held by countries not reporting in the CRS.

From other OECD Secretariat sources

- OPEC and Eastern European lending;
- Inter-company lending;
- Multilateral lending (for non-DRS countries).

There are several elements of estimation in the integrated debt data in the OECD/BIS survey. First, some of the CRS data on guaranteed export credits in Form 3 (but not the data in Form 3A) include, in addition to disbursed credits, undisbursed credits or credit lines and, for a few reporting countries, the interest due over the entire life of the credits. In order to arrive at figures for disbursed credits only for each borrowing country, the OECD makes estimates to exclude undisbursed amounts and future interest due, using internal evidence in the forms from the reporting country concerned. The amounts involved, once quite large, are now negligible, following the gradual improvement in reporting specifications.

Second, it is not possible to eliminate all the overlaps that exist between the figures reported to the BIS and the OECD in respect of officially-guaranteed supplier credits in cases where such credits are acquired by banks and are considered as external claims. For the United Kingdom and the United States adjustments have been made to the OECD data which eliminate these overlaps as far as possible, but for the other creditor countries where overlaps exist no such adjustment has yet been possible. The error involved is nil or negligible for all debtors combined. For any one debtor, it may involve under-counting or double-counting, but is in any case negligible in relation to that debtor's total debt vis-à-vis all countries.

In extending the OECD/BIS nucleus to derive comprehensive debt figures for each borrowing country, two elements of estimation arise from the comparison of data reported by the borrowing country in the World Bank's DRS with the data concerning each creditor's claims on that borrower as compiled from the creditor sources:

a) For creditor countries for which double-counting (or under-counting) may subsist after collation of the data on bank and supplier credit claims, comparison with the debtor's data on the claims of the creditor reporter for these categories combined enables the error to be rectified or reduced;

b) Until recently, DRS reporters issuing bonds on the international market reported them as such, with no breakdown as between bonds held by banks and bonds held by non-banks. These amounts have been included in the data unmodified. For those creditors whose bank claims data include international bonds and notes, there is double-counting for the debtor concerned. With the separate identification in BIS reports of banks' holdings of securities (see Chapter III, Section 4.3 (Q)), this double-counting will be virtually eliminated.

A final element of estimation concerns the breakdown between short-term and long-term liabilities, but does not affect estimated total liabilities. In comparing the amounts reported in successive BIS surveys to ascertain the amount of long-term bank claims reaching the last year of their life, the figures must be taken as reported in US dollars. To the extent that some part of the liabilities recorded is denominated in a urrency other than the US dollar, and that currency has depreciated or appreciated against the dollar between the two periods, the volume of short-term debt will be overstated or understated. Second, inasmuch as short-term supplier credits may be discounted within the banking system, there is a double-counting possibility similar to that referred to earlier. In this instance, however, it is known that a higher proportion of short-term supplier credits than of long-term supplier credits is rediscounted with central banks and so excluded from reported bank claims, thus minimising the potential distortion due to this factor.

1.3.3. Confidentiality

No restriction is placed on the disclosure of the total ODA, "other official" (OOF) or guaranteed private export credit transactions of a given creditor country with all recipient countries or with major groups of recipient countries, or on the disclosure of total OOF, total official or total guaranteed private export credit transactions of a given debtor country with all creditor countries reporting in the CRS or the extended CRS.

As regards individual transactions, the information concerning individual ODA loans is classified as restricted, but no restriction is placed on the disclosure of ODA aggregates from any one donor to any one recipient. Information compiled from the CRS on individual OOF and guaranteed private export credit transactions with developing countries, and information from the "extended CRS" on official sector transactions with and private guaranteed export credits to countries other than developing countries, is classified as confidential, being made available only to:

- Authorised statistical staff of OECD, the World Bank (for data concerning developing countries) and the BIS (export credit data only);
- The OECD's Trade Committee Group on Export Credits and Export Credit Guarantees;
- For the exclusive purpose of cross-checking debt statistics, the non-DAC partner country to a transaction, providing the authority of the reporting country has been obtained beforehand.

2. RELATIONSHIP TO THE CORE DEFINITION

2.1. General

The OECD subscribes to the core definition established by the Group as the concept most adequately describing total external debt. For practical reasons connected with the particular reporting method employed, and its partial derivation from systems set up for other purposes, there are a number of minor deviations between the figures appearing in OECD publications and those which would be obtained by strict application of the core definition.

The figures collected by the OECD in the Creditor Reporting System relate to debt arising from the following types of transaction:

- Bilateral official development assistance (ODA) loans, including debt reorganisation classified as ODA and loans repayable in inconvertible local currency;
- Direct official export credits;
- Official debt reorganisation lending not classified as ODA;
- Other official lending;
- Export credits guaranteed by an official agency in the creditor country, with separate data for;
    - Supplier credits (credits extended by an exporter);
    - Financial credits (credits extended by a bank or other financial institution directly to a foreign buyer).

(The above sub-categories also include leasing arrangements, revolving credits and lines of credit).

2.2. Core Items Excluded or Imperfectly Covered

The main core item excluded is official loans made out of local currency balances, with amortization stipulated in local currency or repayable in local currency at the borrower's option.

2.3. Non-Core Items Collected or Published

Data are reported to OECD on undisbursed amounts, and on the future interest guaranteed by export credit guarantee agencies. These data are usually available separately; if not (see Section 1.3.2.) they are estimated. They are not published.

The published data on export credit claims include guaranteed leasing transactions indistinguishably. Some of these would be excluded on virtually any convention concerning the threshold for inclusion in the core definition (see Chapter VII, Section 2.1.2.1.), but even if none were eligible, the overstatement of "core" debt would be of the order of 1 per cent overall.

2.4. Other Points Concerning Relationship to Core Definition

2.4.1. Residence

In the DCD's systems, reporting is on the basis of IMF balance-of-payments norms, including residence. Strict respect of this criterion, however, would diminish the analytical utility of the derived material in two specific instances. In the published data (including those published in the OECD/BIS survey) on the debt of offshore banking centres, the figures on a residence basis are reduced by neglecting the (substantial) claims of banks on banks. This is on the grounds that the borrowing banks have taken up the funds only to re-lend them externally and that to include these amounts would distort the external indebtedness of the economy proper, as distinct from its banking sector.

A similar view is taken in preparing the overall statistics (but not in the BIS/OECD survey) where the immediate beneficiary of a loan or credit is a "flag of convenience" or "brass plate" company. The principle applied in these cases is to treat non-operational companies as "transparent" and to regard the residence as being that of the ultimate user of the credit.

The reports on export credits in the CRS include indistinguishably amounts of credit extended by lenders in other countries but guaranteed by the reporting agency. In this case, the debt as such is accurately recorded, but there could be small distortions in the assignment of amounts by creditor country.

2.4.2. Maturity

The OECD debt reporting in the CRS covers both long-term and short-term claims, and in many statistical tables a breakdown is shown between claims with an original maturity of one year or less and over one year. Among other things, this permits direct comparison and collation with data in the DAC reporting system, which relate to loans with a maturity of over one year.

2.4.3. Undisbursed or Contingent Amounts

The CRS, since its starting-point is individual commitments, with subsequent disbursements being reported in relation to those commitments, provides data on both disbursed and undisbursed amounts. The published debt statistics pertain only to the disbursed amounts.

Future interest is excluded from data in the public domain.

90

2.4.4. Treatment of Certain Types of Instrument

2.4.4.1. Equity and Intra-group Lending

Lending to overseas subsidiaries is included, to the extent that it is guaranteed. As already mentioned, however, non-operational companies of a "flag of convenience" or "brass-plate" nature are treated as being "transparent", i.e., it is the ultimate beneficiary of the transaction which is taken into account and the non-operational companies are ignored.

2.4.4.2. Leasing

Claims resulting from guaranteed leasing arrangements are automatically but indistinguishably included (see Section 2.3).

2.4.4.3. Loans Repayable in Local Currency

Cross-border loans repayable in local currency are included in the debt figures, even if the repayments are to an account in the lender's name in the borrowing country. By contrast, loans out of such local currency balances, repayable in local currency, are not recorded.

2.4.4.4. Military

Private and official export credits for military purposes are indistinguishably included in the CRS system, so that the corresponding debt is included in OECD figures. In addition, published official data on governmental claims on military account are included where available. As pointed out elsewhere, however, some lending and borrowing countries refuse to reveal information on military transactions.

3. OTHER QUESTIONS REGARDING CONTENT

3.1. Method of Currency Conversion

Most of the CRS data are reported in national currency, which until recently was assumed for practical purposes also to be the currency of repayment (or, more accurately, the currency in which the claim is denominated). However, data by currency of denomination are now being reported by a growing number of countries. For conversion of flow data into dollars, the currency used in the OECD's statistical tables, the OECD Secretariat uses period-average exchange rates (an exception is that in some data on individual transactions circulated to the Group on Export Credit and Export

91

Credit Guarantees, the data are converted into SDRs at the daily exchange rate applicable at the date of commitment). For debt stock data, including those in the BIS/OECD survey, end-period rates are used.

3.2. Treatment of Arrears

Arrears of principal are reported separately by most creditors and treated as part of outstanding debt (this is in most cases the direct result of the statistical method applied). Arrears of interest are reported in the CRS for official and officially guaranteed credits. Arrears classified by the Secretariat as outstanding short-term debt are kept in the data until they are discharged, rescheduled or written off. In this last case, the total debt stock is reduced, thereby inducing a possible asymmetry vis-à-vis debtor statistics, where the amount will be removed from the record only if the write-off is in connection with forgiveness (see Section 3.3).

3.3. Treatment of Debt Reorganisation

The categories of debt reorganisation recognised are those listed in Section 3.4 of Chapter II and their impact on the debt stock data is in principle as described in that section. To summarise, rescheduling and refinancing leave the principal outstanding unchanged, but if interest has been capitalised the amount of debt shown will rise. In the case of write-off, debt is reduced in creditor source data, but not in debtor data; repudiation reduces debt shown in debtor sources but not necessarily in creditor data; forgiveness reduces the debt shown in both sources. With the exception noted below, the debt stock data reflect the sector changes occurring when refinanced debt is assumed by a new debtor, or taken over by a different creditor.

The data actually collected have not been fully comprehensive as regards refinancing. Where a loan to refinance debt is extended by a party other than the original claimant and which is not a reporter to the CRS, the debt outstanding is recorded at a lower figure. Reporting changes now taking place will remedy this understatement through the combination of two approaches: the receipt by the original reporter of disbursements on the new loan (which is amortization from that reporter's point of view) will be identified separately, and the corresponding amount of debt reorganisation lending imputed. In this case, the sector to which the new lender belongs cannot usually be identified. The second approach will be to extend the coverage of the system to encompass reports by bodies, not hitherto in the system, extending refinancing loans.

Data on debt reorganisation are received in the CRS when the lender (or the party effecting a rescheduling) reports a commitment. In the case of multilateral debt reorganisations in, e.g., the Paris Club, this means that the record may be completed only after a considerable time, as the bilateral implementing agreements are concluded.

4. SECTORING

4.1. Country Coverage

Data published by the OECD for individual borrowing countries are shown aggregated over groups of creditors. The standard breakdown is between OECD creditor countries and capital markets, use of IMF credit, multilateral sources, and other creditor countries.

The breakdown published on the debtor side is extremely comprehensive, with the tables normally showing 159 countries, including CMEA and other countries not on the DAC list of developing countries (see specimen tables at the end of this chapter and Appendix 7).

4.2. Types of Debtor/Creditor

The term "official sector" on the creditor side refers to governments, including state or local governments, and embraces also transactions effected by their executing agencies, including export credit guarantee and insurance agencies. All other transactors are regarded as private. The data received in the CRS further identify whether a given aggregate relates to a transaction with a "public" or a "private" borrower (this information is used solely in collating CRS and DRS data) (see Section 1.3.2). The definition of "public" and "private" is the same as that used by the World Bank.

4.3. Types of claim

Considerable detail is provided in the OECD publications concerning the type of claim as well as the type of creditor. (See the specimen tables at the end of the chapter).

5. SPECIAL FEATURES

5.1. Data for Calculating "Net Debt" and Flows

Virtually all the debt stock data collected by the OECD in the CRS relate to gross debt, so that data on net debt, which have not so far been presented, can be calculated only by drawing on figures for reporters' liabilities to each borrowing country taken from other sources. As regards flow data, the systems used by the OECD provide both gross and net figures for most categories of transaction ("net" here referring to allowance for repayments of principal). The record on net flows is completed for the banking sector, where necessary, by referring to data for the change in stock between the two dates,

93

adjusted to allow for a) flow data from the CRS record of banks' export credit transactions and b) changes between the two dates in the value of the currency of denomination vis-à-vis the numeraire (the US dollar).

5.2. Data on Debt Service

Debt service is regularly included in the OECD reporting systems. The quality of these data is not the same as that of the figures on debt. For work to be done in this area, see Chapter III.

5.3. Debt Service Projections

Information on the projected debt service for officially-supported credits (including repayments scheduled in respect of as yet undisbursed amounts and interest payment liabilities maturing in the course of the period) is reported in Form 3, looking ahead eight years. Taken in conjunction with Form 1 information on official loans, this means that projected debt service for many developing countries, especially the poorer ones, is known for the bulk of the currently outstanding debt.

5.4. Other

The annual publication *Geographic Distribution of Financial Flows to Developing Countries* contains data for individual developing countries and significant country groupings concerning the flows of official loans from individual industrialised countries and other groups, together with the country's total receipts of various forms of official and private lending.

NOTES AND REFERENCES

1. The Members of the OECD are: Australia, Austria, Belgium, Canada, Denmark, Finland, France, the Federal Republic of Germany, Greece, Iceland, Ireland, Italy, Japan, Luxembourg, the Netherlands, New Zealand, Norway, Portugal, Spain, Sweden, Switzerland, Turkey, the United Kingdom and the United States. The Commission of the European Communities takes part in OECD work and Yugoslavia participates in many of its activities.

2. Taking over from the Organisation for European Economic Co-operation, which had been created in 1948 to rebuild and restructure the economies of Europe with the help of United States Marshall Plan aid.

3. Not all OECD Member countries belong to the Development Assistance Committee, which consists of Australia, Austria, Belgium, Canada, Denmark, Finland, France, the Federal Republic of Germany, Ireland, Italy, Japan, the Netherlands, New Zealand, Norway, Sweden, Switzerland, the United Kingdom, the United States and the Commission of the European Communities. The IMF and the World Bank are permanent observers.

4. Earlier title: the Expanded Reporting System.

5. See footnote 3.

6. Greece, Portugal, Spain.

7. Grants, and loans conveying a grant element of 25 per cent or more, using a 10 per cent discount rate.

PUBLICATIONS

A. Regular Publications Containing Debt Statistics

1. External Debt Statistics

- Frequency, date of publication: annual, late in year

Obtainable from:

- OECD
  Publications Service
  2, rue André Pascal
  75775 Paris Cedex 16
  France

  (Or from sales agents listed at the back of any OECD publication)

- Price: FF50 or $10

Data shown for last two available end-years.

2. Statistics on External Indebtedness: Bank and Trade-Related Non-Bank External Claims on Individual Borrowing Countries and Territories

- Frequency, date of publication: half-yearly (six to seven months after the date to which the figures relate)

Obtainable from:

- BIS (see Chapter IV, Publications Section)

and

- Development Co-operation Directorate, OECD
  2, rue André Pascal
  75775 Paris Cedex 16
  France

- On request, free of charge.

Data shown for latest three end-half-years.
Also available on micro-computer diskette (FF800 or $105).

(For details, contact:

- OECD
  Data Dissemination and Reception Unit
  2, rue André Pascal
  75775 Paris Cedex 16
  France

3. *Financing and External Debt of Developing Countries*

   – Frequency, date of publication: annual, 6 months after end of year for which estimates presented, with the detailed statistical record up to the preceding end-year.

   Obtainable from:

   – OECD
   Publications Service
   2, rue André Pascal
   75775 Paris Cedex 16
   France

   (Or from sales agents listed at the back of any OECD publication)

   – Price (FF100 or $21).

B.   Other Publications Containing Debt or Debt-Related Statistics

1. *Financial Statistics*

   – Monthly

   Obtainable from:

   – OECD
   Publications Service
   2, rue André Pascal
   75775 Paris Cedex 16
   France

   (Or from sales agents listed at the back of any OECD publication)

   – On request, free of charge.

2. *Geographical Distribution of the Flow of Financial Resources to Developing Countries*

   – Frequency, date of publication: annual, 13-15 months after latest year covered by the statistics

   Obtainable from:

   – Publications Service, OECD
   2, rue André Pascal
   75775 Paris Cedex 16
   France

   (Or from sales agents listed at the back of any OECD publication)

   – Price (FF195 or $39)

Also available on micro-computer diskette (FF1400 or $185)
For details, contact:

- OECD
  Data Dissemination and Reception Unit
  2, rue André Pascal
  75775 Paris Cedex 16
  France

3. *The Export Credit Financing System in OECD Member Countries, Third Edition, Paris 1987*

Obtainable from:

- OECD
  Publications Service
  2 rue André Pascal
  75775 Paris Cedex 16
  France

  (Or from sales agents listed at the back of any OECD publication)

- Price (FF110 or $22).

$ million

Table 2: DEBT AND LIABILITIES OUTSTANDING AT END DECEMBER 1985

| | | OECD Countries and capital markets | | | | | | Multilateral | | | | |
	ODA	Non bank trade claims Total	Non bank trade claims Long-term	Guaranteed bank claims	Other bank claims Total	Other bank claims Long-term	Non bank deposits	Concessional	Non concessional	Other claims	Use of Fund Credit	TOTAL
SAUDI ARABIA	–	3 310	1 665	203	10 310	2 038	330	–	162	–	–	14 153
SENEGAL	287	625	507	167	430	146	43	400	13	401	241	2 756
SEYCHELLES	23	16	8	6	40	22	–	7	17	7	–	111
SIERRA LEONE	82	92	85	16	232	53	–	130	17	47	78	694
SINGAPORE	77	1 003	823	216	2 367	1 947	–	9	131	201	–	4 004
SOMALIA	267	209	205	–	138	115	–	378	129	477	142	1 749
SOUTH AFRICA	–	1 110	414	1 967	18 568	8 687	150	–	–	–	818	22 464
SRI LANKA	1 405	210	185	229	615	463	–	699	56	164	321	3 849
SUDAN	427	2 013	1 804	352	1 269	485	–	898	146	2 563	665	8 333
SURINAME	2	14	8	9	16	8	–	6	–	11	–	58
SWAZILAND	58	22	21	13	68	55	–	33	73	–	10	276
SYRIA	371	372	182	77	1 143	73	–	129	380	1 637	–	4 109
TAIWAN	86	2 499	2 330	307	5 396	2 225	–	–	142	589	–	9 019
TANZANIA	465	597	226	109	329	200	–	798	262	996	21	3 578
THAILAND	1 758	1 449	1 326	360	9 613	6 650	467	341	2 757	594	1 020	18 360
TOGO	43	432	344	19	126	79	14	258	32	21	63	1 008
TONGA	15	1	0	–	–	–	–	9	–	–	–	25
TRINIDAD & TOBAGO	8	492	434	183	973	882	42	17	25	–	–	1 739
TUNISIA	1 268	1 110	940	713	980	689	439	134	660	531	–	5 836
TURKEY	3 588	4 553	3 941	1 330	5 705	5 081	551	641	4 174	2 013	1 326	23 882
TURKS & CAICOS I.	–	0	–	–	86	26	–	0	–	–	–	87
UGANDA	32	127	103	24	22	6	–	388	86	204	282	1 165
UN. ARAB EMIR.	1	323	139	209	8 304	895	709	–	14	17	–	9 576
URUGUAY	61	85	62	44	2 639	1 997	–	18	277	310	350	3 785
U.S.S.R.	–	9 309	7 710	6 386	14 781	7 980	–	–	–	–	–	30 476
VANUATU	3	42	40	21	60	40	–	1	–	–	–	128
VENEZUELA	12	1 366	1 050	307	41 395	24 470	–	36	38	400	–	43 553
VIET NAM	363	142	50	23	378	250	–	173	–	4 376	31	5 486
WALLIS & FUTUNA	2	1	1	–	–	–	–	–	–	–	–	4
YEMEN	106	112	53	69	327	117	89	387	66	1 317	11	2 484
YEMEN, DEM.	19	138	119	10	12	12	–	329	–	995	15	1 625
YUGOSLAVIA	435	2 040	1 569	2 034	13 224	10 452	–	64	2 179	1 171	2 108	23 255
ZAIRE	781	2 725	2 588	101	698	417	–	579	118	238	721	5 961
ZAMBIA	677	785	645	156	688	203	11	266	465	733	762	4 544
ZIMBABWE	276	152	122	347	690	467	24	55	198	162	264	2 169
(FOR REF.) TOTAL DEVELOPING COUNTRIES	74 584	132 273	102 903	55 088	568 647	400 126	34 095	42 115	65 930	71 155	34 568	1 078 456
CMEA COUNTRIES	–	22 616	16 471	14 540	51 378	31 210	–	–	1 628	8 363	1 831	100 355

Source: *External Debt Statistics.*

TABLE I (continued)

Breakdown by borrower of bank and trade-related non-bank short

and long-term external claims of the reporting countries

(in millions of US dollars)

Borrowing country or territory (1) Jun. 87	External bank claims		Non-bank trade-related credits (3)	Total (a)+(c)
	Total (a)	of which: identified guaranteed claims (2) (b)	(c)	(d)
46. Finland.........	17,605	135	277	17,882
47. Gabon...........	1,407	597	507	1,915
48. Gambia..........	49	43	32	81
49. German Dem.Rep(6)	12,502	1,543	1,760	14,262
50. Ghana..........	421	104	73	494
51. Gibraltar.......	247	1	10	257
52. Greece..........	14,348	637	1,600	15,948
53. Grenada.........	12	1	7	19
54. Guatemala.......	477	156	193	670
55. Guiana, French...	–	–	1	1
56. Guinea..........	203	51	147	350
57. Guinea-Bissau....	16	1	17	33
58. Guyana..........	66	3	36	102
59. Haïti...........	33	6	37	70
60. Honduras........	325	87	231	556
61. Hong Kong.....(4)	9,663	1,927	984	10,647
62. Hungary.........	10,853	266	375	11,228
63. Iceland.........	1,481	37	54	1,535
64. India..........	8,330	629	1,829	10,159
65. Indonesia.......	18,172	3,171	5,112	23,284
66. Iran...........	1,296	107	2,331	3,627
67. Iraq...........	8,435	2,933	4,086	12,521
68. Israel.........	5,699	1,104	10,017	15,716
69. Ivory Coast......	3,478	559	623	4,101
70. Jamaica........	540	150	245	785
71. Jordan..........	1,639	252	890	2,528
72. Kampuchea.......	–	–	7	7
73. Kenya..........	1,163	360	488	1,651
74. Kiribati.......	–	–	–	–
75. Korea, Dem.P.Rep.	658	–	417	1,075
76. Korea, Rep.......	29,889	2,025	5,704	35,592
77. Kuwait.........	7,867	18	1,563	9,431
78. Laos............	21	–	6	27
79. Lebanon......(4)	1,120	54	136	1,256
80. Liberia.....(4,5)	9,982	368	200	10,183
81. Libya...........	655	4	1,053	1,708
82. Macao...........	1,095	–	1	1,096
83. Madagascar......	235	56	151	386
84. Malawi.........	84	14	37	121
85. Malaysia........	11,588	753	1,471	13,059
86. Maldives........	15	1	2	17
87. Mali...........	53	12	49	102
88. Malta..........	104	–	40	144
89. Mauritania......	115	51	47	162
90. Mauritius........	98	16	25	123
91. Mexico..........	76,029	3,513	4,680	80,708
92. Mongolia........	–	–	1	1
93. Morocco.........	5,461	1,648	1,846	7,306
94. Mozambique......	350	92	295	645
95. Namibia.........	3	–	–	3
96. Nauru..........	64	–	–	64
97. Nepal..........	85	69	12	97
98. Neth.Antilles (4)	7,191	321	62	7,253
99. New Zealand......	12,130	179	500	12,630
100. Nicaragua.......	578	43	152	731
Pays ou territoire emprunteur (1) Jun. 87	Créances bancaires extérieures		Crédits non bancaires liés à des opérations commerciales (3)	Total (a)+(c)
	Total (a)	dont: montant identifié de créances garanties (2) (b)	(c)	(d)

Ventilation par emprunteur des créances extérieures à court et à long terme des pays

déclarants, liées à des opérations bancaires et à des opérations commerciales non bancaires

(en millions de dollars des Etats-Unis)

TABLEAU I (suite)

Source: Statistics on External Indebtedness.

US $ Million

	1975	1981	1982	1982	1983	1984	1985
GROSS DEBT							
Long term							
I. OECD countries and capital markets	8126	9858	10106	10324	10268	10730	13706
ODA	7274	8751	7940	7899	7728	6726	8255
Official/off. supported	841	955	1635	1467	1127	1900	2063
Official export credits	..	..	..	204	260	733	906
Guaranteed supplier credits	..	..	..	761	494	668	610
Guaranteed bank credits	..	..	..	502	373	498	546
Financial markets	11	132	491	959	1413	2105	3388
Banks	9	100	450	927	1383	1975	3120
Bonds	2	32	41	32	30	130	268
Other private	–	20	40	–	–	–	–
II. Multilateral	3245	6720	9126	9126	10355	11253	12746
of which: concessional	3063	6050	7909	7909	8756	9481	10754
non-concessional	182	670	1217	1217	1599	1772	1992
III. Non-OECD Creditor countries	1100	1604	1305	1258	1207	1272	1501
CMEA	364	311	256	256	302	294	401
OPEC	706	1252	1027	980	885	861	819
Other countries and unspecified	30	41	21	21	20	117	281
Subtotal: Long term debt	*12471*	*18183*	*20537*	*20708*	*21829*	*23256*	*27953*
of which: concessional	11356	16332	17117	17076	17599	17291	20166
non-concessional	1114	1851	3420	3632	4230	5965	7787
Short term							
Subtotal: Short term debt	..	..	..	*2397*	*2049*	*2434*	*3605*
Banks	..	..	..	1513	1437	1811	2747
Export credits	..	..	..	884	612	623	858
Total external debt excluding IMF credit	..	..	..	*23105*	*23878*	*25689*	*31558*
Total external debt including IMF credit	..	..	..	**25384**	**27576**	**29610**	**35760**
Other identified liabilities	..	..	..	422	447	470	623
Total identified debt	..	..	..	**25806**	**28023**	**30080**	**36383**
SERVICE PAYMENTS							
Long term							
I. OECD countries and capital markets	656	1003	1162	962	1145	1100	1422
ODA	283	520	458	466	439	443	420
Official/off. supported	371	450	644	301	575	409	777
Financial markets	2	30	50	195	132	248	225
Other private	–	3	10	–	–	–	–
II. Multilateral	113	193	252	252	341	391	481
of which: concessional	70	92	98	98	118	140	180
III. Non-OECD creditor countries	92	199	235	235	240	189	213
Subtotal: Service payments, long term debt	*861*	*1394*	*1649*	*1450*	*1726*	*1679*	*2116*
of which: concessional	433	788	773	781	762	720	600
Total service payments excl. IMF credit	**861**	**1394**	**1649**	**1644**	**1948**	**1918**	**2363**
Amortization, long term debt	..	..	..	802	1065	898	1249
Interest, long term debt	..	..	..	647	661	781	867
Interest, short term debt	..	..	..	194	222	239	247
Total service payments incl. IMF credit	..	..	..	**1714**	**2173**	**2377**	**2857**

Source: Financing and External Debt of Developing Countries.

101

Chapter VII

THE WORLD BANK'S DEBT STATISTICS

1. ORIGINS OF DEBT STATISTICAL ACTIVITIES AND METHODS USED

1.1. Membership and General Objectives

The International Bank for Reconstruction and Development, like the International Monetary Fund, was established in 1945 following the Bretton Woods Conference. The World Bank Group comprises the International Bank for Reconstruction and Development (IBRD) and its affiliates, the International Finance Corporation (IFC), established in 1956, and the International Development Association (IDA), established in 1960.

The World Bank has a world-wide membership of 150 countries, including most of the world's industrial and developing countries, and including Hungary, Poland and Romania among the centrally-planned economies. Together with its affiliates, it makes loans and credits and provides technical assistance to developing countries for the purpose of promoting economic progress.

1.2. The World Bank's Interest in Debt Statistics

1.2.1. Objectives Pursued

The World Bank's interest in debt statistics is both analytical and operational.

At the analytical level, debt is clearly of major concern to the Bank in its capacity as a leading international source of information and analysis on the economic situation of the developing countries. The World Bank is unique in receiving primary information on the long-term external debt of developing countries in the form of loan-by-loan data reported by its borrowing members. Building on these reported data, the Bank estimates total external indebtedness for developing countries.

The evolution of the Bank's debt expertise stems from its operational needs. The IBRD raises the bulk of the funds needed for its operations on world capital markets. Continued access to the capital markets is to a great extent dependent on the Bank's

102

ability to maintain its reputation as a reliable borrower, and this in turn requires close monitoring, not just of the individual projects it finances, but of the borrowing countries' overall external financial situation. Even in the case of the IDA, the Bank's "soft-loan" affiliate which lends to the poorest countries[1], and whose funds are made available to it by its more developed members, it remains of great importance to maintain its reputation for effective assessment of developing country risk.

The Bank's concern with borrowers' creditworthiness is reflected in its Articles of Agreement. Article III, Section 4, lists seven basic conditions on which the Bank may make a loan or extend a guarantee. One is that:

– "... the Bank shall pay due regard to the prospects that the borrower ... will be in a position to meet its obligations under the loan."

The practical application of this condition is contained in the Bank's operational guidelines and procedures. In the "General Conditions Applicable to Loan and Guarantee Agreements" and the "General Conditions Applicable to Development Credit Agreements", which are incorporated by reference as part of the conditions of each loan and credit, this requirement is elaborated and interpreted as follows:

a) Under Section 9.02, the borrower is required to furnish the Bank all such information that the Bank shall reasonably request with respect to financial and economic conditions in its territory, including information on the borrowing country's balance of payments and external debt.

b) Under Article II, external debt is defined for purposes of the "General Conditions" as "any debt which is or may become payable other than in the currency of the country which is the Borrower or the Guarantor".

The Bank has compiled information on member countries' foreign exchange liabilities ever since 1946. Over this period, policies and practices have evolved concerning the interpretation of these requirements in relation to actual debt reporting. The system described in this chapter is the present culmination of the process.

1.2.2. Use Made of Debt Information

As suggested above, the primary use of debt statistics within the Bank is to analyse the debt-servicing capacity of member countries in relation to the Bank's own lending activities. Debt statistics are also used very extensively in analysing the economic prospects, including external financing constraints, of the developing countries. The Bank's country economists prepare balance-of-payments projections under alternative assumptions about country performance, world economic prospects, financial market conditions and prospective terms of new borrowing.

In the early days, the external debt data compiled by the Bank were used for internal purposes only, and not published. In 1965, the Bank's Annual Report included for the first time summary figures and some commentary on the debt of the developing countries. A more important step was taken the following year when the Bank began to publish, with strict regard for confidentiality, an annual statistical compendium providing key debt indicators for individual countries. The *World Debt Tables*, as this compendium is now called, has expanded steadily over the years in detail, scope and coverage. The analytical information on specific categories of debt has increased; the categories themselves have expanded from their original concentration on public and publicly-guaranteed debt to become a comprehensive survey of the reporting countries' external debt; and the number of countries reporting under the Bank's Debtor Reporting System (DRS) has continued to grow. The *World Debt Tables* is now regularly prefaced by a survey article interpreting international lending developments of the past year and calling attention to major policy issues in external debt management.

Debt information is also published, but in less comprehensive form, in the statistical annex of the Bank's World Development Report. Full details of these publications will be found at the end of this chapter.

1.3. Collection Method

1.3.1. Main Source

The Bank's principal means for monitoring long-term debt is the Debtor Reporting System (DRS), set up in 1951. It is based on the reports of long-term external indebtedness from 109 countries that borrow from the World Bank. Like the publications discussed in the previous section, the DRS has evolved considerably over time, expanding the range of information required and the number of countries it covers.

These reports made by borrowing countries are of two kinds: *a)* loan-by-loan data on long-term debt of the public sector and debts guaranteed by the public sector; and *b)* summary reports on the long-term debt of the private sector that is not publicly guaranteed.

The data are supplied on special reporting forms (see Appendix 9).

a) For public and publicly-guaranteed debt:

- *Form 1*: Report of individual new loan commitments (quarterly);
- *Form 1A*: Repayment schedule for new loans (used only when repayment terms are irregular) (quarterly);
- *Form 2*: Report on the status of debt outstanding at the end of the year and transactions recorded during the year (annual);
- *Form 3*: Corrections to previously submitted Forms 1, 1A and 2 (quarterly).

b) For private non-guaranteed debt:

- *Form 4*: Aggregate figures on the stock of debt, transactions during the year and future debt service payments (annual).

Should these reports not be received within three months of their respective due dates, the debtor country is considered not current for reporting purposes, and this may affect its eligibility for borrowing from the Bank.

Within one month of the end of each calendar quarter, countries are required to submit *Forms 1 and 1A* regarding new loans signed during that three-month period. Form 1 asks for a range of data on new loan commitments which makes it possible to organise statistics in a variety of formats for purposes of analysis. The following information is requested:

- Commitment date;
- Amount and currency of the loan;
- Creditor country;
- Name and type of creditor;
- Name and type of debtor;
- Economic sector, or purpose of the loan;
- Repayment terms: interest rate and type (variable or fixed), dates of first and last principal and interest payments, and frequency of payments. (In cases where the repayment schedules are not of standard type, a report has to be made on Form 1A giving details of the actual repayment schedule.)

The information contained on Form 1 is used to set up a loan record in the DRS data base. Files of loan records are established for each debtor country.

Within three months following the end of each year, countries must file Form 2, giving information on the status of each outstanding loan, including all transactions during the year. The following information is requested for each loan:

- The disbursed debt outstanding;
- The remaining undisbursed balances for loans not fully disbursed;
- Arrears (if any) of principal and interest.

The Form 2 report also includes information on transactions during the year:

- Commitments and disbursements received;
- Debt service payments actually made;
- Cancellations and write-offs.

The normal reporting period for Form 2 reports is the calendar year. A few countries currently report on a fiscal year basis, but the World Bank favours calendar year uniformity in order to maintain inter-country comparability in the data base. Countries normally report in the currency of repayment.

In 1970, DRS reporting was extended to incorporate private non-guaranteed long-term debt, using reporting Form 4. Loan-by-loan detail is not required, in part because of the sensitivities of private lenders and borrowers and in part because many countries are unable to collect detailed information on commitments. Reports are submitted annually along with the Form 2 report. Aggregated data are requested for:

- Disbursed debt outstanding at the year-end;

and for all of the following transactions undertaken during the reporting year:

- Disbursements;
- Interest payments;
- Principal repayments.

Most countries now acknowledge the importance of collecting private non-guaranteed debt information. Detailed data are available, however, only in countries that have registration requirements covering private debt, most commonly in connection with exchange controls. Where formal registration of foreign borrowing is not mandatory, countries mostly rely on balance-of-payments data and on financial surveys. To ensure an adequate response rate, such surveys are usually limited to requests for summary data such as are normally available in corporate balance sheets and income statements.

For more than half the countries reporting through the DRS private non-guaranteed debt is either nil or negligible. For the rest, the data collection difficulties just discussed have resulted in incomplete reporting, and for end-1985 data Form 4 (or equivalent) reports were received from only 20 countries. This number will increase over the next few years, in response to the greater formal emphasis the Bank now attaches to reporting private non-guaranteed debt. In the meantime, Bank staff use other information sources to generate the missing debt numbers for all countries where private non-guaranteed debt is believed to be significant.

1.3.2. Additional Sources and Use of Estimation

As the example of private non-guaranteed debt indicates, considerable additional work is needed in order to arrive at reliable and comprehensive figures on total external debt. This work is of two kinds: a) improving the quality of the reported data and b) filling gaps in country coverage or content.

For reported data, problems of the kind associated with private non-guaranteed debt are exceptional. The loan-by-loan character of public and publicly-guaranteed debt reporting, and the long period over which such reporting has been established, mean that the reliability of the Bank's data is in general extremely high for the countries covered by the DRS. Nevertheless, variations in quality exist in the data base between countries, owing to the difficulties some of them experience in compiling accurate, complete and timely data, and may in some cases also exist within countries between different categories of debt.

The Bank has three main methods of improving the quality of reported data, often used in combination. First, there are the cross-checks deliberately built into the DRS itself, especially between the quarterly reports and the annual summaries, and between the reports for successive periods.

The second is to supplement the reported data by internal action. One important aspect of this is the use of the Bank's own accounting records to capture information on loans made by the Bank. Countries participating in the DRS do not file Form 1 and 2 reports on loans received from the IBRD and IDA. Still more important are the data collecting missions mounted by the Bank's International Finance Division to countries whose reporting is deemed below adequate standards. The Division also provides technical assistance to countries to improve their debt management systems in order to raise reporting standards in the longer run.

The third involves drawing on, and cross-checking with, the data collected by other organisations. In a few instances this means direct incorporation of the data into the

106

DRS: the loan records of the Inter-American Development Bank and of the Asian Development Bank are drawn on in exactly the same way as those of the IBRD and IDA. The Bank also uses International Monetary Fund data to compile its Use of IMF Credit information. In other cases the transfer is indirect. A major example is the use made by the Bank of the OECD/DAC Creditor Reporting System (CRS), jointly sponsored by the World Bank, which provides loan-by-loan reports on official lending that are the mirror image of the DRS reporting Forms 1 and 2. (The CRS is described in detail in Chapter VI.) Occasionally, when debtor country information is not available, CRS data are inserted directly into the DRS data files. Other typical sources for cross-checking data include the US Eximbank and Agency for International Development (USAID) reports.

Where reporting under the DRS leaves gaps in the coverage of a country's external debt position, estimation techniques are used by the staff of the International Finance Division to fill those gaps. This is the case for all countries with respect to short-term debt (debt with an original maturity of 1 year or under), since the DRS only covers long-term debt.

The preferred source of short-term data is again the debtor country and in many instances World Bank and IMF economic missions are able to obtain data compiled by the central bank of the country. When direct debtor country information is not available, however, creditor-source data are assembled that give order-of-magnitude indications of the level of short-term debt outstanding. The most important source is the BIS's semi-annual series showing the maturity distribution of commercial banks' claims on developing countries. By deducting from claims due in one year those that a year earlier had a maturity of between one and two years, an estimate of short-term liabilities by original maturity can be calculated. Combining those estimates with data on officially-guaranteed supplier credits compiled by the OECD gives a "lower bound" estimate of a country's short-term debt, which is then adjusted in the light of any available additional information.

In the case of private non-guaranteed debt that is not reported, the standard estimation approach starts from a calculation of the stock of debt outstanding, using available creditor source data. Figures on guaranteed export credits, obtained from the CRS, are supplemented by loan-by-loan information on official lending to private borrowers and by information on non-insured commercial bank lending to the private sector. Balance-of-payments flow data provide useful guidelines in the process of building a time-series, including transactions, since private non-guaranteed debt can be treated as the residual between total net long-term borrowing and net long-term borrowing recorded in the DRS for public and publicly-guaranteed debt.

By these means a picture of total external debt is built up for countries reporting under the DRS which is comprehensive except to the extent that the coverage of the DRS itself differs from the core definition. Such differences are small, and are discussed in Section 2.

For developing countries outside the DRS reporting net, the International Finance Division estimates total debt numbers in order to support its estimate of the total debt of developing countries published in the World Debt Tables. Individual estimates are not published.

1.3.3. Confidentiality

The loan-by-loan debt information is reported to the Bank by its members in confidence. Only summary data, which do not reveal individual loan details, are circulated outside the Bank's International Finance Division. Over the years, conventions have been established covering the form and character of the information published or otherwise made available for general use. These conventions provide for the release of a wide range of analytical information at different levels of aggregation, best illustrated in the specimen country pages of the World Debt Tables at the end of this chapter.

2. RELATIONSHIP TO THE CORE DEFINITION

2.1. General

The World Bank has been collecting stock and flow data for developing countries' external indebtedness for almost four decades and has sought over that period to ensure internal consistency in its definitions and compilation procedures, and compatibility with other statistical systems, notably the IMF's Balance of Payments. Its concern with the analytical application of the data has influenced the detail of the information required from reporters and its presentation in the Bank's publications. That emphasis has resulted in few significant differences from the concept of external debt embodied in the core definition, and the Bank welcomes the more standardized approach this concept now represents.

The Bank employs the concept of the "Total External Debt" of a country, which is the sum of:

- Long-Term Debt
  - *of which*:
    - Public and publicly guaranteed
    - Private non-guaranteed
  - Use of Fund Credit
  - Short-Term Debt

While formal definitions of external debt have been used for particular purposes, for example the definition under Article II of its "General Conditions Applicable to Loan and Guarantee Arrangements" quoted earlier in Section 1.2.1, the Bank has not adopted a unique definition of external debt for all purposes. Its reporting manual for DRS reporters defines in detail the distinctions between categories of external debt, but does not specifically define external debt itself.

2.2. Core Items Excluded or Imperfectly Covered

Loans to non-residents repayable in the borrower's own currency have been included in the information required from reporters under the DRS, but these data have not to date been included in the data on external debt published by the Bank.

Arrears of capital and interest are also required to be reported under the DRS, but this information has only partially and indirectly been reflected in the published statistics. The stock of long-term debt recorded in the DRS is reduced only by a principal payment actually made, not by one due. Failure to make a payment therefore leaves the stock of debt unchanged, including the arrears indistinguishably in the total. Arrears of interest on long-term debt are not included and not shown. In principle, the published figures for short-term debt currently follow the same convention, incorporating known arrears of principal but not of interest.

Notes and coins held by non-residents are not captured by the DRS and are therefore not included in the published statistics.

2.3. Non-Core Items Collected or Published

In its use of debt statistics to analyse creditworthiness, the Bank has always had a large concern with projecting future flows associated with external borrowing. Particularly important in this respect are data relating to committed but undisbursed debt. In respect of public and publicly-guaranteed debt, for which such information is available through the DRS, the World Debt Tables publishes data for "Debt Outstanding, including Undisbursed". The undisbursed portion, however, is not included in the published figures for "Total External Debt".

Marketable foreign currency debt, e.g., Euro-bonds, raises potential problems in adhering to the core definition. Such debt is reported through the DRS at the time of issue, and remains fully outstanding in the data base until partial or complete repayment takes place. Transfers of ownership through market transactions which result in part of the debt being held in the country of issue are not currently captured in the data.

2.4. Other Points Concerning Relationship to Core Definition

2.4.1. Residence

The Bank adheres to the conventions of the BOP Manual (see Appendix 2), taking residence as a matter of location rather than nationality. External debt is that owed by entities physically located in the reporting country; foreign creditors are those located outside the reporting country, irrespective of nationality. This means, for example, that debts to branches of foreign banks located within the reporting country are regarded as internal debts. Similarly, where banks of the reporting country have overseas offices, those offices are not residents of the reporting country and the debts of those offices, accordingly, are excluded from its DRS returns.

2.4.2. Maturity

The DRS itself provides information on long-term debt only, but short-term debt is also published in the World Debt Tables and included in the country totals. Long-term debt, for the purposes of DRS reporting, is defined as debt with an original or extended maturity of more than one year, measured from the date the loan agreement is signed to the date on which the last payment is due. There are a number of borderline distinctions that have to be made to judge whether debts should or should not be treated as long-term. For example, lines of credit are excluded if the term of repayment of the individual drawings under the credit line is one year or less and deposits with the central bank of reporting countries are included only if the term of the deposit is extended to more than one year.

2.4.3. Undisbursed or Contingent Amounts

Information on commitments of public and publicly-guaranteed debt, as well as on disbursements, is collected through the DRS. See Section 2.3 above for the treatment of the undisbursed portion of loan commitments in the World Debt Tables. Information on frame agreements, arrangements which authorise a series of individual loans up to a specified amount, is also collected through the DRS, but related loan data do not appear in the published statistics until actual commitments and disbursements take place.

2.4.4. Treatment of Certain Types of Instrument

2.4.4.1. Equity and Intra-Group Lending

While ordinary equity investment carries no contractual repayment obligation and is therefore excluded from the DRS, external long-term lending to overseas subsidiaries is included as part of the host country's external debt and reported as such. A separate line for "Foreign Parents" as lending source is shown in the private non-guaranteed debt data published in the World Debt Tables. This treatment differs from the BOP treatment of such lending.

2.4.4.2. Leasing

The World Bank regards "financial leases" as debt to be reported through the DRS. It has not laid down its own definition of a financial lease, and until a commonly-agreed definition has been established, will continue to discuss borderline cases individually with reporters.

2.4.4.3. Loans Repayable in Local Currency

The DRS collects and stores information on debts repayable in local currency, but these amounts are not included in the standard tables in the *World Debt Tables* or other World Bank publications, which confine themselves to debts repayable in foreign currency.

2.4.4.4. Military

No distinction is made between debt incurred for military goods and services and for other transactions, but it is known that not all countries fully report the debt incurred for military purposes.

3. OTHER QUESTIONS REGARDING CONTENT

3.1. Method of Currency Conversion

Since debt data are normally reported to the World Bank in the currency of repayment, they have to be converted into a common currency (usually US dollars) in order to produce summary tables. Stock figures (e.g., the amount of debt outstanding) are converted using end-period exchange rates, as published in the IMF's *International Financial Statistics* (line "ae"). Flow figures are converted at annual average exchange rates (line "rf"). This difference in methodology can give rise to difficulty in comparing flow data with movements in stocks, especially when exchange rates have moved sharply in the course of the year.

3.2. Treatment of Arrears

The Bank collects data on arrears in respect of both capital and interest. Principal in arrears is included, but not identified, in the amount of long-term debt outstanding as published in the World Debt Tables. Interest in arrears is excluded from long-term debt outstanding, unless and until it is capitalised under a debt reorganisation agreement.

3.3. Treatment of Debt Reorganisation

The World Bank's interest in debt reorganisation is to capture accurately the effect of different types of reorganisation on both debt stocks and debt flows, consistent with the circumstances under which the reorganisation takes place. Whether or not a flow has taken place is sometimes difficult to determine, but is important in the presentation of statistical series used in debt analysis. Four principal types of debt reorganisation are distinguished:

a) Forgiveness of debt;
b) Refinancing, under which a new loan is provided to meet part or all of the principal payments due on the original loans;
c) Rescheduling, under which a change in the terms of the existing debt takes place;
d) Consolidation of short-term debt into long-term debt.

In the DRS, these four types are dealt with as follows:

a) **Forgiveness**:   Forgiveness occurs where both debtor and creditor agree to a reduction in the amount of a loan outstanding without actual repayment taking place. Other systems frequently use the term "cancellation" in this context, but cancellation has a special meaning in the DRS, applying only where committed but undisbursed loan amounts are extinguished. The World Bank uses the term "write-off" for forgiveness. Write-offs are recorded in the DRS in the year in which they take place. Only outstanding principal balances (including arrears) may be written off, since the DRS (in conformity with the core definition) does not consider future interest payments as debt. If the entire balance of the loan is written off, the loan is treated as closed. Write-offs in the DRS result in adjustments to the stock of debt but do not involve flows.

b) **Refinancing**:   Refinancing can occur under very different circumstances, with very different implications for debt flows. Where countries have free access to international capital markets they will often take advantage of favourable borrowing conditions to prepay existing debts incurred on less advantageous terms and replace them with new loans at current market rates. The DRS employs a concept of "voluntary" refinancing in these circumstances, and records transactions in respect of the commitment and disbursement of the new loan or loans and also in respect of the repayment of the old loan or loans. These transactions enter into debt flows in the year in which the refinancing takes place. By contrast, refinancing may also take place in circumstances where the country does not have free access to capital markets. In such circumstances refinancing is an alternative to rescheduling, undertaken by agreement between debtor and creditor to avoid imminent default, and is treated as an "involuntary" refinancing by the World Bank. The Bank does not consider that genuine flows have taken place and the DRS does not record commitment, disbursement and repayment transactions. The distinction between "voluntary" and "involuntary" refinancings is not always easily defined: readers will find a more extensive description under the title "Accounting for Debt Restructuring" in the *World Debt Tables*, 1984-85 edition.

c) **Rescheduling**:   In the DRS, the affected principal payments for each debt covered by the rescheduling agreement are transferred to a new loan. With effect from the beginning of the consolidation period, the outstanding balances of the rescheduled loans are reduced by the amount of principal rescheduled. The impact is therefore not on the recorded volume of outstanding debt, since the reduction in the amount of the existing loans is exactly balanced by the newly-created loan or loans, but on the future principal repayment schedules recorded in the data base. The repayment terms of the original loans are adjusted so that they do not project principal payments due during the consolidation period of the rescheduling. The newly-created loans are amortized in accordance with the terms of the

112

rescheduling agreement and bear interest at their respective moratorium interest rates (the interest charged on the rescheduled debt). Since rescheduling involves a transfer of maturities from one loan to another (as recorded in the DRS) and not new lending, no figures for commitments and disbursements are entered in the DRS.

d) **Consolidation of Short-Term Debt**: As with rescheduling, the consolidation of short-term debt into long-term debt in a debt reorganisation is treated as a transfer of debts. A new debt is created that reflects the debt consolidation, but there are no entries for commitments and disbursements, as such entries are reserved as far as possible to represent the flow of new financial resources to developing countries. The increase in long-term debt under this form of debt reorganisation is balanced by an equivalent decrease in short-term debt. (A similar accounting procedure applies to the transfer of private non-guaranteed debt in a debt reorganisation to debt of a debtor country government or public sector agency.)

The DRS also reflects the changes in creditor and debtor status that can result from rescheduling. When insured commercial credits are rescheduled, the classification of the creditor of the rescheduled amounts changes from suppliers or banks to official bilateral, reflecting the assumption of the assets by the credit insurance agencies of the individual creditor countries. The debts to the original creditors are reduced and a new obligation is created to the official creditor agencies. On the debtor side, where the central government accepts responsibility for the payment of rescheduled debt previously owed by private enterprises, this will be reflected in transfers between debtor categories in the DRS. The reimbursement of these debts by the original debtors to the government (normally through the central bank) is considered an internal transaction.

4. SECTORING

4.1. Country Coverage

The *World Debt Tables* contain country tables for 109 individual countries, who are [with one exception[2]] borrowing members of the World Bank. Eligibility for borrowing is determined by the level of per capita income, the cut-off point for which is regularly reassessed. In mid-1987, countries with 1985 per capita incomes of $2 850 or less were eligible for lending by the IBRD, while those with per capita incomes of $790 or less were eligible for IDA concessional credits.

The World Debt Tables also contain summary data pages organised on a geographic regional basis and by economic and financial criteria (e.g., middle-income oil-importers, major borrowers), as well as tables showing totals for all countries reporting under the DRS. A full list of these countries and of the summary groups is contained in Appendix 7.

4.2. Types of Debtor/Creditor

Borrowers are grouped in the World Debt Tables according to whether they are *a)* public sector or publicly-guaranteed borrowers or *b)* private borrowers without a public sector guarantee.

The standard classification of public and publicly-guaranteed borrowers in the DRS Manual gives the following debtor sectoring:

a) Central government (debts that will be serviced from the budget of the central government);

b) Central bank (defined as the agency that issues currency and holds the country's international reserves);

c) Public corporations (business-type entities, i.e., producing services or a product for sale, wholly owned by the government);

d) Mixed enterprises [those business-type entities in which the public sector owns more than 50 per cent but less than 100 per cent of the common (voting) stock];

e) Official development banks (non-monetary financial intermediaries, controlled by the reporting country public sector, primarily engaged in making long-term loans on terms that are beyond the capacity of other financial institutions);

f) Local government (all political entities below the level of central government);

g) Guaranteed private borrowers (private borrowers whose debts are guaranteed against default by the debtor country government or by a public sector agency of that government).

As a gloss on the above sectoring, the public sector is defined, for DRS purposes, as:

a) Central government including ministries and other administrative departments;

b) Political sub-divisions, such as states, provinces and municipalities;

c) The central bank;

d) Autonomous institutions, financial and non-financial, where:

i) the budget of the institution is subject to the approval of the government of the reporting country; or

ii) the government owns more than 50 per cent of the voting stock or more than half of the members of the board of directors are government representatives; or

iii) in case of default, the state would become liable for the debt of the institution.

This definition is identical with that used in the OECD's Creditor Reporting System.

The debtor classification of non-guaranteed private borrowers (those covered by Form 4 reports) is: commercial banks (deposit-money banks), direct investment enterprises, and all others.

114

On the creditor side, the DRS divides holders of public and publicly-guaranteed debt into official creditors (international organisations, governments and government agencies) and private creditors (exporters, private banks and other financial institutions, bonds, and nationalisations).

The classification in Form 4 for private non-guaranteed debt is between: private banks and other financial institutions, foreign parents and affiliates, exporters and other private sources; and official sources (governments and international organisations).

4.3. Types of Claim

The DRS collects a wide variety of information on the terms and characteristics of individual loan agreements, but does not categorise claims by standard types. Average terms for new commitments on loans committed during the year are published in the World Debt Tables, together with memorandum items showing the proportion of public debt contracted on concessional terms[3] and the proportion contracted at variable rates of interest. See specimen tables at end of the chapter.

5. SPECIAL FEATURES

5.1. Data for Calculating "Net Debt" and Flows

The DRS does not collect information on the external assets of its reporting countries. Where a reporting country is itself a creditor of another reporting country, that information will be captured, but in general the DRS focuses on the concept of gross debt.

The DRS seeks comprehensive information on long-term loan transactions, and detailed data on flows are published in the *World Debt Tables.*

5.2. Data on Debt Service

As a sub-set of its data on flows, the *World Debt Tables* publishes detailed debt service information, on the basis of payments actually made during a reporting year. It publishes projections of future debt service (see next section), and it also includes historic debt service ratios.

5.3. Debt Service Projections

A particular feature of the DRS reporting is that it stores the information necessary to project future debt service payments on the outstanding debt, including undisbursed, of reporting countries as of the latest reporting date. There are three main elements in

115

such projections: *a)* undisbursed commitments; *b)* future principal repayments; and *c)* future interest payments. These are treated within the DRS as follows:

- *a)* **Undisbursed commitments:** All undisbursed commitments are disbursed within the DRS projection routine according to one of two methods: pro forma disbursement profiles based on observed experience are used to approximate the disbursement pattern of many standard loan types; specific disbursement schedules are used where the debtor country has its own timetable for utilising individual loans and has reported this on DRS Form 1A.

- *b)* **Principal repayments:** future principal repayments are projected according to the terms of the individual loan contracts, both on the existing stock of debt outstanding and on the projected disbursements from the undisbursed loan amounts.

- *c)* **Interest payments:** future interest payments are calculated on the stock of debt outstanding plus projected future disbursements minus future projected repayments of principal. The DRS has the capability to project interest on floating-rate debt across the range of future interest rates. In the *World Debt Tables*, however, future interest service is projected on the basis of interest rates prevailing at the latest reporting date.

Debt service projections are published for the eight-year period extending beyond the latest reporting date in the *World Debt Tables*. These projections do not take account of any new loans committed or debt reorganisation implemented after the reporting date.

5.4. Other

Reflecting its concern with the analytical use of debt data, the *World Debt Tables* includes in its country data pages several major economic aggregates (e.g., gross national product), together with a range of standard debt ratios and indicator charts.

NOTES AND REFERENCES

1. The International Development Association (IDA) lends on highly concessional terms to the poorest countries among the Bank's membership. New IDA loans have maturities of 35-40 years, including a ten-year grace period. An annual service charge of 0.75 per cent is charged on disbursed balances outstanding.

2. Because of its importance as a financial centre, Hong Kong reports to the Bank under the DRS even though it is not a borrower from the Bank and not required to do so.

3. Loans are considered to be on concessional terms when their original grant element is 25 per cent or above. Grant elements are calculated on a discount factor of 10 per cent. (A full explanation of the basis of the calculation will be found in the notes to the *World Debt Tables*.)

PUBLICATIONS

A. Regular Publications Containing Debt Statistics

1. World Debt Tables

- Frequency, date of publication: annual, January/February;

Obtainable from:

- Publications Sales Unit
  World Bank
  1818 H Street, N.W.
  Washington D.C. 20433

- Price $125

Data shown for eight years: (1987-88 edition) 1975, 1980-86; projected debt service for 1987-94.

Also available on magnetic tape.

2. World Debt Tables – Supplements

- Frequency, date of publication: up to three times a year (normally in March, June and August)

Obtainable from:

- As above
- Price: included in subscription to World Debt Tables

Contains statistical tables showing updates of the external debt of selected reporting countries.

Also available on magnetic tape.

3. World Development Report

- Frequency, date of publication: annual, around July.

Obtainable from:

- Publications Sales Unit
  World Bank
  1818 H Street, N.W.
  Washington D.C. 20433

- Price $12.75.

TOTAL ALL COUNTRIES[1]

(US$ Millions)

	1975	1980	1981	1982	1983	1984	1985	1986
TOTAL EXTERNAL DEBT (EDT)	..	**579,398.5**	**672,010.1**	**745,192.4**	**807,830.6**	**876,833.1**	**949,073.9**	**1,021,166.4**
Long-Term Debt	**161,944.9**	**433,631.9**	**498,011.4**	**556,885.3**	**639,356.2**	**713,812.4**	**783,600.4**	**870,709.3**
Public and Publicly Guaranteed	126,160.8	359,102.6	402,555.3	454,664.7	528,040.9	603,198.8	682,392.8	780,435.3
Private Nonguaranteed	35,784.1	74,529.3	95,456.1	102,220.6	111,315.3	110,613.5	101,207.6	90,274.0
Use of IMF Credit	**4,868.1**	**9,446.6**	**14,844.9**	**20,208.1**	**30,429.3**	**33,402.5**	**37,599.4**	**40,215.9**
Short-Term Debt	..	**136,320.0**	**159,153.8**	**168,099.0**	**138,045.1**	**129,618.2**	**127,874.1**	**110,241.2**

PUBLIC AND PUBLICLY GUARANTEED LONG-TERM DEBT

	1975	1980	1981	1982	1983	1984	1985	1986
Debt Outstanding, including Undisbursed	**180,758.6**	**496,230.8**	**549,920.9**	**607,748.3**	**680,614.6**	**748,721.2**	**838,744.1**	**939,814.8**
Official Creditors	109,527.5	257,420.8	281,322.3	304,112.0	329,425.2	363,137.6	408,296.8	465,303.3
Multilateral	36,090.6	100,353.4	116,670.0	132,878.9	147,800.4	179,206.0	201,662.0	204,220.6
IBRD	17,925.3	45,523.7	53,649.1	61,446.1	70,562.1	76,326.2	83,209.9	92,231.1
IDA	9,675.9	21,310.6	24,145.7	27,030.7	29,161.2	31,499.2	36,506.2	41,476.6
Bilateral	73,436.9	157,067.3	164,652.4	171,233.1	181,624.9	183,931.6	206,634.8	261,082.7
Private Creditors	71,231.1	238,810.0	268,598.6	303,636.3	351,189.4	385,583.5	430,447.3	474,511.5
Suppliers	20,004.2	32,725.5	34,076.2	35,308.6	38,143.7	37,435.9	41,878.9	44,228.9
Financial Markets	51,226.9	206,084.5	234,522.4	268,327.7	313,045.7	348,147.6	388,568.3	430,282.6
Debt Outstanding & Disbursed (DOD)	**126,160.8**	**359,102.6**	**402,555.3**	**454,664.7**	**528,040.9**	**603,198.8**	**682,392.8**	**780,435.3**
Official Creditors	71,884.9	162,462.9	180,870.9	199,448.8	222,241.3	256,508.1	295,014.0	343,157.9
Multilateral	18,507.3	52,513.3	61,436.4	72,716.9	83,030.9	112,442.7	129,675.0	126,470.9
IBRD	9,299.2	22,077.3	26,382.8	31,271.2	36,963.8	42,879.1	47,969.0	54,110.3
IDA	5,586.2	11,874.3	13,796.3	16,288.0	18,536.9	20,825.5	24,157.6	27,872.9
Bilateral	53,377.5	109,949.6	119,434.5	126,731.9	139,210.4	144,065.4	165,339.1	216,686.9
Private Creditors	54,275.9	196,639.7	221,684.4	255,215.9	305,799.6	346,690.7	387,378.8	437,277.4
Suppliers	12,760.6	23,177.8	22,382.8	23,574.9	26,718.0	27,230.6	31,684.1	34,417.8
Financial Markets	41,515.3	173,461.9	199,301.6	231,641.0	279,081.6	319,460.1	355,694.7	402,859.6
Commitments	**44,754.0**	**99,727.4**	**107,096.6**	**108,531.8**	**95,574.4**	**81,376.4**	**82,220.5**	**72,191.9**
Official Creditors	21,655.0	45,850.3	42,347.2	40,459.4	39,505.1	37,349.4	33,972.9	40,596.8
Multilateral	8,065.7	19,893.0	20,332.3	20,626.1	21,796.7	20,826.5	22,473.0	27,200.2
IBRD	3,898.4	7,978.2	9,744.3	9,994.3	11,977.1	9,268.7	11,666.6	14,577.6
IDA	1,719.0	4,361.6	3,084.0	3,150.8	2,533.9	3,250.4	3,598.5	3,216.8
Bilateral	13,589.3	25,957.4	22,014.9	19,833.4	17,708.5	16,522.9	11,499.9	13,396.5
Private Creditors	23,099.0	53,877.1	64,749.4	68,072.4	56,069.2	44,027.0	48,247.5	31,595.2
Suppliers	6,218.9	6,245.4	9,074.2	7,281.3	9,073.3	6,550.8	5,019.9	3,327.0
Financial Markets	16,880.1	47,631.6	55,675.2	60,791.1	46,995.9	37,476.2	43,227.6	28,268.2
Disbursements	**33,534.5**	**82,385.6**	**91,003.9**	**94,768.0**	**86,308.6**	**79,078.9**	**77,100.3**	**75,130.3**
Official Creditors	15,123.6	28,399.8	32,887.6	32,307.9	32,778.5	33,055.4	30,558.8	36,883.6
Multilateral	4,289.7	11,162.6	11,927.6	14,509.9	15,258.2	16,472.2	16,875.4	20,701.8
IBRD	2,038.0	4,593.7	5,655.3	6,667.2	7,864.5	8,646.0	8,474.6	10,230.4
IDA	1,116.4	1,580.1	1,983.2	2,560.2	2,367.9	2,556.1	2,875.3	3,142.3
Bilateral	10,833.9	17,237.2	20,960.1	17,798.1	17,520.3	16,583.2	13,683.4	16,181.9
Private Creditors	18,410.9	53,985.8	58,116.3	62,460.0	53,530.1	46,023.5	46,541.5	38,246.7
Suppliers	4,108.2	5,839.9	6,078.5	6,565.2	8,080.4	6,693.4	5,987.9	4,854.0
Financial Markets	14,302.7	48,145.9	52,037.8	55,894.8	45,449.8	39,330.2	40,553.5	33,392.7
Principal Repayments	**9,071.0**	**30,297.4**	**34,536.3**	**36,024.1**	**35,164.1**	**36,749.8**	**44,044.5**	**48,164.7**
Official Creditors	3,087.7	7,330.1	8,451.5	9,648.4	10,985.9	11,447.7	14,078.4	17,384.5
Multilateral	616.1	1,693.0	2,044.4	2,615.1	4,155.0	4,240.5	5,267.7	6,397.0
IBRD	445.3	1,051.0	1,341.7	1,778.8	2,184.6	2,825.1	3,377.2	4,042.2
IDA	15.3	31.0	59.6	72.3	57.0	91.2	115.3	134.8
Bilateral	2,471.6	5,637.0	6,407.1	7,033.3	6,830.9	7,207.2	8,810.7	10,987.5
Private Creditors	5,983.4	22,967.3	26,084.8	26,375.7	24,178.2	25,302.1	29,966.1	30,780.2
Suppliers	2,500.5	4,741.1	5,086.4	5,178.9	4,859.6	4,829.4	4,792.1	5,661.4
Financial Markets	3,482.9	18,226.2	20,998.3	21,196.9	19,318.6	20,472.7	25,174.0	25,118.7
Net Flows	**24,463.5**	**52,088.2**	**56,467.6**	**58,743.8**	**51,144.5**	**42,329.2**	**33,055.8**	**26,965.6**
Official Creditors	12,035.9	21,069.7	24,436.1	22,659.6	21,792.6	21,607.7	16,480.4	19,499.1
Multilateral	3,673.7	9,469.6	9,883.2	11,894.8	11,103.1	12,231.7	11,607.7	14,304.8
IBRD	1,592.7	3,542.7	4,313.6	4,888.4	5,679.9	5,820.9	5,097.4	6,188.2
IDA	1,101.1	1,549.1	1,923.5	2,503.1	2,295.6	2,464.9	2,760.0	3,007.4
Bilateral	8,362.3	11,600.1	14,552.9	10,764.8	10,689.5	9,376.0	4,872.8	5,194.4
Private Creditors	12,427.5	31,018.5	32,031.5	36,084.3	29,352.0	20,721.4	16,575.4	7,466.5
Suppliers	1,607.6	1,098.8	992.1	1,386.3	3,220.8	1,864.0	1,195.8	-807.5
Financial Markets	10,819.9	29,919.7	31,039.4	34,697.9	26,131.2	18,857.5	15,379.5	8,274.0

Source: World Debt Tables.

TOTAL ALL COUNTRIES[1]
(US$ Millions)

	1975	1980	1981	1982	1983	1984	1985	1986
Interest Payments (INT)	**5,521.3**	**25,384.1**	**31,252.3**	**36,305.1**	**36,506.3**	**40,212.1**	**44,951.1**	**47,675.8**
Official Creditors	2,174.8	6,220.4	7,057.8	8,146.2	8,971.3	9,991.7	11,610.8	15,340.1
Multilateral	851.8	2,611.7	2,790.5	3,248.7	4,070.9	4,627.4	5,377.2	7,635.0
IBRD	630.4	1,812.3	1,886.6	2,194.0	2,649.6	3,128.9	3,550.9	5,193.4
IDA	34.6	79.0	91.8	108.0	129.3	162.9	188.1	236.6
Bilateral	1,323.0	3,608.7	4,267.3	4,897.5	4,900.5	5,364.3	6,233.6	7,705.0
Private Creditors	3,346.5	19,163.7	24,194.5	28,158.9	27,534.9	30,220.4	33,340.3	32,335.7
Suppliers	623.1	1,577.2	1,588.7	1,648.6	1,678.1	1,827.0	2,181.0	2,269.8
Financial Markets	2,723.4	17,586.5	22,605.8	26,510.4	25,856.8	28,393.5	31,159.3	30,065.9
Net Transfers	**18,942.2**	**26,704.2**	**25,215.3**	**22,438.7**	**14,638.2**	**2,117.0**	**-11,895.3**	**-20,710.2**
Official Creditors	9,861.2	14,849.3	17,378.3	14,513.3	12,821.2	11,616.0	4,869.6	4,159.1
Multilateral	2,821.9	6,857.9	7,092.7	8,646.1	7,032.3	7,604.4	6,230.5	6,669.7
IBRD	962.3	1,730.4	2,427.0	2,694.4	3,030.3	2,692.0	1,546.6	994.8
IDA	1,066.5	1,470.1	1,831.7	2,395.1	2,166.3	2,302.0	2,571.9	2,770.9
Bilateral	7,039.3	7,991.4	10,285.6	5,867.3	5,789.0	4,011.7	-1,360.9	-2,510.7
Private Creditors	9,081.0	11,854.8	7,837.0	7,925.3	1,817.0	-9,499.0	-16,764.9	-24,869.2
Suppliers	984.5	-478.4	-596.6	-262.2	1,542.6	37.0	-985.1	-3,077.3
Financial Markets	8,096.5	12,333.2	8,433.6	8,187.6	274.4	-9,536.0	-15,779.8	-21,791.9
Total Debt Service (TDS)	**14,592.3**	**55,681.4**	**65,788.6**	**72,329.3**	**71,670.4**	**76,961.9**	**88,995.6**	**95,840.5**
Official Creditors	5,262.4	13,550.5	15,509.3	17,794.6	19,957.2	21,439.4	25,689.2	32,724.6
Multilateral	1,467.8	4,304.7	4,834.9	5,863.8	8,225.9	8,867.8	10,644.9	14,032.0
IBRD	1,075.7	2,863.3	3,228.3	3,972.8	4,834.1	5,954.0	6,928.0	9,235.6
IDA	49.9	110.0	151.5	165.1	201.6	254.1	303.4	371.4
Bilateral	3,794.6	9,245.8	10,674.4	11,930.8	11,731.3	12,571.5	15,044.3	18,692.6
Private Creditors	9,329.9	42,131.0	50,279.3	54,534.7	51,713.1	55,522.5	63,306.4	63,115.9
Suppliers	3,123.7	6,318.3	6,675.1	6,827.5	6,537.8	6,656.3	6,973.1	7,931.2
Financial Markets	6,206.2	35,812.7	43,604.2	47,707.2	45,175.4	48,866.2	56,333.3	55,184.7
AVERAGE TERMS OF NEW COMMITMENTS								
All Creditors								
Interest (%)	6.9	9.2	11.1	10.5	9.2	9.1	8.0	6.9
Maturity (years)	16.5	15.8	14.2	14.1	13.9	15.5	15.9	16.4
Grace Period (years)	5.4	4.9	4.6	4.4	4.3	5.0	5.4	5.0
Grant Element (%)	19.8	8.9	-1.2	1.3	6.8	7.7	13.2	19.0
Official Creditors								
Interest (%)	5.2	5.6	6.4	7.5	7.3	7.1	6.5	6.4
Maturity (years)	25.2	23.5	21.1	22.0	21.7	22.6	23.1	21.3
Grace Period (years)	8.0	6.2	5.4	5.8	5.6	5.7	5.8	5.5
Grant Element (%)	35.2	32.5	24.8	20.1	20.0	22.4	25.9	24.9
Private Creditors								
Interest (%)	8.6	12.3	14.1	12.3	10.5	10.9	9.0	7.5
Maturity (years)	8.3	9.2	9.6	9.4	8.4	9.5	10.9	10.0
Grace Period (years)	3.0	3.8	4.1	3.7	3.4	4.5	5.1	4.4
Grant Element (%)	5.3	-11.1	-18.2	-10.0	-2.5	-4.7	4.2	11.4
MEMORANDUM ITEMS								
Concessional Public DOD (%)	41.9	27.8	26.7	25.4	22.9	20.5	20.8	21.9
Variable Rate Public DOD (%)	19.5	34.7	37.9	39.3	44.2	44.4	43.3	46.5

	1987	1988	1989	1990	1991	1992	1993	1994
PROJECTED PUBLIC DEBT SERVICE[2]	**130,334.7**	**134,583.5**	**130,974.5**	**127,783.0**	**116,762.5**	**102,284.2**	**87,614.0**	**72,451.6**
Principal	78,190.2	84,885.3	85,901.3	87,546.3	82,562.3	74,085.3	64,879.8	53,966.2
Interest	52,144.5	49,698.2	45,073.2	40,236.7	34,200.2	28,198.9	22,734.2	18,485.4
Official Creditors	**43,021.7**	**45,466.8**	**47,369.6**	**51,055.7**	**49,129.8**	**47,599.8**	**42,985.1**	**39,706.1**
Principal	23,705.2	25,408.2	27,658.5	31,774.4	31,413.3	31,783.8	29,129.9	27,613.3
Interest	19,316.5	20,058.6	19,711.1	19,281.3	17,716.5	15,816.1	13,855.2	12,092.9
Private Creditors	**87,313.0**	**89,116.6**	**83,604.9**	**76,727.3**	**67,632.7**	**54,684.4**	**44,628.9**	**32,745.4**
Principal	54,485.0	59,477.1	58,242.8	55,772.0	51,149.0	42,301.5	35,749.9	26,352.9
Interest	32,828.0	29,639.5	25,362.2	20,955.4	16,483.7	12,382.9	8,879.0	6,392.5

	1975	1980	1981	1982	1983	1984	1985	1986
TRANSACTIONS WITH THE IMF								
Use of IMF Credit	4,868.1	9,446.6	14,844.9	20,208.1	30,429.3	33,402.5	37,599.4	40,215.9
Purchases	2,501.8	4,404.3	7,934.9	7,282.8	13,488.9	7,474.9	4,075.4	4,487.6
Repurchases	293.5	2,192.5	1,815.3	1,251.4	2,048.2	2,397.4	3,804.0	6,275.1

TOTAL ALL COUNTRIES[1]
(US$ Millions)

	1975	1980	1981	1982	1983	1984	1985	1986
MAJOR ECONOMIC AGGREGATES								
Gross National Product (GNP)	1,037,572.7	2,046,732.2	2,157,983.5	2,087,525.8	2,008,795.6	2,035,568.5	2,036,172.1	2,130,885.2
Exports of Goods & Services (XGS)	171,757.4	447,196.2	470,415.2	440,839.8	434,393.9	471,571.6	463,018.3	450,235.7
Imports of Goods & Services (MGS)	224,343.4	550,108.2	602,047.9	569,760.4	521,815.8	533,843.9	540,613.1	529,215.0
International Reserves (RES)	63,065.9	185,574.9	152,422.5	146,952.6	143,128.8	149,556.6	157,531.2	145,318.5
PRINCIPAL RATIOS								
Total External Debt								
EDT/XGS (%)	..	129.6	142.9	169.0	186.0	185.9	205.0	226.8
EDT/GNP (%)	..	28.3	31.1	35.7	40.2	43.1	46.6	47.9
RES/EDT (%)	..	32.0	22.7	19.7	17.7	17.1	16.6	14.2
RES/MGS (months)	3.4	4.0	3.0	3.1	3.3	3.4	3.5	3.3
Public and Publicly Guaranteed Debt								
DOD/XGS (%)	73.5	80.3	85.6	103.1	121.6	127.9	147.4	173.3
DOD/GNP (%)	12.2	17.5	18.7	21.8	26.3	29.6	33.5	36.6
TDS/XGS (%)	8.5	12.5	14.0	16.4	16.5	16.3	19.2	21.3
TDS/GNP (%)	1.4	2.7	3.0	3.5	3.6	3.8	4.4	4.5
INT/XGS (%)	3.2	5.7	6.6	8.2	8.4	8.5	9.7	10.6
INT/GNP (%)	0.5	1.2	1.4	1.7	1.8	2.0	2.2	2.2
RES/DOD (%)	50.0	51.7	37.9	32.3	27.1	24.8	23.1	18.6

PUBLIC LONG-TERM DEBT INDICATORS

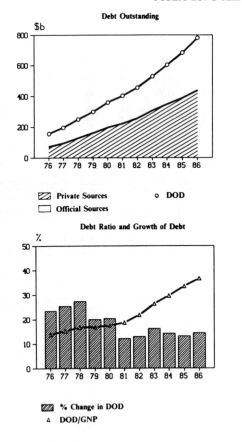

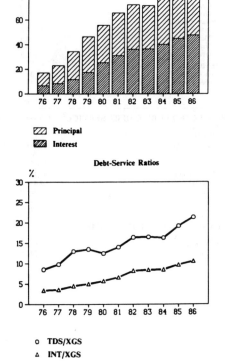

SYNOPTIC TABLES

- Main features of debt statistics of:
    - IMF;
    - BIS, OECD, World Bank;
    - Sectorisation of information in standard debt statistics.

MAIN FEATURES OF DEBT STATISTICS

Institution	IMF	IMF	IMF	IMF
Collection System	Balance of Payments Statistics	Government Finance Statistics (GFS)	International Banking Statistics (IBS)	International Financial Statistics (other than IBS, and including Money and Banking Statistics)
Creditor or debtor:	Debtor	Debtor	Debtor and creditor	Debtor
Brief description of method:	Country sources, quarterly, through balance-of-payments reporting forms	Country sources, annually, through government financial statistics reporting forms	Country sources, monthly through financial institutions' reporting and quarterly from 31 banking centres	Country sources, monthly through financial institution reporting forms (combined with BOP and GFS data)
Additional sources:	Other organisations	Other organisations	Other organisations	Other organisations
Relations to core definition				
General:	Consistent	Consistent	Consistent	Consistent
Residence principle:	Strictly applied	BOP principles strictly applied	As in BOP	As in BOP
Main exclusions:	None	Debt of the non-government sector	Claims of non-banks on non-banks	None
Main additions:	Equity, identified separately	Government-held equity as in BOP	Some equity included	Some equity included
Undisbursed, contingent:	Excluded	Excluded	Excluded	Excluded
Intra-group lending:	Included	Included	Included	Included
Loans repayable in local	Included	Included	Included	Included

	Column 1	Column 2	Column 3	Column 4
Currency conversion:	Contract, transaction or period-average or end-period rates depending on type of data	Transaction, period-average or end-period rates depending on type of data	Period-average or end-period rates depending on type of data	Contract, transaction or period-average or end-period rates depending on type of data
Treatment of arrears:	As liabilities	As liabilities	As liabilities	As liabilities
Debt reorganisation:	Information on debt reorganisation and arrears See Appendix 4			
Net debt and "flows":	Detailed information	Detailed information	Net debt: details available Exchange rate adjusted changes calculated	Some information
Debt service:	Detailed information	Detailed information		
Leasing:	Included on 75% basis	As in BOP	As in BOP	As in BOP
Other:	Short-term/long-term breakdown	Maturity: short-term/long term breakdown. Some information on arrears		Some information on maturities

MAIN FEATURES OF DEBT STATISTICS

Institution	BIS	BIS	OECD	IBRD
Collection System	Semi-annual	Quarterly	Creditor Reporting System	Debtor Reporting System
Creditor or debtor:	Creditor	Creditor	Creditor	Debtor
Brief description of method:	Balance-sheet-based reports from financial institutions in 17 industrialised countries, largely on a consolidated basis	Balance-sheet-based reports from financial sector institutions in 18 industrialised countries and 6 other financial centres	Transaction-by-transaction reporting, plus periodical status reports	Transaction-by-transaction reporting for public and publicly-guaranteed debt, plus periodical status reports
Additional sources:			Other organisations	Other organisations; country specialists
Relationship to core definition				
General:	Consistent with principle, as applied to banking sector	Consistent with principle as applied to banking sector	Essentially consistent	Consistent
Residence principle:	No: consolidated data	Strictly applied; see other	Strictly applied	Strictly applied
Main exclusions:	Claims of non-bank sector Some trade credits	Claims on non-bank sector Some trade credits		Arrears of interest
Main additions:	Some equity	Some equity	–	–
Undisbursed, contingent:	Reported separately	Excluded	Excluded (undisbursed also collected)	Some figures include undisbursed
Intra-group lending:	Consolidated data: intra-group positions netted out	Frequently included	Included in principle	Included in principle
Loans repayable in local	Included	Included	Included	Collected, not published

Currency conversion:	End-period exchange rates	End-period exchange rates	End-period rates for stocks, period-average for flows	End-period rates for stocks, period-average for flows
Treatment of arrears:	Principal included; treatment of interest varies from country to country	Principal included; treatment of interest varies from country to country	Included	Principal arrears only
Debt reorganisation:	Depends on practices of individual banks	Depends on practice of individual banks	See Chapter VI, 2.2	See Chapter VII, 2.2
Net debt and "flows":	Not available	Data on banks' external assets and liabilities and on exchange-rate adjusted changes are given	Considerable detail on flows	Information on flows
Debt service:	No information	No information	Detailed information	Detailed information
Leasing:	Generally included	Generally included	Guaranteed leasing transactions included	Included in principle
Other:	Detailed breakdown by residual maturity	Positions in foreign currency vis-à-vis residents also recorded	Projections one year ahead, principal only	Detailed debt service projections; debt ratios and related economic variables

SUMMARY OF SECTORISATION PRACTICES

By Debtor Sector		
United Nations SNA	World Bank's Debtor Reporting System	IMF's Money and Banking IBS Classification[1]
Financial sector	Financial sector	Financial sector Banking sector
The central bank	The central bank	Monetary authorities[2]
Other monetary institutions	Other monetary institutions Privately owned and/or controlled Publicly owned and/or controlled	
Other financial institutions	Other financial institutions Privately owned and/or controlled Publicly owned and/or controlled	Other banking institutions
Insurance companies and pension funds	Insurance companies and pension funds Privately owned and/or controlled Publicly owned and/or controlled Unknown (insurance co., pension funds, or other financial institutions)	Nonbank sector Financial non-bank institutions
Nonfinancial sector	Nonfinancial sector	Nonfinancial sector
General government Central government State and local government Social security fund	General government Central government State and local government	General government Central government State and local government
Nonfinancial enterprises Public Private	Nonfinancial enterprises (NFE) Public	Nonfinancial enterprises (NFE) Public Private
Private nonprofit institutions serving households	Private NFE and households	
Households, including private non-financial unincorporated enterprises	Unknown or unclassified institutions	Households

1. Defined according to the Fund's *Draft Guide to Money and Banking.*
2. The Fund's definition of monetary authorities includes the central bank and any other governmental agencies whose function is to issue currency, control credit, manage the country's reserves, and maintain general supervision of the monetary system.

SUMMARY OF SECTORISATION PRACTICES *(cont'd)*

By debtor sector		By creditor sector
BIS Classification	Fund's Balance of Payments Classification	Usual Classification[3]

Banking sector[4]	Deposit money banks
	
	Official sector
	  Central bank
	  General government
	    Central government
	    State and local government
		Official creditors
		  Multilateral (International
		    organisations)[5]
		    Bilateral, includes:
		      (Central government)
		      (State and local government)
		      (Central bank)
		      (Nonfinancial public
		      enterprises)

Nonbank sector[6]	All other sectors
	  (Private enterprises)
	  Nonmonetary financial institutions
	  Nonfinancial enterprises
	  Households and nonprofit
	  organisations
	  Public enterprises
	    Nonmonetary financial
	    institutions
	    Nonfinancial enterprises
		Private creditors
		
		Financial markets
		  (Deposit money banks)
		  (Other financial institutions)
		  (Bonds held by private sector)
		
		Suppliers includes:
		  (Nonfinancial private enterprises)

3. The OECD, the DRS, and the WEO share a similar creditor sectorisation, which is illustrated here. The OECD debt presentation also overlays the creditor classification with a geographic distribution of the data and a maturity breakdown.
4. The institutional division between banks and nonbanks is as reported by the central bank concerned.
5. Multilateral institutions may be of a governmental or financial type. They generally refer to the IMF, World Bank, and multi-country banks such as the European Development Fund, African Development Bank, etc.
6. Further subdivided into Public and Private in the semi-annual system.

Note: The items shown in parentheses are components of the main category noted but are not necessarily identified separately

Appendix I

SPECIAL CASES IN THE APPLICATION OF THE RESIDENCE CRITERION

The application of the residence criterion gives results in a few cases which might require special treatment or a special presentation of the measure of external debt.

The problems arise mainly in connection with   *a)* offshore banking units[1];   *b)* countries sponsoring "flag of convenience" or "brass plate" companies[2];   *c)* bank deposits owned by nationals living abroad (emigrants' deposits) but used in part or totally for domestic expenditure;   *d)* foreign currency deposits of residents; and *e)* accounts owned jointly by, or with joint access of, national and foreign donor governments. This appendix sets out the main issues involved in each case and some of the practices currently used by reporting countries concerning the inclusion of these items in external debt.

A.   Countries sponsoring offshore banking units

A major reason for the difficulty in classifying the liabilities of offshore banking units in external debt statistics is the varying relationships of these units with the host economy. Some offshore banks have very limited financial relationships with the host country and banks may, in such countries, be limited by law almost entirely to dealing with non-residents; others may have significant transactions with residents, especially with local banks and the government. Moreover, the relationship of the host authorities to offshore banking units differs from case to case. One example is where the host monetary authorities act as lender of last resort; however, this responsibility will usually lie with the government of the country in which the parent bank is located. Authorities may treat offshore banking units as if they were non-residents in spite of their physical residency, in order to provide better data for monetary analysis where these units have insignificant domestic transactions. Also, where countries choose to hold substantial foreign exchange reserves with offshore banking units, inclusion of the assets and liabilities of offshore banking units in the economy would result in a decline in official foreign exchange reserves unless the country redefined its official reserves to include the foreign exchange holdings of banks.

In the case of these offshore units, the figures on their gross liabilities are likely to be misleading unless accompanied by information on their foreign assets.

Similar considerations might apply to portions of the external bank debt of industrial countries, where banks are engaged in largely extra-territorial deposit-taking and lending. However, in industrial countries, banks dealing in the international market also have complex financial relationships with the domestic economy, and the authorities usually assume a degree of responsibility, at least as lender of last resort, for the external liabilities of at least nationally-owned banks. It is therefore more difficult to assess which assets, or parts of assets, should be shown separately for industrial countries' gross external bank liabilities. In these cases, the banks should be, and are, treated as residents.

128

B. Countries sponsoring "flag of convenience" or "brass plate" companies

The external debt of countries sponsoring "flag of convenience" or "brass plate" companies (other than banks) gives rise to the same considerations as for offshore centres. However, the problems become even more complex, owing to the lack of symmetry between the asset and liability sides of the balance sheets. Under present balance-of-payments (BOP) conventions, such companies are treated as resident. However, they are omitted from the debt statistics of most of the countries sponsoring such companies.

A similar problem occurs for some industrial and developing countries which have established free-trade or "export-processing" zones. The companies in these zones, like "flag of convenience" or "brass plate" companies, are exempted from the country's normal regulations, with customs duties not applied to their imports but levied on transactions between the free-trade zone and the rest of the country. The BOP methodology, with its adherence to the residence criterion, includes any statistics concerning the free-trade zone in the statistics of the country within whose territory the zone lies, whether or not the country itself treats it as a foreign entity.

C. Workers' remittances and emigrants' deposits

Classification difficulties also arise in connection with certain specific deposits, primarily deposits in domestic and foreign currencies by non-residents.

The basic residence criterion in the BOP methodology, e.g., the location of the general interest of the depositor, does not in practice give an unequivocal guide to the residence of some depositors, and an arbitrary twelve-month rule for distinguishing between residents and non-residents has been used.

Several countries do not include deposits with domestic banks by nationals living abroad (workers' remittances and emigrants' deposits, deposits by sailors) in their measure of external debt, regardless of whether they are in foreign or domestic currency and regardless of the period spent abroad. In many cases, these deposits show the characteristics of domestic deposits, and withdrawals appear to be mostly or entirely for domestic use, e.g., members of the non-resident's family are often authorised to use these deposits. In these cases the foreign currency deposit is maintained as a hedge against depreciation. From the macro-economic perspective of the country concerned, when these accounts are used by local designees, they should probably be viewed as part of the monetary aggregates, since they influence domestic expenditure decisions. However, under the residence criterion, these deposits are formally part of the external debt, and a change in the "deposit" behaviour of nationals living abroad is a potential drain on the foreign exchange holdings of the country. Depending on the foreign exchange regulations, the change could result in a decline in new deposits and/or withdrawal of present deposits. The current Balance of Payments Manual (Fourth Edition) does not address the question of access by residents.

There are cases where strict adherence to the residence criterion is difficult or not strictly correct. Some countries have practical problems in determining whether the "emigrant" is still abroad, since account-holders are allowed to keep their special "emigrant's" account once it has been established. For these countries, emigrants' deposits are held by both residents and non-residents in unknown proportions. Even when residence is known, strict adherence to the one-year rule of thumb can be questioned in cases where, for example, sailors are away for more than twelve months on a ship registered under a flag other than that of their home country. The financial interests of the sailors are presumably still in the home countries and so their deposits should be excluded from the external debt measures. This is also the case in countries in which the emigrants' deposits behave in the same manner as domestic deposits.

D. Deposits in foreign currencies by residents

According to the residence criterion, deposits in foreign currencies by residents should not be included in external debt. However, the influence these deposits could have on the foreign exchange holdings of countries make them interesting for analytical purposes and information concerning them constitutes a useful complement to external debt data.

E. Joint accounts of donor and local governments (counterpart funds)

There are a number of instances in which donor governments provide commodity aid which is sold in the market and generates local currency balances. In certain cases these balances are deposited with the central bank under the joint control of the donor and recipient governments. Such balances, often called counterpart funds, present some problems with respect to their classification as external debt or restricted domestic deposits. The BOP treats the original transfer of the goods as a loan unless there is clear evidence that the transaction is in fact an unrequited transfer. It is normal practice to treat the balance with the banking system as neither a foreign liability to the donor government nor a deposit of the recipient government as long as there is joint control; the balances, where important, should be classified separately.

NOTES AND REFERENCES

1. This is of prime interest for offshore banking centres where the balances of the offshore banking units are large compared with the size of the host economy.
2. Countries sponsoring "flag of convenience" or "brass plate" companies are countries with favourable tax rules and regulations attracting part or whole companies having their main business outside the country. The term "flag of convenience" comes from the fact that these companies were originally mainly in shipping, but they are now often engaged in production or services.

130

RESIDENTS OF AN ECONOMY AS DEFINED IN THE BOP MANUAL

1. Definition of Residents

52. The residents of an economy comprise the general government, individuals, private nonprofit bodies serving individuals, and enterprises, all defined in terms of their relationship to the territory of that economy. Included with the territory of an economy are its territorial seas and those international waters beyond its territorial waters over which the economy has or claims to have exclusive jurisdiction; overseas territories and possessions may or may not be regarded as separate economies. (Paragraph numbers are the numbers in the BOP Manual.)

53. The concept of residence underlying the definitions and rules adopted for this Manual is intended to be essentially the same concept that is used in the United Nations' *A System of National Accounts* (SNA). The following discussion concentrates on elaborating the aspects of residence that are especially pertinent in a balance of payments context; in particular, it defines the residence of entities in terms of the sectors or parts thereof that are relevant in applying the classification scheme recommended in Chapter 8. Any differences from the wording of the corresponding passages in the SNA should not be taken as recommending a different coverage for the residents of an economy.

2. General Government

54. The general government agencies that are residents of an economy include all departments, establishments, and bodies of its central, state, and local governments located in its territory and the embassies, consulates, military establishments, and other entities of its general government located elsewhere.

55. The general government of an economy covers all agencies of the public authorities not classified elsewhere: *a)* government departments, offices, and other bodies, irrespective of whether they are covered in ordinary or extraordinary budgets, or in extrabudgetary funds, that engage in administration, defense, and regulation of the public order, promotion of economic growth and welfare and technological development, provision of education, health, cultural, recreational, and other social and community services free of charge or at sales prices that do not fully cover their costs of production; *b)* other non-profit organisations primarily serving government bodies themselves; *c)* social security arrangements for large sections of the community imposed, controlled, or financed by the government, including voluntary social security arrangements for certain sections of the community and pension funds that are considered to be part of the public social security schemes; *d)* unincorporated government

enterprises that mainly produce goods and services to the public, but that operate on a small scale; and *e)* public saving and lending bodies that are financially integrated with a government or that lack the authority to acquire financial assets or incur liabilities in the capital market.

56. Embassies, consulates, military establishments, and other entities of a foreign general government are to be considered as extraterritorial by the economy in which they are physically located. The construction of embassies, structures and other works in extraterritorial enclaves by resident producers of the economy in which the enclaves are located is part of the production and exports of that economy. Wages and salaries paid to locally recruited staff of foreign diplomatic, military, and other establishments are payments to residents of the economy in which these establishments are located.

57. International bodies that do not qualify as enterprises (see paragraph 63), comprising most political, administrative, economic, social, or financial institutions in which the members are governments, form part of foreign general government for balance-of-payments purposes. Such bodies are not considered residents of any national economy, including that in which they are located or conduct their affairs. The employees of these bodies are, nevertheless, residents of a national economy, specifically, of the economy in which they are expected to have their abode for one year or more. In most cases, that economy will be the one in which the given international unit is located or in which the employees are engaged in technical assistance, peace keeping, or other activities on behalf of the international organisation. It follows that the wages and salaries paid by the international organisations to their own employees are payments to residents of the economy in which those employees are stationed for one year or more.

58. In contrast, enterprises that are owned jointly by two or more governments are not treated as international bodies but are, like other enterprises, considered to be residents of the economies on whose territories they operate.

3. Individuals

59. The concept of residence adopted for individuals is designed to encompass all persons who may be expected to consume goods and services, participate in production, or engage in other economic activities in the territory of an economy on other than a temporary basis. These are the persons whose general centre of interest is considered to rest in the given economy.

60. In particular, the resident individuals of an economy are considered to comprise all persons living within the territory of the given economy except the following:

a) Visitors (tourists) i.e., persons in the given economy for less than one year, specifically for recreation or holiday, medical care, religious observances, family matters, participation in international sports events and conferences or other meetings, and study tours or other student programmes;

b) Crew members of vessels or aircraft who do not live in the given economy but who are stopping off or laying over there;

c) Commercial travellers who are to be in the given economy for less than one year and employees of non-resident enterprises who have come to the economy for less than one year for the purpose of installing machinery or equipment purchased from their employer;

d) Employees of foreign governments and international bodies who are on a mission of less than one year in duration;

e) Official diplomatic and consular representatives, members of the armed forces, and other government personnel of a foreign economy (together with their dependents) who are stationed in the given economy;

f) Seasonal workers, i.e., persons who are, and will be, in the given economy explicitly for the purpose of seasonal employment only.

61. The categories of individual enumerated above are to be considered residents of the economy in which they normally live, that is, have their general centre of interest. Border workers – persons who cross the border between two economies daily, or slightly less frequently but regularly, because they work in one economy but have their abode in the other economy – are residents of the economy in which they have their abode, not of the economy in which they are employed.

4. Private Non-profit Bodies Serving Individuals

62. All private non-profit bodies classed as serving individuals are resident economic entities of the economy in whose territory the bodies are located or conduct their affairs. Such bodies are not entirely, or mainly, financed and controlled by organs of general government, and they furnish educational, health, cultural, recreational, and other social and community services to individuals either free of charge or at sales prices that do not fully cover their costs of production.

5. Enterprises

a) General definition

63. Resident enterprises are the actual or notional units that engage in *i)* production of goods and services on the territory of a given economy, *ii)* transactions in land located within the territory of that economy, or *iii)* transactions in leases, rights, concessions, patents, copyrights, and similar non-financial intangible assets issued by the government of that economy.

b) Types of enterprise

64. Enterprises are either privately owned and/or controlled or publicly owned and/or controlled and include both monetary and non-monetary institutions.

65. Private enterprises include *i)* incorporated enterprises, e.g., corporations, joint stock companies, limited liability partnerships, co-operatives, or other forms of business association recognised as independent legal entities by virtue of registration under company and similar acts, laws, or regulations; *ii)* unincorporated enterprises, including those owned by non-residents; and *iii)* non-profit institutions and associations mainly serving business enterprises and entirely, or mainly, financed and controlled by them. The private monetary institutions are deposit money banks, i.e., banks having liabilities in the form of deposits payable on demand that are transferable by cheque or otherwise usable in making payments; such banks may alternatively be characterised as the commercial institutions whose demand deposit liabilities are important or form a large proportion of their total liabilities.

66. Public enterprises are *i)* public corporations (incorporated by virtue of company acts or other public acts, special legislation, or administrative regulations) that hold and manage the financial assets and liabilities, as well as the tangible and non-financial intangible assets, involved in their business, and *ii)* large, unincorporated government enterprises; both types sell to the public most of the goods or services they produce. The principal public monetary institution is usually the central bank, which is the publicly owned and/or controlled monetary authority; it issues currency and sometimes coin, and is commonly the chief holder of the international reserves

of the country. The central bank also has liabilities in the form of the demand deposits of other banks and often of the government. Other public monetary institutions are deposit money banks.

6. Special Implications of Definition of an Enterprise

a) Break-up of single entities

67. The general rule governing the determination of the residence of enterprises (see paragraph 63) often makes it necessary to divide a single legal entity (e.g., a parent company operating in one economy and its unincorporated branch operating in another economy) or a single establishment (e.g., a pipeline or railway spanning the territory of two or more economies) into two or more separate enterprises. Each of these enterprises is to be regarded as a resident of the economy on whose territory its operations are carried out. The costs and proceeds of the separate units are to be calculated as if the units bought and sold at market prices, even though some, most, or all of what they receive from or transfer to the other units of the complex of which they form a part may be omitted from their records or entered only at a nominal value. The balance of payments entries should reflect the allocation to each member of the complex of an appropriate share of any common operating costs, including head office expenses and charges in respect of mobile equipment. The net income of the units should be shown as accruing to the economy where the head office is located.

b) Mobile equipment

68. Situations involving mobile equipment – for instance, aircraft, ships, highway and railway rolling stock, fishing vessels, and gas and oil drilling rigs – often seem to present problems of residence. These problems, however, can be partly illusory; it must be kept in mind that it is not the residence of the mobile equipment that is to be decided but rather the residence of the enterprise that employs the equipment in its productive activities. The resident status of all enterprises is in fact to be governed by the same rule (see paragraph 63), whether the capital equipment that they use is immovable or mobile; an enterprise is a resident of the economy on whose territory it engages in production.

69. Mobile equipment thus presents a problem of principle – in the sense that the residence of the enterprise operating it cannot logically be inferred from the above rule – only when it is used in production outside the territory of any national economy, i.e., in international waters or air space. Mobile equipment that merely moves between the territories of two or more economies should, in accordance with the above rule, be regarded as being operated by a separate enterprise in each of the economies where it is used in production. As a practical matter, however, equipment that moves frequently between the territories of various economies also poses a problem very similar to that of equipment used in international waters or air space. Therefore, a supplementary rule of thumb to deal with both of these cases is recommended in this Manual. This rule is that mobile equipment that is operated on more than one national territory during the course of the year, or outside any national territory, is to be attributed to a single enterprise with a determinate residence. That enterprise is considered to be the operator for aircraft, ships, highway and railway rolling stock, fishing vessels, gas and oil drilling rigs, or other mobile equipment that is not used for production primarily on the territory of any one economy for as much as a year or is used in international waters or air space.

70. In the decision on the residence of an enterprise conceived in accordance with the above rule, attention should be given to such attributes as the flag of registration of the equipment, the

economy of incorporation of the company directing its operations, the residence of the owners of that company, and for an unincorporated enterprise the residence of the entity responsible for its operations. In addition, such circumstances as the fact that the equipment is subject to the laws, regulations, and protection of a particular economy, or that it is linked more closely to one economy than to others, could if necessary be taken into account.

71. In rare instances, considerations such as those in the preceding paragraph could point to more than one economy as being the residence of the enterprise operating, say, a transportation system or fishing fleet. In the case of an enterprise of that sort which is jointly organised and owned by residents of more than one economy, its transactions should be attributed to enterprises in the economies of each of its owners in proportion to the owner's share in the financial capital of the joint enterprise.

c) Residence of enterprises engaged in installation

72. Without exception, a transaction should be attributed to the economy of the principal on whose behalf a transaction is undertaken and not to the economy of the agent representing or acting on behalf of that principal. However, the services rendered by the agent to the enterprise he represents should be attributed to the economy of which the agent is a resident.

73. Problems of defining the residence of an enterprise are encountered where employees of a resident enterprise of an economy go abroad in order to install machinery or equipment that the enterprise has sold to non-residents. In these instances, the installation services should be considered to be services that have been provided by the resident enterprise to a non-resident if the work of installation is carried out entirely, or primarily, by the employees in question and they complete the installation in less than one year. However, if a significant portion of the work of installation is performed by residents of the economy where the machinery or equipment is installed, the work of installation is likely to be substantial and will probably take a significant time to complete. Such services should then, in principle, be attributed to an enterprise resident in that economy.

e) Leased goods

74. The general rule determining the residence of an enterprise applies whether it is using its own or leased capital goods. If such goods have been obtained under a financial leasing arrangement, the rule for determining the attribution of ownership of those goods should also be consulted (see paragraph 217).

Appendix 3

LIST OF IMF FACILITIES

1. The Nature of Countries' Liabilities to the Fund

Members of the Fund may draw on the Fund's ordinary and borrowed resources to meet their balance-of-payments needs. In addition, members have access to resources that have been administered by the Fund on behalf of its members. When a member uses the Fund's ordinary and borrowed resources, it uses its currency to purchase currencies of other member countries or SDRs held by the General Resources Account of the Fund. Access to administered resources has taken the form of direct loans. Resources under the new Structural Adjustment Facility, which is based on the repayments of Trust Fund Loans, is also provided in the form of direct loans; however, these loans are included under the use of Fund resources.

The financial resources of the Fund are made available through a range of facilities which differ mainly in regard to the type of underlying balance-of-payments problem they seek to address and the degree of conditionality attached to them. Purchases of Fund resources generally take place through a stand-by arrangement under the credit tranche policy which is designed to provide short-term balance of payments assistance, or under an extended Fund facility which is designed to take account of balance-of-payments difficulties that arise from problems that can only be corrected over a longer period.

Members of the Fund may draw on the Fund's ordinary resources under "tranche" policies, with purchase of up to 100 per cent of their quota, or the extended Fund facility with purchase of up to 165 per cent of their quota (including the first credit tranche). In addition, there are two facilities for special purposes – the facility for compensatory financing of export fluctuations (established in 1963 and expanded in coverage in 1981 to compensate for fluctuations in cereal import costs) and the buffer stock financing facility (established in 1969). Members may also make use of temporary facilities established by the Fund with borrowed resources. These have included the oil facility, for 1974 and 1975, to help members meet the increased cost of imports of petroleum, and a supplementary financing facility which was established in 1978, and replaced by a policy of enlarged access to the Fund's resources in 1981, to enable the Fund to provide supplementary financing in conjunction with the use of the Fund's ordinary resources to all members facing serious payments imbalances that are large in relation to their quotas.

The amount of assistance under the enlarged access policy is determined according to guidelines adopted by the Fund from time to time. Present guidelines specify limits of 90-110 per cent of quota annually or 270-330 per cent over a three year period. At the same time, a limit of 400-440 per cent of quota (net of scheduled repurchases), applies on the cumulative net use of both ordinary and borrowed resources. Drawings under the special facilities are not included under this cumulative limit and members can, under these facilities, purchase an additional 45 per cent of quota in the case of the buffer stock financing facility, and 105 per cent of quota in the case of the compensatory financing facility.

Within a prescribed time, a member must reverse the transaction by buying back its own currency with SDRs or currencies specified by the Fund. Repurchases of ordinary resources under stand-by arrangements are required to be made within three to five years after the date of purchase, and within four and a half to ten years under the extended Fund facility. Resources used under the supplementary financing facility and enlarged access policy have to be repurchased within three and a half to seven years. In addition, a member is normally expected to repurchase earlier if its balance of payments and reserve position improve. The expectation of repurchase is based on the level of a members' gross external reserves and on the changes in these reserves in the most recent six-month period. It amounts to 1.5 per cent of gross reserves plus (or minus) 5 per cent of the increase (or decrease) of gross reserves in the latest six-month period for which data are available. However, the Fund does not expect any one repurchase to be in excess of 4 per cent of the members' gross reserves. In addition, repurchases are not expected to exceed 10 per cent of gross reserves during the year or to reduce gross reserves below a level of 250 per cent of quota.

The Fund levies charges, which are payable periodically, on the use of its resources. A service charge of 0.5 per cent of the amount of purchase is payable on each purchase other than reserve tranche purchases. The Fund also charges a stand-by fee of 0.25 per cent payable at the beginning of each twelve month period on the undrawn balance of a stand-by or extended arrangement. The fee is refunded proportionately to purchases made under the arrangement. The rate of charge for purchases in the credit tranches and under the extended Fund facility, the compensatory financing facility, and the buffer stock financing facility is determined at the beginning of each financial year on the basis of the estimated income and expenses of the Fund during the year and a target amount of net income; the rate of charge effective on January 16th 1986 was 7.87 per cent a year. Finally, there are separate charges for the use of the supplementary financing facility and of borrowed resources under the enlarged access policy, under which charges are equal to the cost of borrowing by the Fund plus a margin of 0.2-0.325 per cent a year.

The Structural Adjustment Facility (SAF) was established to provide balance-of-payments assistance to low-income developing countries on concessional terms. The SDR 2.7 billion in Trust Fund reflows (see below) expected to become available during 1985-91 are made available to eligible members at an interest rate of half of 1 per cent and provide for a five year grace period, with semi-annual repayments to be made over the subsequent five years.

With the exception of reserve tranche purchases, which comprise the use by a member of its own resources, drawings on the Fund's own resources, including resources under the SAF, and on the facilities financed by borrowing resources are accounted in Fund statistics as "use of Fund credit".

Members also had access through the Fund to resources that are administered by the Fund on behalf of its members. These have taken the form of direct loans denominated in SDRs and are accounted in the Fund's accounts as "Trust Fund loans".

a) The use of Fund credit

The use of Fund credit may be defined as the net use by a member of its conditional drawing rights in the Fund. It is the outstanding stock of credit owed by a member country to the Fund. The use of Fund credit, other than through the SAF, is completed through the exchange of domestic currency in return for other currencies or SDRs; it effectively raises the foreign exchange reserves of the purchasing country without altering the total of resources of the Fund. Rather, a purchase results in an increase in the Fund's holdings of the purchasing member's currency and a corresponding decrease in the Fund's holdings of other currencies or SDRs. A member is required to repurchase its own currency according to repayment conditions for the particular drawing facility in question. In addition, it is expected to complete repurchases earlier than scheduled if its balance-of-payments situation improves sufficiently.

b) Trust Fund loans

The Trust Fund was established in May 1976 as a temporary facility to provide special balance-of-payments assistance to developing countries. The resources of the Trust Fund were derived from profits from the sale by public auction of a portion of the Fund's gold, supplemented by transfers by some of the beneficiaries of direct distributions of gold sale profits and income from investment of assets. During the period January 1977 through March 1981, Trust Fund loans were made on concessional terms to eligible members who qualified for assistance if they could demonstrate a balance-of-payments need and that an effort was being made to strengthen their external position. Given that Trust Fund loans are direct loans, they do not require the purchase of Trust Fund resources with the member country's own currency.

The Trust Fund was terminated as of 30th April 1981 and since then the responsibilities of the Fund as trustee have been confined to the receipt and disposition of interest and loan repayments and the completion of any unfinished business of the Trust Fund. Amounts accruing to the Trust Fund from interest and loan repayments are transferred to the Special Disbursement Account. In December 1980, the Fund's Executive Board decided to commit up to SDR 750 million of these assets to the supplementary financing facility subsidy account to reduce the cost for low income developing country members of using the supplementary financing facility and approximately SDR 0.4 billion has been transferred to the Subsidy Account for that purpose. In March 1986, the Fund's Executive Board established the SAF which would base its loans on the remaining Trust Fund reflows.

Appendix 4

BALANCE-OF-PAYMENTS PRESENTATION OF ARREARS AND DEBT REORGANISATION

In the balance-of-payments presentation, separate practices are followed for the accounting of arrears of interest and amortization, debt rescheduling, debt refinancing and debt forgiveness. In practice, a debt reorganisation package, particularly if it is a multi-year arrangement, may combine elements of each of these. In a multi-year arrangement, it is also frequently the case that a rescheduling of obligations due beyond the current accounting period is subject to certain conditions being in place when the obligations fall due. Balance-of-payments accounting practice is to record entries only in the period when the particular conditions have been fulfilled and the debt reorganisation has been concluded.

The balance of payments uses two forms for presenting data: a detailed presentation which includes all the standard components (instruments), as discussed in the BOP Manual, and an aggregate presentation which classifies the standard components into seven standard groups considered relevant for analysing the international economic relationship of reporting countries in a uniform manner. The double-entry system used in balance-of-payments accounting implies that the balance of payments must be in balance and, therefore, arriving at a surplus or deficit in the aggregate presentation requires summing a sub-section of all external transactions and distinguishing the transactions "above the line" from those "below the line". A broad approach is to place below the line only transactions undertaken to compensate for a balance-of-payments deficit on net autonomous transactions, i.e., to compensate for transactions undertaken for their own sake. In the aggregate presentation of the *Balance of Payments Statistics* the "below the line" items are liabilities constituting foreign authorities' reserves, total change in reserves, and exceptional financing.

The relevant balance-of-payments entries for arrears and the various forms of debt reorganisation are summarised in the accompanying table. The balance-of-payments accounting shows payments due or past due below the line in the aggregate presentation, while payments not yet due are shown above the line regardless of whether the changes of the future payments are due to refinancing, rescheduling or debt forgiveness. For example, a refinancing of amortizations that are due comprises in the aggregate presentation debit entries under long-term capital and credit entries under exceptional financing, while a refinancing of amortizations that are not yet due comprises both debit and credit entries under long-term capital.

There are a number of difficulties due to the level of detail at which balance-of-payments data are currently compiled for deriving complete data on arrears and the various forms of debt reorganisation from balance-of-payments accounts. The balance-of-payments categories in which the relevant flows are recorded do not usually distinguish transactions associated with arrears and debt reorganisation from those which are autonomous.

Appendix 4

Balance of payments Accounting for Arrears and Debt Reorganisation

Type of transaction	Balance of Payments Presentation			
	Aggregated		Detailed	
	Credit	Debit	Credit	Debit
Disbursements and Arrears				
Disbursed interest payments	Reserves	Investment income	Reserves	Investment income
Interest arrears	Exceptional financing	Investment income	Short-term capital	Investment income
Disbursed amortization:				
Short-term	Reserves	Short-term capital	Reserves	Short-term capital
Long-term	Reserves	Long-term capital	Reserves	Long-term capital
Amortization arrears:				
Short-term	Exceptional financing	Short-term capital	Short-term capital	Short-term capital
Long-term	Exceptional financing	Long-term capital	Long-term capital	Long-term capital
Rescheduling				
Payments due:				
Interest	Exceptional financing	Investment income	Long-term capital	Investment income
Amortization	Exceptional financing	Exceptional financing	Long-term capital	Long-term capital
Payments past due:				
Interest	Exceptional financing	Exceptional financing	Long-term capital	Short-term capital
Amortization	Exceptional financing	Exceptional financing	Long-term capital	Short-term capital
Payments not yet due:				
Amortization	Long-term capital	Long-term capital	Long-term capital	Long-term capital
Refinancing				
Payments due:				
Interest	Exceptional financing	Investment income	Long-term capital	Investment income
Amortization	Exceptional financing	Long-term capital	Long-term capital	Long-term capital
Payment not yet due:				
Amortization	Long-term capital	Long-term capital	Long-term capital	Long-term capital
Debt Forgiveness				
Payments due:				
Interest	Exceptional financing	Investment income	Unrequited transfers	Investment income
Amortization	Exceptional financing	Long-term capital	Unrequited transfers	Long-term capital
Payments past due:				
Interest	Exceptional financing	Exceptional financing	Unrequited transfers	Short-term capital
Amortization	Exceptional financing	Exceptional financing	Unrequited transfers	Short-term capital
Payments not yet due:				
Amortization	Unrequited transfers	Long-term capital	Unrequited transfers	Long-term capital

The Fund uses the following terminology concerning debt refinancing and debt rescheduling: *i)* debt refinancing is either a roll-over of maturing debt obligations or the conversion of existing or future debt-service payments into a new medium-term loan; *ii)* debt rescheduling covers formal deferment of debt-service payments with new maturities applying to the deferred amounts.

Where the reorganisation takes the form of refinancing, what takes place in practice is that a new loan is arranged to cover the timely repayment of the original debt; thus the original contract is extinguished and replaced by a new one. As can be seen in the table, if the payments are not yet due, the entire accounting is indistinguishable from a normal repayment and an unrelated new loan in the balance-of-payments statistics. When a debt rescheduling takes place, the terms of the original loan, possibly even the creditor, are being changed. Rescheduling of official and officially-guaranteed debt is generally carried out under the auspices of the Paris Club, while rescheduling and/or refinancing of debt to international banks is often carried out under the auspices of a bank advisory committee, often called the London Club. These arrangements, particularly under the Paris Club, might result in a resectorisation, which could lead to problems of correctly capturing the data. For example, if the central bank of the debtor country assumes the debt of a non-bank, but the bank lender continues to report it under debt to non-banks, the total debt of the country will be overestimated when the reports of the debtor country are used together with the international banking statistics for the estimation.

Where the reorganisation takes the form of debt forgiveness, the balance-of-payments practice is to treat the amount of debt forgiven as an unrequited transfer to the debtor, with the consequence that the liability is reduced by the same amount.

In the case of a debt write-off, the creditor chooses to treat the sum as a bad debt, without extinguishing the debtor's repayment obligations; this does not give rise to a balance-of-payments entry.

Appendix 5

INSTITUTIONAL ARRANGEMENTS FOR DEBT RELIEF

Developing countries renegotiate their debts in two multilateral fora: the Paris Club for debts to governments and for officially guaranteed private export credits, and ad hoc commercial bank advisory committees for debts to banks not officially guaranteed.

Paris Club

The Paris Club is an informal intergovernmental group convened to renegotiate debts to official creditors. Its chairman and secretariat are provided by the French Treasury. Initially, the Paris Club only covered officially guaranteed private export credits, but now debts to governments, including concessional credits and some military loans, are also included. Countries that are members of the Organisation for Economic Co-operation and Development are the principal members, but other creditor countries with similar claims are encouraged to participate in the meetings, though no Eastern European creditor has yet participated. Occasionally, a meeting of official creditors will be designated as a "creditor group meeting" and not a Paris Club meeting.

Interest, as well as principal, may be rescheduled. The consolidation period is typically twelve to eighteen months (but may be longer under a MYRA), and rescheduled debt is repaid between eight and ten years. After the Paris Club Agreed Minute has been signed, debt relief becomes effective only when bilateral implementing agreements negotiated with the individual participating signatory creditor countries establish the list of debts covered by the rescheduling and the interest charge on rescheduled debt (the so-called "moratorium interest rate").

Commercial Bank Advisory Committees

These are often referred to in the press as London Club agreements, but there is no regular group that meets with debtor countries, as is the case with the Paris Club, nor do these meetings always take place in London. A special advisory committee, representing the major creditor banks, is formed for each negotiation. Membership in the advisory committee is based on the size of individual banks' exposure and the need to spread representation among key creditor countries. Normally, only principal is rescheduled, and arrears are expected to be repaid when the restructuring agreement goes into effect.

In addition to restructuring outstanding loan maturities, commercial bank creditors may provide new money (normally extended in proportion to existing exposure) and maintain or extend short-term credit facilities. The advisory committee and the debtor-country government must first reach an agreement in principle for a restructuring, which must then be signed by all creditor banks. The agreement goes into effect when a specified proportion of creditors signs the agreement and other conditions are met, e.g., the payment of arrears.

142

In an effort to eliminate uncertainties associated with year-by-year reschedulings, commercial banks have concluded multi-year restructuring agreements (MYRAs) with selected debtor countries consolidating principal payments due over a three-to-five year period. Debt restructured under MYRAs is typically repayable over much longer periods than under conventional year-by-year agreements. The average original maturity for MYRAs with middle-income countries has been twelve and a half years, in contrast with seven years for previous reschedulings. In September 1986, the maturity on the Mexican MYRA was extended from fourteen to twenty years.

Countries receiving MYRAs are, in principle, perceived to be working their way out of the payment difficulties that led to their debt-servicing problems. Formal arrangements to monitor economic performance are an essential part of MYRAs. The debtor country is required to have an upper-credit tranche programme in place with the IMF or to arrange for enhanced surveillance by the IMF, whose reports may be transmitted by the debtor-country government to bank creditors.

Other Creditors

Debts to governments not participating in the Paris Club are renegotiated individually. On occasion, the debtor country will also meet with representatives of commercial (non-bank) creditors not covered by official export credit insurance and thus falling outside the Paris Club. The Paris Club requires that the terms of rescheduling by all of these creditors (and by commercial banks) be at least as favourable to the debtor country as the agreement with official creditors.

BIS REPORTERS: COUNTRIES PROVIDING DATA FOR THE BIS QUARTERLY AND SEMI-ANNUAL REPORTING SYSTEMS

Industrialised reporting countries	Quarterly system	Semi-annual system
Austria	×	×
Belgium	×	×
Canada	×	×
Denmark	×	×
Finland	×	×
France	×	×
Germany (Federal Republic)	×	×
Ireland	×	×
Italy	×	×
Japan	×	×
Luxembourg	×	×
Netherlands	×	×
Norway	×	
Spain	×	×
Sweden	×	×
Switzerland	×	×
United Kingdom	×	×
United States	×[1]	×
Other banking centres		
Bahamas	×	
Bahrain	×	
Cayman Islands	×	
Hong Kong	×	
Netherlands Antilles	×	
Singapore	×	

1. The United States authorities also provide data on positions of US bank branches located in Panama.

Appendix 7

CONTENTS OF COUNTRY GROUPS REPORTED ON IN STATISTICAL TABLES

A. BANK FOR INTERNATIONAL SETTLEMENTS

Data for the individual countries in a group are invariably presented in tables in which a total is shown for that group.

B. INTERNATIONAL MONETARY FUND

Classification of Countries

Industrial countries: (classification used since December 1979)

Australia	Germany, Fed. Rep. of*	New Zealand
Austria	Iceland	Norway
Belgium	Ireland	Spain
Canada*	Italy*	Sweden
Denmark	Japan*	Switzerland
Finland	Luxembourg	United Kingdom*
France*	Netherlands	United States*

(The countries asterisked are referred to collectively as the *major industrial countries.*)

Developing countries: all other Fund members (as of 1st January 1986) together with certain essentially autonomous dependent territories for which adequate statistics are available. Regional breakdowns: see IFS (in this classification, Egypt and Libyan Arab Jamahiriya are part of the Middle East, not Africa).

Fuel exporters (exports in SITC 3 over 50 per cent of total in 1980):

Algeria	Iraq	Saudi Arabia
Bahrain	Kuwait	Syrian Arab Rep.
Congo	Libyan Arab Jamahiriya	Trinidad and Tobago
Ecuador	Mexico	Tunisia
Gabon	Nigeria	United Arab Emirates
Indonesia	Oman	Venezuela
Iran, Islamic Rep. of	Qatar	

Primary product exporters, (exports of agricultural and mineral primary products other than fuel + SITC 0, 1, 2, 4 and diamonds and gemstones over 50 per cent of total in 1980):

Afghanistan	Côte d'Ivoire	Liberia	Solomon Islands
Argentina	Djibouti	Madagascar	Somalia
Bangladesh	Dominican Rep.	Malawi	South Africa
Belize	Equatorial Guinea	Malaysia	Sri Lanka
Benin	Ethiopia	Mali	St. Christopher
Bhutan	Fiji	Mauritania	and Nevis
Bolivia	Gambia, The	Mauritius	Sudan
Bostwana	Ghana	Morocco	Suriname
Brazil	Guatemala	Mozambique	Swaziland
Burma	Guinea	Nicaragua	Tanzania
Burundi	Guinea-Bissau	Papua New Guinea	Thailand
Cameroon	Guyana	Paraguay	Togo
Central African Rep.	Haiti	Peru	Turkey
Chad	Honduras	Philippines	Uganda
Chile	Jamaica	Rwanda	Uruguay
Colombia	Kenya	Sao Tomé and Principe	Viet Nam
Comoros	Lao People's	Senegal	Zambia
Costa Rica	Dem. Rep.	Sierra Leone	Zimbabwe

(of which: mineral exporters):

Bolivia	Jamaica	Peru	Zaire
Bostwana	Liberia	Sierra Leone	Zambia
Chile	Mauritania	South Africa	Zimbabwe
Guinea	Morocco	Suriname	
Guyana	Niger	Togo	

Agricultural exporters: other non-fuel primary product exporters that are not mineral exporters.

Exporters of manufactures: exports of manufactures SITC 5-8 less diamonds and gemstones over 50 per cent of total in 1980):

China	India	Poland	Singapore
Hong Kong	Israel	Romania	Yugoslavia
Hungary	Korea		

Service and remittance countries: receipts from services (such as tourism) and private transfers (such as workers' remittances) at least 50 per cent of their exports of goods and services):

Antigua and Barbuda	Egypt	Nepal	St. Vincent
Bahamas	Greece	Netherlands Antilles	Tonga
Barbados	Jordan	Pakistan	Western Samoa
Burkina Faso	Kampuchea. Dem.	Panama	Yemen Arab Rep.
Cape Verde	Lebanon	Portugal	Yemen, People's
Cyprus	Lesotho	Seychelles	Dem. Rep. of
Dominica	Malta	St. Lucia	

Non-fuel exporters: primary product exporters, exporters of manufactures, and service and remittance countries taken together.

Capital exporting developing countries (developing countries that, on average, recorded a current account surplus during the period 1979-81 and were aid donors over the same period):

Iran, Islamic Rep. of	Libyan Arab	Oman	Saudi Arabia
Iraq	Jamahiriya	Qatar	United Arab Emirates
Kuwait			

Capital importing countries: all other developing countries. *Of which: Market borrowers* (countries which obtained at least two thirds of their external borrowings from 1978 to 1982 from commercial creditors):

Algeria	Congo	Korea	Philippines
Antigua and	Côte d'Ivoire	Malaysia	Portugal
Barbuda	Cyprus	Mexico	Singapore
Argentina	Ecuador	Nigeria	South Africa
Bahamas	Gabon	Panama	Trinidad and Tobago
Bolivia	Greece	Papua New Guinea	Uruguay
Brazil	Hong Kong	Paraguay	Venezuela
Chile	Hungary	Peru	Yugoslavia
Columbia	Indonesia		

Official borrowers: Countries, except China and India, which obtained two thirds or more of their external borrowings from 1978 to 1982 from official creditors:

Afghanistan	Fiji	Maldives	St. Vincent
Bahrain	Gambia, The	Mali	Sudan
Bangladesh	Ghana	Malta	Swaziland
Bhutan	Grenada	Mauritania	Syrian Arab Rep.
Burkina Faso	Guatemala	Nepal	Tanzania
Burma	Guinea	Netherlands Antilles	Togo
Burundi	Guinea-Bissau	Nicaragua	Tonga
Cape Verde	Guyana	Pakistan	Uganda
Central African Rep.	Honduras	Rwanda	Viet Nam
Chad	Jamaica	Sâo Tomé and	Western Samoa
Comoros	Jordan	Principe	Yemen Arab Rep.
Djibouti	Lao People's Dem.	Senegal	Yemen, People's Dem.
Dominica	Rep.	Seychelles	Rep. of
Dominican Rep.	Liberia	Sierra Leone	Zaire
El Salvador	Madagascar	Somalia	Zambia
Equatorial Guinea	Malawi	St. Lucia .	

Diversified borrowers: all other capital importing developing countries that are not market or official borrowers, with China and India.

Other Analytical Groups

Capital importing fuel exporters (also referred to as "indebted fuel exporters"): the 12 fuel exporters that are not capital exporters.

15 heavily indebted countries:

Argentina	Côte d'Ivoire	Peru
Bolivia	Ecuador	Philippines
Brazil	Mexico	Uruguay
Chile	Morocco	Venezuela
Colombia	Nigeria	Yugoslavia

Low-income countries: per capita GDP, as estimated by the World Bank $410 or less in 1980:

Afghanistan	Comoros	Lao People's Dem.	Rwanda
Bangladesh	Equatorial Guinea	Rep.	Sâo Tomé and
Benin	Ethiopia	Madagascar	Principe
Bhutan	Gambia, The	Malawi	Sierra Leone
Burkina Faso	Ghana	Maldives	Somalia
Burma	Guinea	Mali	Sri Lanka
Burundi	Guinea-Bissau	Mauritania	Sudan
Cape Verde	Haiti	Mozambique	Tanzania
Central African Rep.	India	Nepal	Togo
Chad	Kampuchea, Dem.	Niger	Uganda
China	Kenya	Pakistan	Viet Nam
			Zaire

Small or smaller low-income countries: above group, less China and India.

Sub-Saharan Africa: all African countries (as defined in IFS) except Algeria, Morocco, Nigeria, South Africa, and Tunisia.

Other groups (classification in use from 1980-1984)

Oil exporting developing countries (1978-80 average) oil exports (net of any imports of crude oil) both at least two thirds of total exports and at least 100 million barrels a year:

Algeria	Kuwait	Qatar
Indonesia	Libyan Arab Jamahiriya	Saudi Arabia
Iran, Islamic Rep. of	Nigeria	United Arab Emirates
Iraq	Oman	Venezuela

Non-oil developing countries: all others, of which: *net oil exporters*: (oil exports exceeded oil imports in most years of the 1970's)

Bahrain	Gabon	Syrian Arab Rep.
Bolivia	Malaysia	Trinidad and Tobago
Ecuador	Mexico	Tunisia
Egypt	Peru	

Net oil importers: all other non-oil developing countries.

Except where otherwise specifically indicated, the Union of Soviet Socialist Republic and other non-member countries of Eastern Europe, Cuba, and North Korea are excluded from tables, as are a number of small countries or territories for which trade and payments data are not available.

148

C. OECD

a) Debtor Groups

Low income (* = Least developed)	Lower middle income	Upper middle income
Afghanistan*	Angola	Algeria
Anguilla	Belize	Antigua and Barbuda
Bangladesh*	Cameroon	Argentina
Benin*	Congo	Aruba
Bhutan*	Cook Islands	Bahamas
Bolivia	Costa Rica	Bahrain
Botswana*	Cote d'Ivoire	Barbados
Burkina Faso*	Cuba	Bermuda
Burma	Dominica	Brazil
Burundi*	El Salvador	Brunei
Cape Verde*	Grenada	Cayman Islands
Central African Rep.*	Guatemala	Chile
Chad*	Jamaica	Colombia
China	Korea, Dem.	Cyprus
Comoros*	Mauritius	Dominican Republic
Djibouti*	Morocco	Ecuador
Egypt	Nicaragua	Falkland Islands
Equatorial Guinea*	Nigeria	Fiji
Ethiopia*	Pacif. Isl. (Trust Tr.)	Gabon
Gambia*	Papua New Guinea	Gibraltar
Ghana	Peru	Greece
Guinea*	Philippines	Guadeloupe
Guinea-Bissau*	St. Kitts-Nevis	Guiana
Guyana	St. Lucia	Hong Kong
Haiti*	St. Vincent and Gr.	Iran
Honduras	Swaziland	Iraq
India	Thailand	Israel
Indonesia	Tonga	Jordan
Kampuchea	Tunisia	Korea
Kenya	Turkey	Kuwait
Kiribati*	Vanuatu	Lebanon
Laos*	Wallis & Futuna	Libya
Lesotho*	Zimbabwe	Macao
Liberia		Malaysia
Madagascar		Malta
Malawi*		Martinique
Maldives*		Mexico
Mali*		Montserrat
Mauritania*		Namibia
Mayotte		Nauru
Mongolia		Netherlands Antilles
Mozambique		New Caledonia
Nepal*		Niue

C.   OECD *(cont'd)*

a) Debtor Groups

Low income (* = Least developed)	*Lower middle income*	*Upper middle income*
Niger*		Oman
Pakistan		Panama
Rwanda*		Paraguay
Sao Tomé & Principe*		Polynesia, French
Senegal		Qatar
Sierra Leone*		Reunion
Solomon Islands		Saudi Arabia
Somalia*		Seychelles
Sri Lanka		Singapore
St. Helena		St. Pierre & Miquelon
Sudan*		Suriname
Tanzania*		Syria
Togo*		Taiwan
Tokelau		Trinidad & Tobago
Turks & Caicos Islands		United Arab Imirates
Tuvalu*		Uruguay
Uganda*		Venezuela
Vanuatu*		Virgin Islands
Viet Nam		Yugoslavia
Western Samoa*		
Yemen*		
Yemen, Dem.*		
Zaire		
Zambia		

As well as developing countries and territories as defined above by income group, and shown in *Financing and External Debt of Developing Countries,* indebtedness of further countries is shown in external debt statistics. These are: CMEA (Bulgaria, Czechoslovakia, Germany Dem. Rep., Hungary, Poland, Romania and USSR) Albania, Andorra and South Africa. The joint OECD/BIS publication, *Statistics of External Indebtedness,* shows data for all the above countries and in addition for Australia, Finland, Iceland, New Zealand and Norway.

b) Creditor Groups

DAC Member countries are as follows: Australia, Austria, Belgium, Canada, Denmark, Finland, France, Germany (FR), Ireland, Italy, Japan, Netherlands, New Zealand, Norway, Sweden, Switzerland, United Kingdom and United States.

The creditor group "OECD" includes DAC Members and also Greece, Iceland, Luxembourg, Portugal, Spain and Turkey.

CMEA creditors are CMEA debtors (see above) and also Albania, Korea PDR and Mongolia.

OPEC (Organisation of Petroleum Exporting Countries): Algeria, Ecuador, Gabon, Indonesia, Iran, Iraq, Kuwait, Libya, Nigeria, Qatar, Saudi Arabia, United Arab Emirates (including Abu Dhabi) and Venezuela.

D. WORLD BANK

Classification by Income Group[1]

Low-income Africa	Low-income Asia	Middle-income Importers	
Benin, People's Republic of	Bangladesh	Argentina	Lesotho
	Burma	Bahamas	Liberia
Burkina Faso	China	Barbados	Malaysia
Burundi	India	Belize	Malta
Cen. African Rep.	Maldives	Bolivia	Mauritania
Chad			
	Nepal	Botswana	Mauritius
Comoros	Pakistan	Brazil	Morocco
Equatorial Guinea	Vanuatu	Cape Verde	Nicaragua
Ethiopia		Chile	Panama
Gambia, The	*Oil Exporters*	Colombia	Papua New Guinea
Ghana			
	Algeria	Costa Rica	Paraguay
Guinea	Cameroon	Côte d'Ivoire	Peru
Guinea Bissau	Congo, People's Rep. of the	Cyprus	Philippines
Kenya		Djibouti	Portugal
Madagascar	Ecuador		
Malawi	Egypt, Arab Rep. of	El Salvador	Seychelles
		Fiji	Singapore
Mali	Gabon	Greece	Solomon Islands
Niger	Indonesia	Grenada	St. Vincent
Rwanda	Mexico	Guatemala	Swaziland
Sao Tomé & Prin.	Nigeria		
Senegal	Oman	Guyana	Thailand
		Haiti[2]	Tunisia
Sierra Leone	Syrian Arab Rep.	Honduras	Turkey
Somalia	Trinidad & Tobago	Hong Kong	Uruguay
Sudan	Venezuela	Hungary	Western Samoa
Tanzania			
Togo		Israel	Yemen Arab Rep.
		Jamaica	Yemen, People's Dem. Rep. of
Uganda		Jordan	
Zaire		Korea, Rep. of	Yugoslavia
Zambia		Lebanon	Zimbabwe

1. "Low-income" refers to countries in which 1985 GNP per capita was no more than $400. "Middle-income" refers to countries in which GNP per capita was $401 or more.
2. Haiti, with GNP per capita of $350 in 1985, is the only low-income Latin American country reporting under the DRS. To preserve the regional integrity of the other low-income classifications, it is included in "middle-income oil importers".

Classification by Geographic Region

Africa, South of the Sahara

Benin, People's
  Republic of
Botswana
Burkina Faso
Burundi
Cameroon

Cape Verde
Central Af. Rep.
Chad
Comoros
Congo, People's Rep.
  of the
Côte d'Ivoire
Djibouti
Equat. Guinea
Ethiopia
Gabon

Gambia, The
Ghana
Guinea
Guinea-Bissau
Kenya

Lesotho
Liberia
Madagascar
Malawi
Mali

Mauritania
Mauritius
Niger
Nigeria
Rwanda

Sao Tomé & Prin.
Senegal
Seychelles
Sierra Leone
Somalia

East Asia and Pacific

China
Fiji
Hong Kong
Indonesia
Korea, Rep. of

Malaysia
Papua New Guinea
Philippines
Singapore
Solomon Islands

Thailand
Vanuatu
Western Samoa

Africa, South of the Sahara (cont'd)

Sudan
Swaziland
Tanzania
Togo
Uganda

Zaire
Zambia
Zimbabwe

Latin America and the Caribbean

Argentina
Bahamas
Barbados
Belize
Bolivia

Brazil
Chile
Colombia
Costa Rica
Dominican Rep.

Ecuador
El Salvador
Grenada
Guatemala
Guyana

Haiti
Honduras
Jamaica
Mexico
Nicaragua

Panama
Paraguay
Peru
St. Vincent
Trinidad & Tobago

Uruguay
Venezuela

North Africa and the Middle East

Algeria
Egypt, Arab Rep. of
Jordan
Lebanon
Morocco

Oman
Syrian Arab Rep.
Tunisia
Yemen Arab Rep.
Yemen, People's
  Dem. Rep. of

South Asia

Bangladesh
Burma
India
Maldives
Nepal

Pakistan
Sri Lanka

Europe and the Mediterranean

Cyprus
Greece
Hungary
Israel
Malta

Portugal
Romania
Turkey
Yugoslavia

Major Borrowers[1]

Argentina	Egypt, Arab Rep. of	Israel	Mexico
Brazil	India	Korea, Rep. of	Turkey
Chile	Indonesia	Malaysia	Venezuela

1. Disbursed and outstanding long-term debt above $17 billion in 1985.

Highly Indebted Countries

Argentina	Costa Rica	Mexico	Philippines
Bolivia	Côte d'Ivoire	Morocco	Uruguay
Brazil	Ecuador	Nigeria	Venezuela
Chile	Jamaica	Peru	Yugoslavia
Colombia			

Private Non-guaranteed Debt: Reporting

Africa, South of the Sahara	*East Asia and Pacific*	*Latin America and the Caribbean*	*South Asia*
Cameroon	Korea, Rep. of	Brazil	India
Mauritius	Philippines	Chile	Pakistan
Senegal	Thailand	Colombia	Sri Lanka
Zimbabwe	Vanuatu	Dominican Republic	
		Honduras	*Europe and the Mediterranean*
		Paraguay	
		Uruguay	Turkey
			Yugoslavia

Private Non-guaranteed Debt: Non-reporting

Africa, South of the Sahara	*East Asia and Pacific*	*Latin America and the Caribbean*	*North Africa and the Middle East*
Côte d'Ivoire	Fiji	Argentina	Egypt, Arab Rep. of
Kenya	Hong Kong*	Bolivia	Morocco*
Niger	Indonesia	Costa Rica	Tunisia
Nigeria	Malaysia	Ecuador	
Tanzania	Papua New Guinea	El Salvador	*Europe and the Mediterranean*
Zaire*	Singapore*	Guatemala	
Zambia		Jamaica	Greece
		Mexico	Israel
		Peru	Portugal
		Venezuela	

* Individual country data are not published, but estimates are included in all totals and regional aggregates.

Appendix 8

FORMS USED IN THE OECD'S CREDITOR REPORTING SYSTEM

IBRD / OECD
CREDITOR REPORTING SYSTEM

Form 1 B **DESCRIPTION OF INDIVIDUAL OFFICIAL LOAN COMMITMENT**
[For definitions and instructions see reverse of the form and DAC(83)29]

010. Reporting Country : ....
011. CRS Identification No. : ....
012. Compilation Date : ....

```
1   0
|   |   |   |   |   |   |           |   |   |
1       4       7                   25
```

013. Extending Agency [a] : ....

014. Recipient Country : .... 015. Commitment Date : ....

016. Name of Borrower : ....

017. If not an official entity, name of guarantor : ....

020. Amount : .... 021. In thousands of : ....(currency)[b]

022. Estimated Grant Element (%) : ....

023. Nature of submission : Initial report □ 1 if supplementary report : Change in amount committed □ 2
Revision of terms □ 3 Other (describe in notes) □ 4

024. Classification : ODA □ 1 Other □ 8

Expected disbursement dates : 025. first .... 026. final ....

PURPOSE AND RELATED INFORMATION :
030. Check if : project □ 1 or if non-project □ 2 : supplies □ technical co-operation □ debt reorganisation □ or other purpose □ covered by the commitment.
031. Describe briefly :

032. Suggested code | | | | | | |

Specific Amount :
034. Technical co-operation ....
035. Maintenance .... 036. of which to be spent locally ....
038. Other recurrent costs .... 039. of which to be spent locally ....

Local costs : 040. Intended or estimated amount .... 041. Conditions : No special arrangements □ 1
Subject only to overall programme ceiling □ 2 May not be financed □ 3 May account for a maximum of .... % of commitment □ 4

Eligible sources of supply : 050. Amount tied .... 051. Amount untied ....
Tying status of remainder . 052. Suggested code .... 053. Amount ....
Description :

TERMS :
Repayment schedule : 060. based on : Total commitment □ 1 Each disbursement □ 2
061. Type : Equal principal payments □ 1 Annuity □ 2 Lump sum □ 3 Other □ 4 (Describe in notes : Form 1.1 may be supplied)
062. Number of service payments per annum....... 063. Interest rate ....% Non-interest charges : 064. Amount ....
or 065. ....% and give description in notes. Repayment dates : 066. first .... 067. final ....

ASSOCIATED FINANCING
070. The transactions below are associated in law □ 1 in fact □ 2 with the transaction identified above. 071. Taken together all these transactions constitute a package that is □ 1 is not □ 2 subject to the DAC Guidelines on Associated Financing.

ODA grant : 073. Amount : .... CRS identification No. : ....
074. of which Technical Co-operation amount : ....
OOF loan (non-export credit) : 075. Amount : .... CRS identification No. : ....
Official export credit to buyer, over 5 years : 076. Amount : .... CRS identification No. : ....
5 or under 5 years : 077. Amount : ....
Guaranteed private export credit, over 5 years : 078. Amount : .... CRS identification No. : ....
5 or under 5 years : 079. Amount : ....
080. Unguaranteed private export credit : .... 081. Bank loan(s) : ....
082. Direct investment : ....

083. **Amount of package** (incl. transaction reported on) : ....
084. Description of package :

Grant element of : 085. Concessional resources and export credits .... %
086. All reported national transactions combined .... %

a. Name of reporting agency if different : ....
b. Currency of repayment if different : (090) ....

NOTES (Give other pertinent information not covered in main body of the form)

67 129

For Secretariat Use
013 |___| 014 |___|
015 |___|
020 |___|
021 |___| 022 |___|
023 |___| 024 |___|
025 |___|
026 |___|
030 |___|
031 |___|
|___|
|___|
|___|
|___|
032 |___|
034 |___|
035 |___|
036 |___|
038 |___|
039 |___|
040 |___|
041 |___|
050 |___|
051 |___|
052 |_|
053 |___|
060 |___| 061 |___| 062 |___|
063 |___|
064 |___|
065 |___|
066 |___|
067 |___|
070 |___| 071 |___|
072 |___|
074 |___|
075 |___|
076 |___|
077 |___|
078 |___|
079 |___|
080 |___|
081 |___|
082 |___|
083 |___|
084 |___|
|___|
|___|
085 |___|
086 |___|
090 |___| 091 |___|
092 |___|
093 |___|
094 |___|
095 |___|

156

IBRD/OECD

Creditor Reporting System (CRS)

Form 2 CURRENT STATUS OF OUTSTANDING OFFICIAL LOANS AND TRANSACTIONS DURING PERIOD

[For definitions and instructions see reverse of the form and DAC(83)29]

1. Reporting country:
2. Year:
3. Compilation date:
5. Currency in which amounts reported (thousands of):
   (millions if yen or lire)

```
0 7 2 0
1        6        23
```

Recipient country and loan identification number (year, number)	(Do not write in this column)		Transactions during year						Status at end of year			
		Commitments	Disbursements	Code	Cancellations or adjustments	Amortization	Interest and other charges received	Undisbursed	Disbursed and still outstanding	Arrears of principal	Arrears of interest
(4)	(6)	(8)	(9)	(10)	(11)	(12)	(13)	(14)	(15)	(16)	(17)
	(5)	(04)										

(1) Code for type of cancellation or adjustment: 1 = write-off or forgiveness of principal. 2 = extinguished through multiple rescheduling. 3 = transfer from extinguished outstanding balances through multiple rescheduling. 4 = change in currency of repayment to local currency. 5 = cancellation from undisbursed. 6 = write-off, forgiveness or cancellation of interest. 7 = loan generated by transfer from balances of one or more other loans. 8 = extinguished through transfer to another loan. 9 = other.

6701s

157

IBRD / OECD

Form 3 A

**Current Status of Outstanding Official Export Credits,
Transactions during Period and Future Payments**[1]

[For definitions and instructions see TC/ECG/83.1 or DAC (83)1]

1. Reporting country :

2. Six month period ended (month, year) :

3. Compilation date :

4. Currency in which reported :

Name of borrowing country	Type of borrower[2]	Transactions during period								Amounts outstanding at end of period				
		Commitments		Disbursements or drawings	Service and other payments received		Adjustments		Total	of which			arrears included in columns 12 and 12(a)	
		Total	of which principal		Total	of which principal				disbursed principal	undisbursed principal		Total	of which principal
(5)	(7)	(8)	(8 a)	(9)	(10)	(10 a)	(11)		(12)	(12 a)	(12 b)		(13)	(13 a)
		3 . 0 . 1	3 . 0 . 2	3 . 0 . 3	3 . 0 . 4	3 . 0 . 5	3 . 0 . 6		3 . 0 . 7	3 . 2 . 0	3 . 2 . 1		3 . 0 . 9	3 . 1 . 0

(Do not write in this column)

1. This form is used to report data to TC./ECG, DAC and IBRD.
2. Enter code 8 or 9 as appropriate : 8 = private non-guaranteed in borrowing country ; 9 = official or officially guaranteed in borrowing country.

J8987

ORIGINAL TO OECD

IBRD / OECD

CONFIDENTIAL

Form 3

Current Status of Outstanding Private Loans and Credits under Official Guarantee or Insurance, Transactions during Period, and Future Payments[1]

[For definitions and instructions see TC/ECG/83.1 or DAC (83)1]

1. Reporting country :

2. Six month period ended (month, year) :

3. Compilation date :

4. Currency in which reported :

9.8 . 0 . 3 . 0 . 3 . 0,0,3 . 9 9 9,99
1   4   7   10   13   16   19

Name of borrowing country	(Do not write in this column)	Type of credit and borrower[2]	Transactions during period									Status at end of period				
			New obligations of buyers or borrowers		Estimated utilisation (Shipments or drawings)		Service and other payments received		Adjustments		Amounts outstanding		of which arrears	
			Total	of which principal			Total	of which principal			Total	of which principal	Total	of which principal
(5)	(6)	(7)	(8)	(8 a)	(9)	(9a)[3]	(10)	(10 a)	(11)		(12)	(12 a)	(13)	(13 a)
	16	6	3 , 0 , 1	3 , 0 , 2	3 , 0 , 3		3 , 0 , 4	3 , 0 , 5	3 , 0 , 6		3 , 0 , 7	3 , 0 , 8	3 , 0 , 9	3 , 1 , 0
			7	7	7		7	7	7		7	7	7	7

1. This form is used to report data to TC / ECG, DAC and IBRD.
2. Enter code 4, 5, 6 or 7 as appropriate : 4 = Supplier credit, private non-guaranteed in borrowing country, 5 = Supplier credit, official or officially guaranteed in borrowing country, 6 = Financial credit, private non-guaranteed in borrowing country, 7 = Financial credit, official or officially guaranteed in borrowing country.
3. Enter code to show whether amounts in column 9 : 1 = include interest, 2 = exclude interest, 3 = partly include interest.

Appendix 9

FORMS USED IN THE WORLD BANK'S DEBTOR REPORTING SYSTEM

FORM NO. 1363 (E)
(12—77) **WORLD BANK DEBT REPORTING SYSTEM**

1. Reporting country:
2. Debt number:

FORM 1: DESCRIPTION OF INDIVIDUAL EXTERNAL PUBLIC DEBT AND PRIVATE DEBT PUBLICLY GUARANTEED

NOTE: Please consult instructions on the reverse side of this form.

---

3. Name of borrower:

---

4. Type of borrower: (mark one)

_____ 1. Central government

_____ 2. Central bank

_____ 6. Public Corporation

_____ 7. Mixed enterprise

_____ 8. Official development bank

_____ 4. Local government

_____ 9. Private

---

5. Name of guarantor in reporting country:

---

6. Are repayments financed from the central government budget?

_____ 1. Yes   2. No

---

7. Economic sector of destination and purpose of the loan:

---

8. Type of interest: (mark one)

_____ 1. Interest free

_____ 2. Interest included in principal

_____ 3. One fixed rate

_____ 4. Two or more rates applying to separate time periods (describe in Item 22)

_____ 6. Variable rates (see instructions; describe rates in Item 22)

---

9. Interest rate or rates:

1. Fixed rate _____

2. First of two rates _____

Second of two rates _____

(If there are two rates, mark Item 8.4 above.)

---

10. Interest payment dates:

1. First _____   2. Final _____

3. Number of payments per annum _____

4. If Item 8.4 is marked, give dates on which rates take effect:

---

11. Commitment charge:

(rate %) _____

---

12. Estimated dates of drawings:

1. First _____   2. Final _____

(Fill in Column 3 of Form 1A if amounts of drawings can be estimated.)

---

13. Name of lender:

---

14. Creditor country:

---

15. Type of credit or creditor: (mark one)

_____ 1. Exporter

_____ 2. Private bank or other financial institution

Is this a syndicated loan? Yes _____   No _____

_____ 4. International organization

_____ 5. Government or public agency

_____ 6. Bond   _____ 8. Nationalization

---

16. Commitment date:

---

17. Amount of commitment:

---

18. Currency in which:

1. Amounts reported _____

2. Debt is repayable _____

---

19. Type of agreement: (mark one)

_____ 0. Normal

_____ 3. Frame agreement

_____ 4. Commitment under frame agreement

_____ 5. Debt relief (see instructions)

_____ Refinancing loan, or

_____ Rescheduling

_____ 6. Other (describe in notes)

---

20. Principal repayments:

1. Pattern of repayments: (mark one)

_____ 1. Equal principal payments

_____ 2. Annuity 1/

_____ 5. Repayable in one lump sum

_____ 6. Other (Form 1A must be supplied)

2. Repayments based on: (mark one)

_____ Total commitment   _____ Each drawing

3. If repayments based on each drawing:

(a) Number of months from drawing to first principal repayment: _____

(b) Number of principal repayments on each drawing: _____

---

21. Principal repayment dates:

1. First _____   2. Final _____

3. Number of payments per annum _____

---

22. Description of terms of principal repayment and interest: (Form 1A should be supplied if principal or interest payments are irregular)

1/ Equal installments of principal plus interest in which the size of the principal repayments increases as the size of the interest payments decreases.

NOTES:

FORM NO. 1365 (E)
(12-77)

WORLD BANK DEBT REPORTING SYSTEM

FORM 2: INDIVIDUAL EXTERNAL PUBLIC DEBTS AND PRIVATE DEBTS PUBLICLY GUARANTEED

CURRENT STATUS AND TRANSACTIONS DURING PERIOD

1. Reporting country:

2. Period ended (month, year):

NOTE: Please consult instructions on the reverse side of this form.

Debt Number	Currency in which amounts reported	(Do not write in this column)	Status at end of period					Transactions during period				
			Drawn and still outstanding	Undrawn balance	Principal in arrears	Interest in arrears	Commitments	Drawings	Cancellations	Principal repaid	Interest paid
(1)	(2)		3	4	5	6	7	8	9	10	11
		13									

Duplicate on all cards

0 1 1 3 1

1   6   10 12

23   28

22

NOTES:

163

GLOSSARY OF TERMS USED IN THIS REPORT

The definitions in the following list are those used currently by the four organisations covered by the report, and, in most cases, by the financial community in general. Where a term is used by one of the organisations in a particular or more restricted sense, this is indicated in the definition.

Accrued interest

Interest which has accumulated but which is not legally due before a specified payment date.

Affiliates

(Of banks): Branches, subsidiaries and joint ventures.

Amortization

Repayment of principal balances during a given accounting period.

Arrears

Amounts of principal and/or interest due but not paid as of the reporting date.

Banking offices

Affiliates and head offices.

Banks

Generally defined as those institutions that are entitled by law to conduct banking business, usually (but not necessarily) including the acceptance of deposits from the general public.

BOP

Balance of Payments; in abbreviated form, refers to the balance-of-payments statistical system operated by the IMF (as in "BOP Manual").

Bridging (Bridge) loan

A short-term advance pending receipt of funds by the borrower from the same or another source.

Buyer (buyer's) credit

Loan obtained by the overseas purchaser of goods or services, with the supplier being paid in cash; also known as financial credit.

Cancellations

(WB): The annulment of undisbursed portions of loans or credits.

Capitalisation

(Of interest): The conversion of accrued or future interest into a capital liability.

Certificates of deposit (CDs)

Negotiable bearer documents representing evidence of a deposit with a bank repayable on a fixed date.

Claims

(Of banks): Financial assets (balance-sheet items only).

Commitment

A contractual obligation to lend a specific sum. (OECD): (of government loans) a firm obligation expressed in an agreement or equivalent contract to furnish funds of a specified amount under specified terms and conditions and for specified purposes.

Commitment, date of

The date on which a loan agreement is signed.

Concessional loans

Loans with a grant element of 25 per cent or more.

Consolidated

(Of a bank's balance sheet): Balance sheet grouping assets and liabilities of parent company and subsidiaries, after elimination of all unrealised profits on intra-group trading and of all intra-group balances.

Contingent (contingency)

Used of a liability which may or may not be incurred, depending on a future event (contingency).

Creditor country

The country in which the lender is resident.

Creditor Reporting System (CRS)

Statistical system operated by the OECD (see Chapter VI, section 1.3.1).

Cross-border operations

Transactions between residents of different countries.

Cross-border positions

Asset and liability positions vis-à-vis banks and non-banks located in a country other than the country of residence of the reporting bank (also referred to as "external" positions).

Currency of repayment

The currency in which payment is due according to the loan agreement.

Debt conversion

Exchange of debt for another liability.

Debt/equity swaps

Transaction in which debt (usually of a country) is exchanged for equity participation in one of the country's firms.

Debt forgiveness

The extinction of a loan, in whole or in part, by agreement between debtor and creditor.

Debtor country

The country in which the debtor is resident.

Debtor Reporting System (DRS)

Statistical system operated by the World Bank (see Chapter VII, section 1.3.1).

Debt relief

Cancellation of unpaid principal (whether or not already due), of interest payments already due, and (OECD) reduction in interest rates.

Debt reorganisation

General term for operations altering the amount or terms of outstanding debt (includes debt relief, rescheduling, refinancing, etc.).

Debt restructuring

Alternative general term for debt reorganisation.

Debt service

The sum of interest payments and repayment of principal.

Debt service ratio

The ratio of debt service payments made by or due from a country to that country's export earnings.

Deposit banks

A term covering deposit money banks and other bank-like institutions accepting deposits.

Deposit money banks (DMBs)

(IMF): Financial institutions other than monetary authorities that have liabilities in the form of deposits payable on demand and transferable by cheque or otherwise in making payment.

Deposits

Sums placed with a financial institution for credit to a customer's account.

Developing countries

See Appendix 7.

Direct investment

Investment made to acquire a lasting interest in an enterprise operating in an economy other than that of the investor, with the aim of having an effective voice in the management.

Disbursement

The placement of resources at the disposal of the borrower.

End-of-period exchange rate

Exchange rate ruling on the final working day of a given period.

Equities

Ownership interests of stockholders in a firm, usually in the form of stock (not bonds).

Equity

The value of the interest of an owner or partial owner in an asset.

Equity participation

Interest in a firm in the form of equities.

Euro-currency

Used of transactions (e.g. deposits) in a currency other than that of the country in which the other party to the transaction is located.

Euro-market

Market for transactions in currencies other than the currency of the country in which the financial institution is located.

European Currency Unit (ECU)

Currency unit of the European Economic Community used primarily for accounting and financial purposes, whose value is based on a "basket" of European Community currencies.

Exceptional financing

(IMF): A special "below-the-line" category in IMF BOP reporting used to accommodate transactions undertaken on behalf of the monetary authorities to compensate for any overall imbalance.

Export credit

A loan for the purpose of trade which is not represented by a negotiable instrument.

Financial credit

See buyer credit.

Financial (finance) lease

See Chapter III, section 2.1.1.2.

Flag of convenience countries

Countries with favourable tax rules and other regulations attracting part or whole companies whose main business (originally shipping, now often production or services) is outside the country.

Floating-rate notes (FRNs)

Negotiable and transferable securities with flexible interest rate, fixed interest periods, and issued in pre-determined and uniform amounts.

Foreign bank

Bank with head office outside the country in which it is located.

Foreign currency transactions

(BIS): transactions denominated in a currency other than the domestic currency of the country in which the banking office is located.

Frame agreement

An arrangement which authorises a series of individual loans up to a specified amount.

Government Finance Statistics (GFS)

Statistical system operated by the IMF (see Chapter V, section 1.3.1). GFSY: Government Finance Statistics Yearbook (IMF publication); GFSM: Government Finance Statistics Manual (IMF publication).

Grant element

Face value of a loan commitment less the sum of the discounted present value of the debt service payments to be made on the loan, using a discount rate of 10 per cent.

Grant-like

(OECD): Used of a transaction where the donor country retains a formal title to repayment but has expressed its intention in the commitment to hold the proceeds of repayment in the borrowing country.

Host country

(Of banks): the country where a bank's foreign affiliate is located; (of private investment) the country in which a direct investor's investment is located.

IMF credit

See Use of Fund Credit.

Interbank positions

Asset and liability positions of banks vis-à-vis other banks.

International banking business

(BIS): Banks' transactions in whatever currency with non-residents and transactions in foreign (non-local) currency with residents.

International Banking Statistics (IBS)

Statistical system operated by the IMF (see Chapter V, section 1.3.1). Also used in a generic sense to refer to the BIS's international banking statistics.

International Capital Markets (ICM)

An IMF "Occasional Paper" containing considerable material on debt (see Chapter V, sections 1.2.2 and 6).

International Financial Statistics (IFS)

Monthly IMF publication containing financial and economic statistics for most countries of the world.

International interbank market

An international money market in which banks lend to each other – either cross-border or locally in foreign currency – large amounts of money, usually for periods between overnight and six months.

International license banks

Alternative term for offshore banking units, referring to the fact that special licenses or other authority are needed for them to operate.

Intra-bank

Refers to transactions between parts of the same bank.

Intra-company

Refers to transactions between parts of the same company or the same group.

Joint venture

(Of banks): A banking enterprise in which two or more parties hold major interests.

Leasing

Renting of an asset for a given period of time, as an alternative to outright purchase. (See Chapter III, section 2.1.1.2).

Long-term

Used of claims with an original or extended maturity of more than one year.

Maturity (original)

Period from commitment or disbursement to final repayment of a loan.

Maturity (residual)

Time remaining to final repayment of a loan.

Maturity structure

(BIS): Breakdown of claims or liabilities according to their residual maturity (also known as "maturity profile" or "maturity distribution").

Multi-year rescheduling agreement (MYRA)

Agreement consolidating principal payments due over a period of several years (generally three to five).

Nationality

(Of banks): Country of residence of head office.

Net debt

See Chapter III, section 2.2.

Net flow

Excess of new lending over amortization receipts.

Non-banks

All entities, other than official monetary authorities and deposit banks. Includes individuals.

Note-issuance facility (NIF)

A medium-term legally-binding commitment under which a borrower can issue a short-term paper in its own name, underwritten by banks which are committed either to purchase any notes the borrower is unable to sell, or to provide credit.

Official creditors

International organisations, governments and government agencies, including official monetary institutions.

Official Development Assistance (ODA)

(OECD): Official assistance for development purposes. Includes grants and concessional loans.

Official development bank

A non-monetary financial intermediary, controlled by the public sector, primarily engaged in making long-term loans that are beyond the capacity of other financial institutions.

171

Officially-guaranteed

(OECD): Used of debt whose repayment is guaranteed by a government or by an entity of the official sector in the creditor's country.

Officially-supported

(OECD): Portmanteau term for "official and officially-guaranteed".

Official monetary institutions

Mainly central banks or related national or international bodies.

Offshore banking centres

Countries with banking sectors dealing primarily with non-residents. For countries reporting to the BIS see Appendix 6.

Offshore banking units (OBUs)

Alternative term for international license banks.

Operational (operating) lease

See Chapter III, section 2.1.1.2.

Other Official Flows (OOF)

(OECD) Flow Statistics: Officially-financed flows other than Official Development Assistance. Debt statistics: also excludes direct official export credits (classified as export credits).

Outside-area countries

(BIS): Countries and territories outside the BIS "reporting area".

Paris Club

Forum of official creditors for negotiating debt restructuring. See Appendix 5.

Period-average exchange rate

Arithmetic average of the reported monthly exchange rates during a given period.

Perpetual

(Of bonds): Of indefinite maturity.

Portfolio investment

Investment other than direct investment.

Provisioning (provisions)

Setting aside of sums (provisions) to meet an eventuality (in the debt context, usually to provide against a doubtful debt).

Public external debt

(WB): An obligation to a non-resident creditor of national or local governments or of enterprises that are at least 50 per cent government-owned.

Publicly-guaranteed

(WB): Used of debt whose repayment is guaranteed by a government or by an entity of the public sector in the debtor country.

Quarterly (reporting) system

One of the two main BIS statistical systems (see Chapter IV).

Refinancing

The extension of a new loan to enable the repayment of all or part of the amounts outstanding on earlier borrowing, possibly including amounts not yet due.

Reporting area

(BIS): The whole group of countries reporting to the BIS (see Appendix 6).

Reporting banks/institutions

(BIS): Generally all those deposit-taking institutions (plus some non-deposit-taking financial institutions specialising in foreign trade finance) within a reporting country which have international assets and liabilities of any size.

Reporting centres/countries

(BIS): The industrial countries and offshore banking centres listed in Appendix 6.

Repudiation

(Of debt): Unilateral disclaiming of a liability by a debtor.

Rescheduling

a) The postponement of all or part of one or more maturities of one or more loans, the creditor and the debtor remaining unchanged;
b) A general term for the outcome of discussions on debt reorganisation for a borrowing country.

Resident

See Appendix 2.

Restructuring

See debt reorganisation.

Revolving credit

A credit with a clause for automatic renewal (under certain conditions).

Revolving Underwriting Facility (RUF)

Medium-term facility on which the borrower can draw at any time of its life, usually certificates of deposit (CDs) or short-term promissory notes.

Rollover (credit)

Renewal of an existing credit (or credits).

Sectoring

Breaking down of external debt according to classifications of various kinds.

Semi-annual (reporting) system

One of the two main BIS statistical systems (see Chapter IV).

Short-term

Used of claims with a maturity of one year or less.

Special Drawing Rights (SDRs)

Special reserve assets, value based on a basket of currencies, issued by the IMF. Also used as a unit of account.

Standby credit

A commitment to lend up to a specified amount for a specific period, to be used only in a certain contingency.

Stock figures

(BIS): Amounts outstanding on a particular date.

Supplier (supplier's) credit

Credit extended by the supplier of goods or services to an overseas purchaser.

Swaps

See Chapter II, Section 3.1.1.2.

System of National Accounts (SNA)

United Nations statistical system of national accounts.

Trade credit

(IMF): Credit extended in connection with the sale or purchase of goods or services (covers both supplier's credits and buyer's credits).

Trade financing

(WB): Equivalent to trade credit.

Trade-related credit

(OECD, BIS): Equivalent to trade credit.

Undisbursed

Used of amounts committed but not yet utilised. (BIS): (of credit commitments): open lines of credit which for the lending banks are legally binding.

Use of Fund Credit (UFC)

Liabilities to the International Monetary Fund resulting from use of the IMF General Resources Account (e.g., drawings under credit tranches, use of the compensatory financing and buffer stock facilities). (See footnote 4 of Chapter II).

Vis-à-vis country

(BIS) Country of location of the counterparty to a financial contract.

World Economic Outlook (WEO)

Annual IMF publication containing information on debt (see Chapter V, sections 1.2.2. and 6).

Write-off

The removal from the creditor's books of disbursed debt and/or of interest arrears.

ANNOTATED BIBLIOGRAPHY

(For details on regular debt statistics publications, see final sections of Chapters IV to VII).

I. GENERAL REFERENCE

I.1. BIS *Manual on Statistics Compiled by International Organisations on Countries' External Indebtedness*, Basle, March 1979, p.109

This manual, which is largely replaced by the present publication, provides information on statistics available from international organisations on external indebtedness as of 1979.

I.2. IMF *Balance of Payments Manual*, Fourth Edition, Washington, 1977

The basic source for all matters connected with the compilation and reporting of balance-of-payments statistics, explaining the fundamental concepts underlying their compilation.

I.3. IMF *A Manual on Government Financial Statistics*, Washington, 1986

This Manual deals with the compilation of statistics on the finances of government and provides a common system of definitions and classifications. It generally follows the lines of institutional sectorisation laid down in the United Nations' SNA, but goes further in differentiating between performance of government and financial institutions in the economy.

I.4. IMF *A Guide to Money and Banking Statistics in International Financial Statistics* (IFS), Draft, 1984 (not available to the public)

Explains the methodology followed in producing the money and banking data published in the IFS.

I.5. IMF *Staff Papers*

A quarterly publication that presents the results of studies by IMF staff on monetary and financial problems.

II. ANALYTICAL STUDIES

II.1. BIS   *The International Interbank Market*

A descriptive study, BIS Economic Paper No. 8, July 1983

II.2. IMF   Joslin Landell-Mills, *The Fund's International Banking Statistics*, Washington, 1986

This pamphlet describes the Fund's international banking statistics project. The data resulting from this project are now published in three pairs of world tables in the IFS. Compilation issues and procedures are discussed in detail, together with the possible uses of the data.

II.3. IMF   Bahram Nowzad and Richard C. Williams, *External Indebtedness of Developing Countries*, Washington, 1981

The paper presents a quantitative account of the major developments in the external debt of developing countries during 1972-1979, and analyses the significant changes in the debt structure. The paper also includes a description of the multilateral debt renegotiations undertaken with official and bank creditors.

II.4. IMF   Staff team headed by E. Brau and R.C. Williams, with P.M. Keller and M. Nowak, *Recent Multilateral Debt Restructuring with Official and Bank Creditors*, Washington, 1983

This paper reviews developments in external indebtedness of developing countries, with emphasis on a description of the arrangements made for restructuring official and commercial bank debt from 1978 to October 1983. The study includes a comparison of this experience with the findings of the 1981 study (see II.3 above).

II.5. IMF   *Foreign Private Investment in Developing Countries*, IMF Research Department, Washington, 1985

The study discusses trends in the size and composition of foreign private investments and in income payments on such investments in the 1970s and early 1980s. It also examines the role of direct investments in the transfer of resources and the possibilities for substitution between direct investments and other forms of resource transfer.

II.6. IMF   E. Brau and C. Puckahtikom, *Export Credit Cover Possibilities and Payments Difficulties*, Washington, 1985

This paper is a special study undertaken to review the policies and practices of the ten major official export credit agencies following the difficulties in servicing external debt experienced since 1982. It deals with the adaptation of approaches in the changed environment and reviews the experience of the agencies with a sample of eleven debtor countries in the period 1980 to mid-1984.

II.7. IMF   K.B. Dillon, C.M. Watson, G.R. Kincaid and C. Puckahtikom, *Recent Developments in External Debt Restructuring*, Washington, 1985

This study is a sequel to the 1981 and 1983 papers on the subject (see II.3 and II.4 above) and deals with the arrangements for restructuring commercial bank and official debt from 1983 to early 1985. The paper reviews the major sources of recent debt-servicing difficulties and discusses approaches that have been taken by debtors and creditors to resolving these problems. It compares the treatment of various groups of creditors and different types of debt.

II.8.   IMF   B. Dillon and Gumersindo Oliveros, *Recent Experience with Multilateral Official Debt Rescheduling*, Washington, 1987

The latest in the series of papers covering this area, describing developments in multilateral debt renegotiations in the 18 months to the end of June 1986. Recently, official creditors have concluded multi-year rescheduling agreements (MYRAs) with countries considered to have made considerable progress in their adjustment efforts.

II.9.   IMF   H. Mahran (ed.), *External Debt Management*, Washington, 1985

This book is the outcome of a seminar on external debt management organised by the Fund in December 1984. The introduction places the seminar in perspective and is followed by a section dealing with the debt problem on a global basis. A final section describes the external debt management experience of individual countries.

II.10. OECD   *Export Credit Financing Systems in OECD Countries*, Paris, 1987

Describes the institutional framework and procedures governing the financing and guaranteeing of export credit transactions. Updates earlier studies of the same topic.

II.11. World Bank   Gordon W. Smith and John T. Cuddington (eds.), *International Debt and the Developing Countries*, 1985

This book contains edited contributions to the World Bank symposium held in April 1984. It examines the theory and recent experience of international lending, its contribution to the growth of developing countries and its role in the international financial system.

II.12. World Bank   Kathie L. Krumm, *The External Debt of Sub-Saharan Africa*, Staff Working Papers, 1985

This study reviews the origins, magnitude and implications of Sub-Saharan Africa's debt problems.

II.13. World Bank   *International Capital and Economic Development,* World Development Report, 1985

Prepared by a World Bank staff team led by Francis Colaço, the 1985 World Development Report focuses on the contribution of international capital to economic development, and reviews both the institutional and the policy environment of international lending.

Published on behalf of the International Monetary Fund, the World Bank, the Bank for International Settlements,
and the Organisation for Economic Co-operation and Development
by OECD PUBLICATIONS, 2, rue André-Pascal, 75775 PARIS CEDEX 16 - No. 44263 1988
PRINTED IN FRANCE
(43 88 02 1) ISBN 92-64-13039-X